I0891360

SOUL CITY

SOUL CITY

Oakland, U.S.A.

Ken Light

Foreword by Ishmael Reed

Heyday, Berkeley, California

Foreword copyright © 2026 by Heyday
All images and other text copyright © 2026 by Ken Light

All rights reserved. Except for brief passages quoted in reviews, no portion of this work may be reproduced or transmitted in any form or by any means, electronic or mechanical, including photocopying and recording, or by any information storage or retrieval system, or be used in training generative artificial intelligence (AI) technologies or developing machine-learning language models, without permission in writing from Heyday.

The images on pages 22–23, 106–7, 116, 130, and 137 were previously published in *What's Going On? 1969–1974*, copyright © 2015 by Ken Light.

Library of Congress Cataloging-in-Publication Data is available.

Cover Photo: Ken Light
Cover Design: Archie Ferguson
Interior Design/Typesetting: Archie Ferguson

Published by Heyday
P.O. Box 9145, Berkeley, California 94709
(510) 549-3564
heydaybooks.com

Printed in China by Regent Publishing Services, Hong Kong
10 9 8 7 6 5 4 3 2 1

Foreword

Before AI-generated visual effects became the trend, photographers could often highlight the human story more effectively than print. The little girl running naked from a napalm attack changed minds about the war in Vietnam, and the visuals of the beating of demonstrators crossing the Pettus Bridge led to civil rights legislation.

When my family and I moved to Oakland in 1979, the city was still a hub of Black Power activism. The mayor was Black; our friend Robert Maynard was the first Black publisher of a major newspaper, the *Oakland Tribune*; the museum director was Black; and the conductor of the symphony was Black.

At the same time, however, industries that provided jobs for thousands of Black people were beginning to close or depart from Oakland, among them Transamerica Delaval and General Electric. As a result, some of our inner-city neighbors sought to earn money illegally. A crack dealer told me that he had had a job at Gerber Products, but the facility had closed.

Ken Light captures Black Oakland in the period between its decline and the election of Jerry Brown, whose "elegant density" attracted tech workers to Oakland, promising easy commutes to San Francisco. In 1980, Black residents made up 47 percent of the city's population. Because of rising housing costs driven by gentrification, in 2024 the percentage of the Black population was reduced to 21.09 percent. Many Blacks found themselves among Oakland's homeless—5,490 people in 2024—adding to the health issues that affect thousands of Black Oaklanders. Pediatrician Michael LeNoir says that some of the health problems incurred by the living conditions of the homeless are spreading to the general population, especially those whose health is already fragile.

You can tell from the posture of two Black women—one carrying a grocery cart holding a watermelon—that they have been deprived of the kind of exercise available to the upscale. A stooped-over Black man walking before the smiling icon of a Coke ad tells the same story. Some of the photos show liquor and cigarette ads, many of which are designed to lure Black consumers.

Other photos show that the Christian faith is still available to some, while the younger generation acquires its proverbs from lyrics and slogans, leading to a decline in church attendance. Some of the Oakland churches have relocated to surrounding towns where Blacks seeking cheaper rents have resettled. If Jesus of Nazareth still appears in these photos, the faith he founded has competition. Many local Blacks are Muslims or have adopted Buddhism. A Black man wearing a Rasta hat poses in front of a statue of Buddha. Buddhism is winning converts among Black artists and intellectuals.

In two of these photos, the Kennedy brothers and Martin Luther King Jr. appear as saints.

Another photo stands out. A Black kid stands next to a sheeted individual, and another kid wears a Barbie doll face. If one views the ghost as a Klansman, the photographer presents the dark side of the American experience.

Other photos showcase the fashion styles of Black residents, particularly the hats, which historically emphasized individuality. The fashion industry has adopted these Black styles.

The hairstyles of those pictured in these photos, once denounced, have also become mainstream. You can discern the political situation of Black America by hairstyles. In these photos, the younger generation wears their hair in an Afro style, while members of the older generation straighten their hair. In a country ruled by those with straight hair, Black hair becomes a political issue. The 1960s and '70s marked a period of political and cultural rebellion among Black Americans; however, the 1980s brought a backlash with the election of Ronald Reagan, who campaigned against Students for a Democratic Society and the Black Panthers. The latter organization drew international attention to the city. People from all over the world were taking Black Panther tours. I was on board during research for my book *Blues City: A Walk in Oakland*.

The newspaper stand is headed for museums as younger generations use social media for information. In one photo, Lionel Wilson, the Black Panthers' choice for mayor, appears on the cover of the *Oakland Tribune*. Elaine Brown, a Black Panther member, described him as the Panthers' Sun Yat-sen. The Black Panthers sought to end police brutality, but even after the outpouring of sympathy following the public execution of George Floyd, police brutality continues. Yet the Panther legend lives on. In 2025, cofounder Bobby Seale had part of a street named for him. His name appears in a photo above the sign Justice Market. The Panthers, with their breakfast programs and other community services, were way ahead of the New York City mayor who promised city-owned grocery stores with low prices. Those glory days have vanished, the Afros with them.

For decades, home ownership has been an issue for Black Americans. For Sale and For Rent signs that appear on the outside of some of the homes in these photos show how vulnerable Black people are to displacement because of redlining's legacy. When the landlords raised the rents in my neighborhood because of gentrification, the Black population was reduced by 50 percent.

Despite the often grim surroundings, which Light effectively portrays in black and white, children continued to ride bicycles, dance, and celebrate Christmas. Halloween too. In one photo, Black kids wear white masks. Is this because they view whites as monsters, a result of listening to their old relatives, refugees from Arkansas, Texas, and Louisiana, who tell them of their horrible treatment at the hands of whites? Light demonstrates how an independent photographer might show all aspects of a group's culture, while photographers who work for the media might stereotype Blacks and Hispanics to flatter white subscribers.

For decades, men and women from other ethnic groups, using film, television, the press, and political campaigns, have blamed Daniel Patrick Moynihan's so-called tangle of pathology, including family dysfunction, on Black Americans. (Based on my research, the conditions in their ethnic groups might be worse. I don't know of any Black man who advocates for honor killings.) Instead, Light shows Black men in the home, loving and caring for their families.

I cringe when I hear privileged white TV men comment about urban crime. Until the 2010s, before my neighborhood was transformed, there were shootouts between crack operations. That began when the Reagan administration tolerated their Contra allies flooding Black neighborhoods with drugs. Despite this atmosphere, most of the Black kids in my neighborhood left to join the middle class. Occasionally, they return to visit us. They don't recognize the neighborhood. Mercedes and BMWs have replaced the American cars that appear in Ken Light's photos.

We used to meet with the police and our representatives at neighborhood crime councils. I confronted a liquor store owner about why he, as a Muslim, was selling liquor. A policeman told me that the question was out of order. The police were supposed to be present only to collect crime statistics, not to butt in. Elderly attendees to these meetings always questioned why the police were so chummy with the crack dealers on the block.

One photo shows Black men in military garb, perhaps to be used as cannon fodder for one of the country's perennial wars. I'm sure that the thousands upon thousands of Black men who've lost their lives from the Revolutionary War to now would be glad to learn that their sacrifice was part of a DEI experiment.

Like Berkeley, Oakland is becoming a white city. But just as we gaze at photos of other historic Black zones that have been razed, Ken Light's photos will remind future generations that there was a time when Blacks lived among deteriorating Victorians, and no matter how miserable the environment, they had pride and they had friends, made love, had jobs, ran businesses, and made much from little, which has been the strategy of Blacks since the slave ships landed. Even under those horrible conditions, Africans created art on those ships.

—ISHMAEL REED

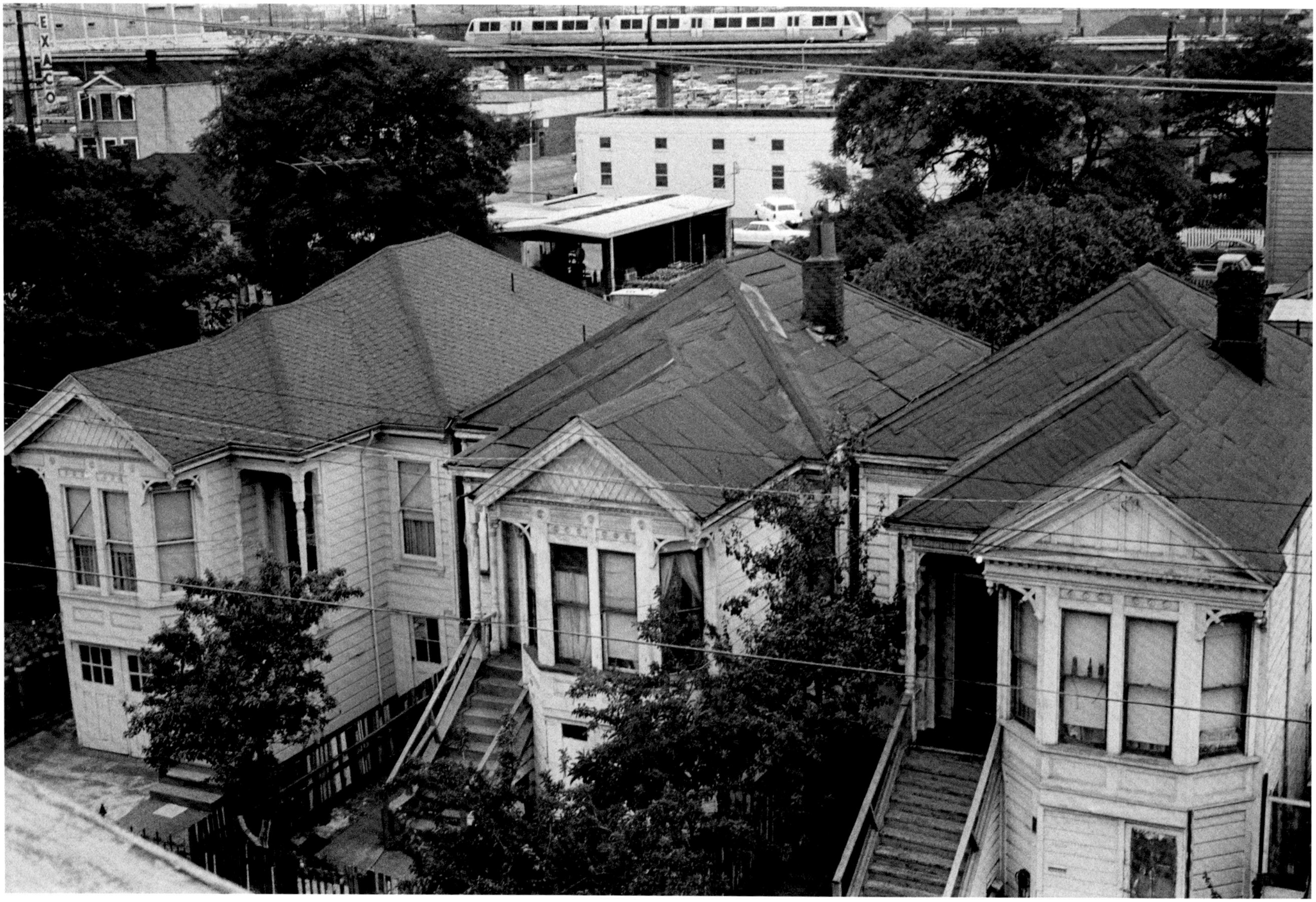
EXACO

Introduction

During the 1940s, an industrial boom filled the San Francisco Bay Area with shipyard jobs supporting the war effort against fascism. Many African Americans migrated from the South and settled in Oakland looking for jobs and a better way of life. These participants in the Second Great Migration came from Texas, Louisiana, Arkansas, and Oklahoma, among other places, driven by the search for jobs in war industries and to escape Jim Crow segregation.

The African American population of Oakland increased by thousands. New residents found jobs at shipyards, foundries, and factories. They worked as welders, riveters, electricians, and manual laborers. There was an office for the Brotherhood of Sleeping Car Porters on Seventh Street in West Oakland, the center of Black commerce. These unionized, well-paying jobs formed the backbone of the local Black middle class. But these migrants faced severe housing discrimination, redlining, and restrictive covenants—forces that concentrated the Black population in the lower part of Oakland, sometimes called "the Bottoms," better known to most of us as West Oakland.

This influx transformed Oakland from a predominantly white city to a thriving Black cultural hub. West Oakland became a major blues center; the clubs around Seventh Street attracted locals, out-of-towners, and military visiting the port. Aretha Franklin, Billie Holiday, T-Bone Walker, Big Mama Thornton, and many local musicians performed there. Along with the vibrant music venues, many new African American–owned businesses enriched the community.

In the 1950s and '60s, wartime jobs dried up as defense-related industries, such as shipbuilding, closed or retooled; there was also a general decline in manufacturing jobs. Black workers were so often "last hired, first fired," and this accelerated.

The building of aboveground track for the Bay Area Rapid Transit system (BART) drove a final nail into the community. BART sent shrieking trains along Seventh Street, the business and cultural hub of the community, from dawn to midnight. Groups of African American residents of West Oakland had mobilized to resist these "urban renewal" projects, to no avail. The Oakland Planning & Building Department estimates that between 5,100 and 9,700 housing units were lost in West Oakland in the 1960s alone. The freeway physically divided the neighborhood, creating a daunting barrier that isolated West Oakland from downtown and other parts of the city. Decades later, the I-980 freeway is recognized by urban planners as a major driver of inequality in West Oakland.

Along its Victorian-lined streets, West Oakland became a center for the Black Panther Party. On April 6, 1968, Little Bobby Hutton, age seventeen, was killed in West Oakland during a shootout with Oakland police. Hutton was shot multiple times after he and Eldridge Cleaver surrendered to police at a house on Twenty-eighth Street. Police violence against West Oakland residents, as well as the community's organized resistance to redevelopment, helped the Panthers' rise. But the FBI cracked down on the Panthers, and by the late 1970s the community had collapsed, isolated by the freeway and ignored by the city.

* * *

Beginning in 1974, I photographed West Oakland for two years with the support of numerous local community organizations. It was my first photographic documentary project in California, as I had myself just arrived in 1973.

I exposed hundreds of rolls of film, even though I didn't have a darkroom or place to develop or print them yet. I was twenty-three, and my photos documenting the turbulence of the late 1960s, the antiwar movement, the feminist and Black Power movements, and rural poverty had been published in the underground press of the era. What I saw in West Oakland moved me. This community, once considered the "Harlem of the West" (along with San Francisco's Fillmore District), was now considered a blight in the city of Oakland, literally cut off by urban renewal projects. The power structure was unconcerned with the current Black residents. The mayor was a Republican. The city had experienced white flight to the suburbs. The loss of this tax base led to a decline in city services, contributing to further urban decay in communities like West Oakland.

I had little support or income, living with my girlfriend, who was on welfare, and her two-year-old son and just beginning to try freelancing on my road as a documentary photographer.

I had migrated to California with dreams, all my possessions packed on top of my car, one hundred dollars, and a Shell Oil card that later tagged me with seven years of bad credit. Eventually I got a part-time job doing layout and paste-up at the *Oakland Post*, the local Black newspaper, which gave me time during the days to cruise the streets of West Oakland.

With the encouragement of community organizations, activists, and the local neighborhood arts program, I was invited into homes and churches, and I photographed life on the street. I became known as the Cameraman. People ran out of their houses waving me down to take a photo of them. I gave them prints, which I made in a community darkroom where I paid by the hour to print and develop the film.

I had recognized that there was a powerful expression of Black identity, heritage, pride, and resilience in this community, what in the 1960s was labeled as Soul. It pushed me to photograph for those two years.

I showed the photos to colleagues, magazines, and some curators, and they mostly said, "Who cares about Black people in Oakland?" After two years with little interest, I stowed the negatives and proof sheets in my file cabinet, where they sat unseen as I continued doing other social-issue documentary projects that have defined my career.

More than fifty years after my West Oakland photography work, the area has undergone seismic changes. Because of the neighborhood's relatively low rents, its remarkable but often neglected Victorian homes, and its proximity to San Francisco, the community has begun to attract a young white middle class. A wave of gentrification is now in full swing. Black and Latino families are being pushed out, and many newer residents don't know the history of the area.

There is still a strong presence of the old community. Lil' Bobby Hutton Park, where the Panthers used to meet, is still thriving with community festivals. Even Esther's Orbit Room, once the last vestige of music in this once bustling community, is being renovated with the hope of revitalizing the Seventh Street corridor. As a Black West Oakland resident and activist told me, "Despite gentrification, we still here."

These photos, I hope, remind us that the homes and streets I visited were full of life and work, hardship and celebration. West Oakland was—and is—alive with community rooted in Soul.

—KEN LIGHT

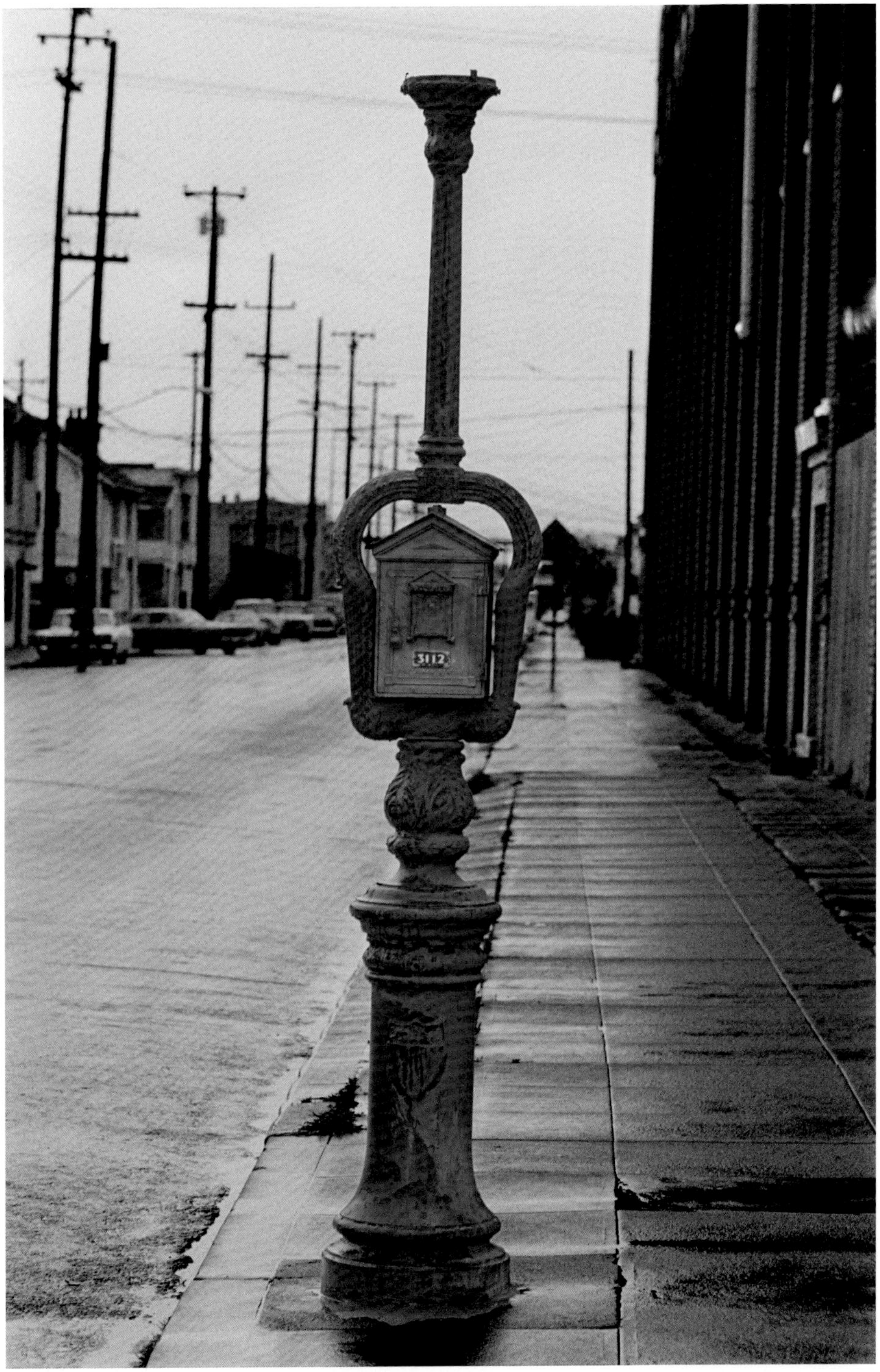
3112

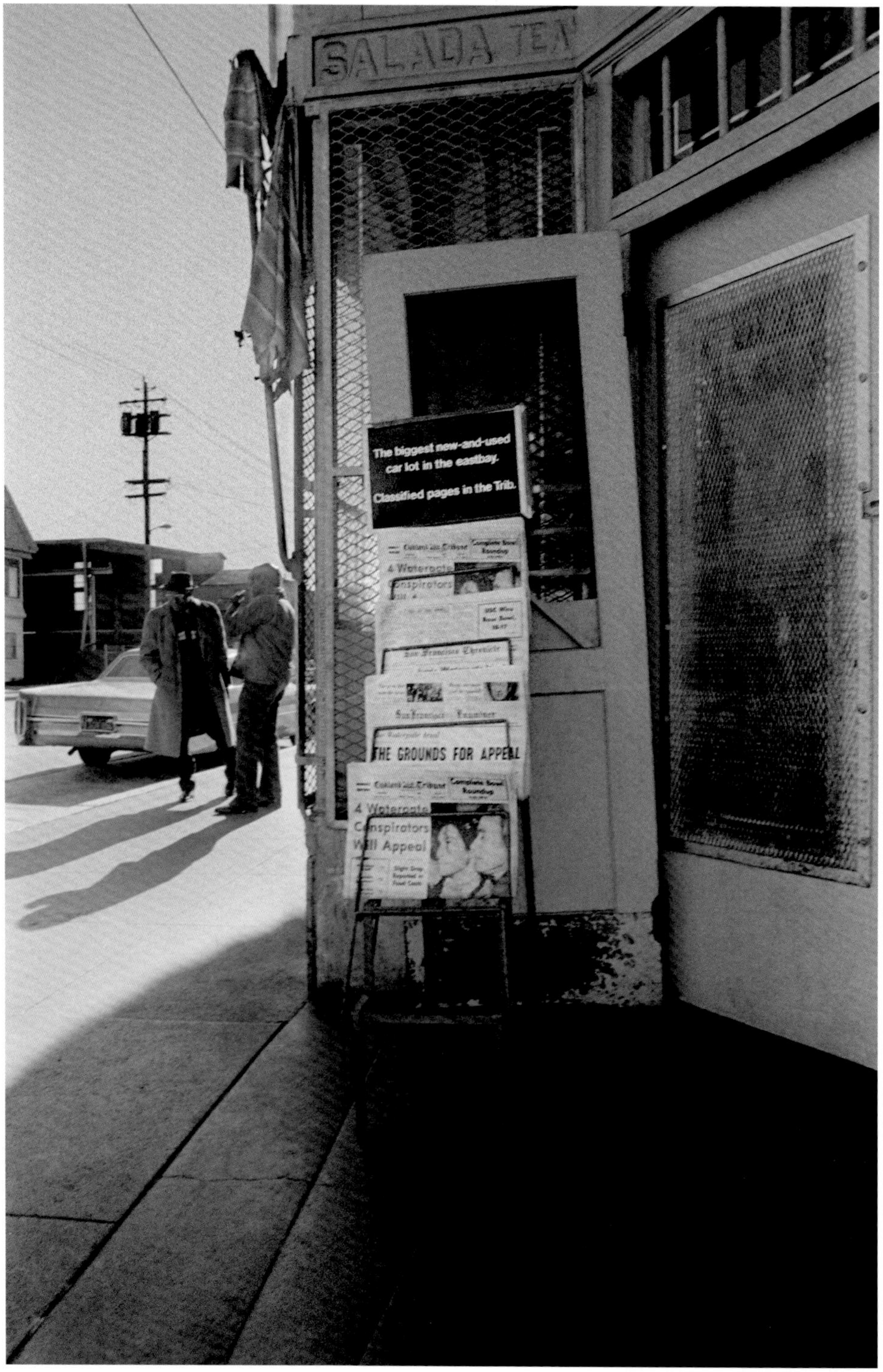
The biggest new-and-used car lot in the eastbay.
Classified pages in the Trib.
THE GROUNDS FOR APPEAL
4 Watergate Conspirators Will Appeal

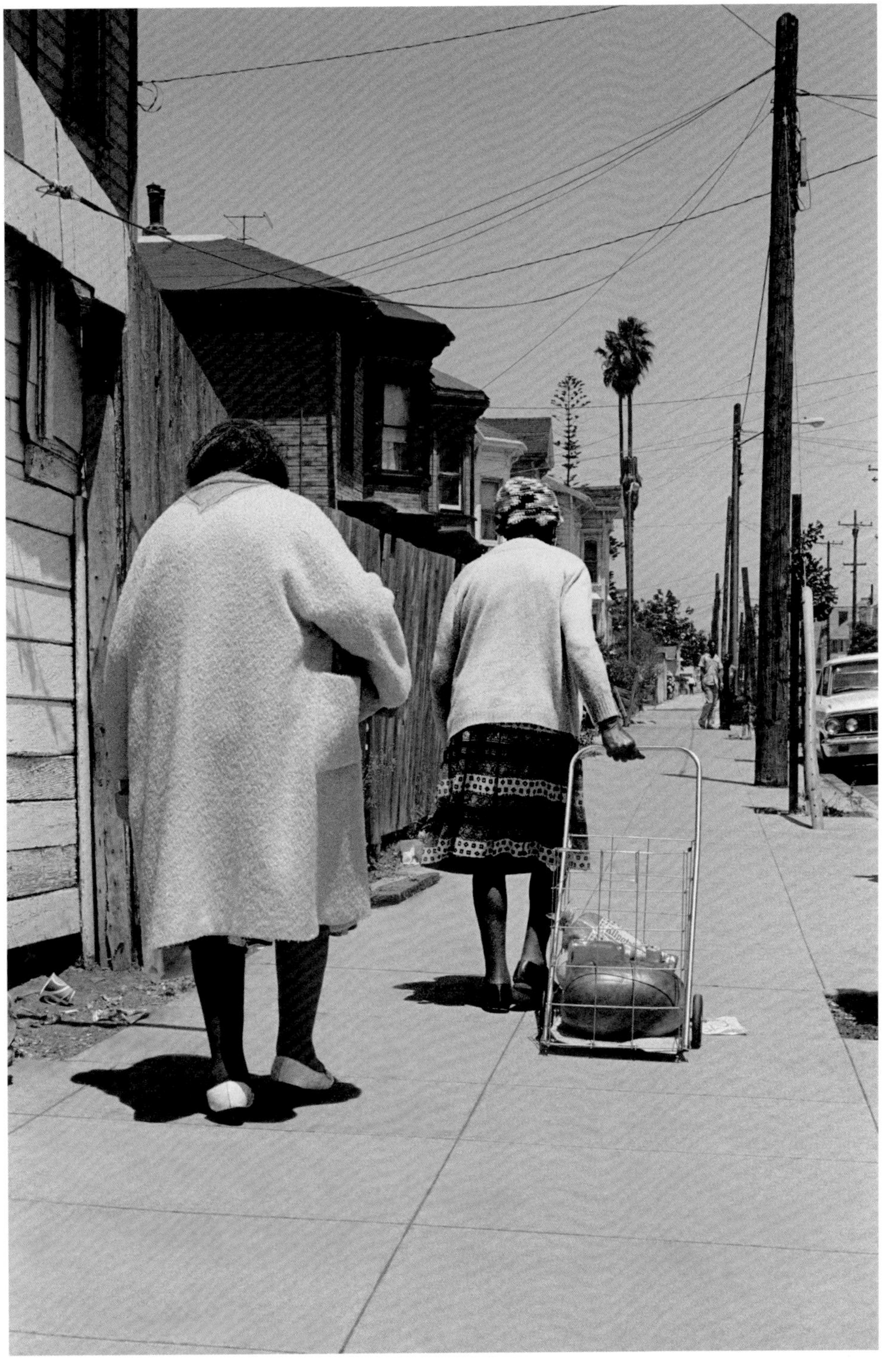

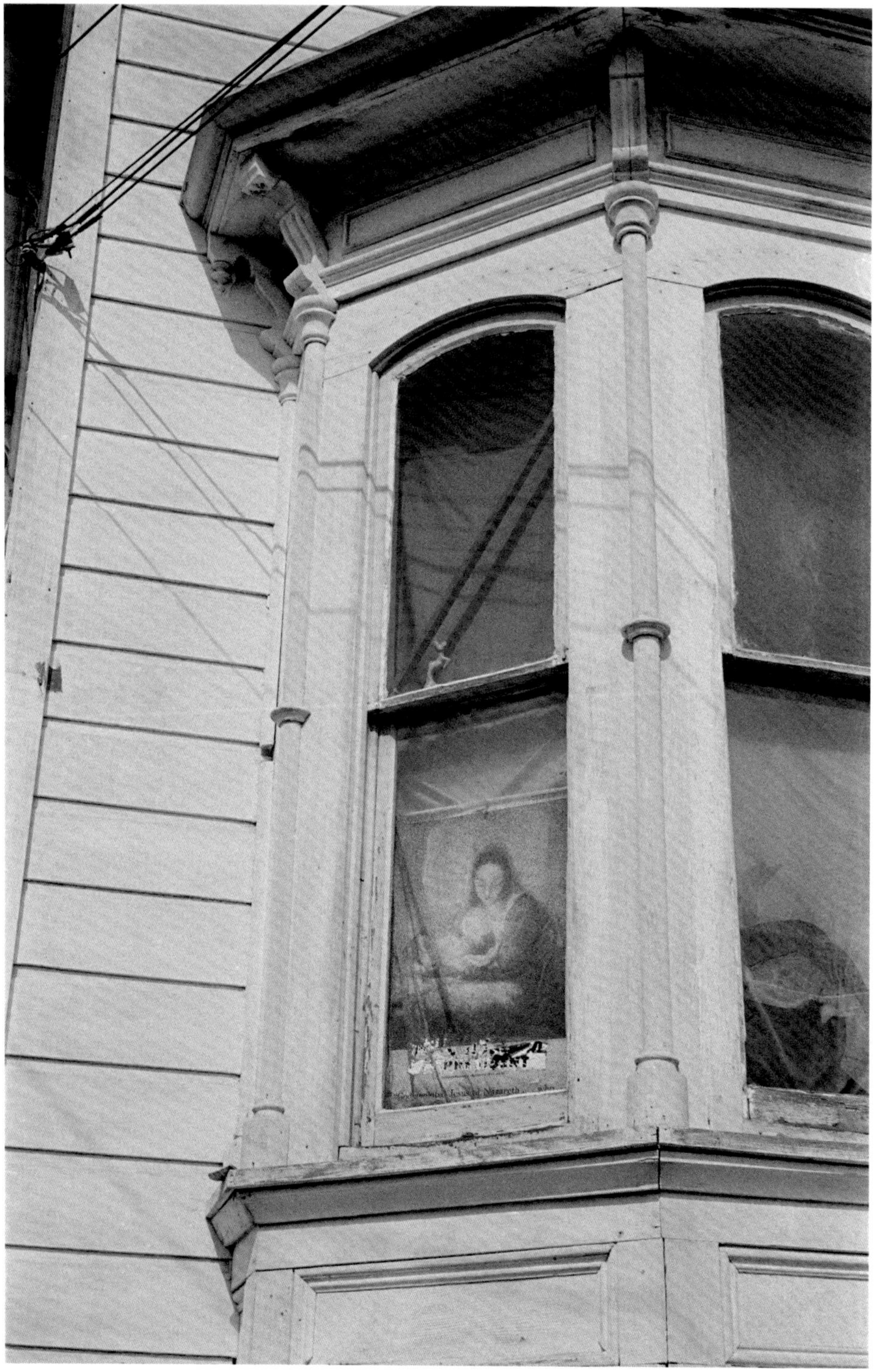

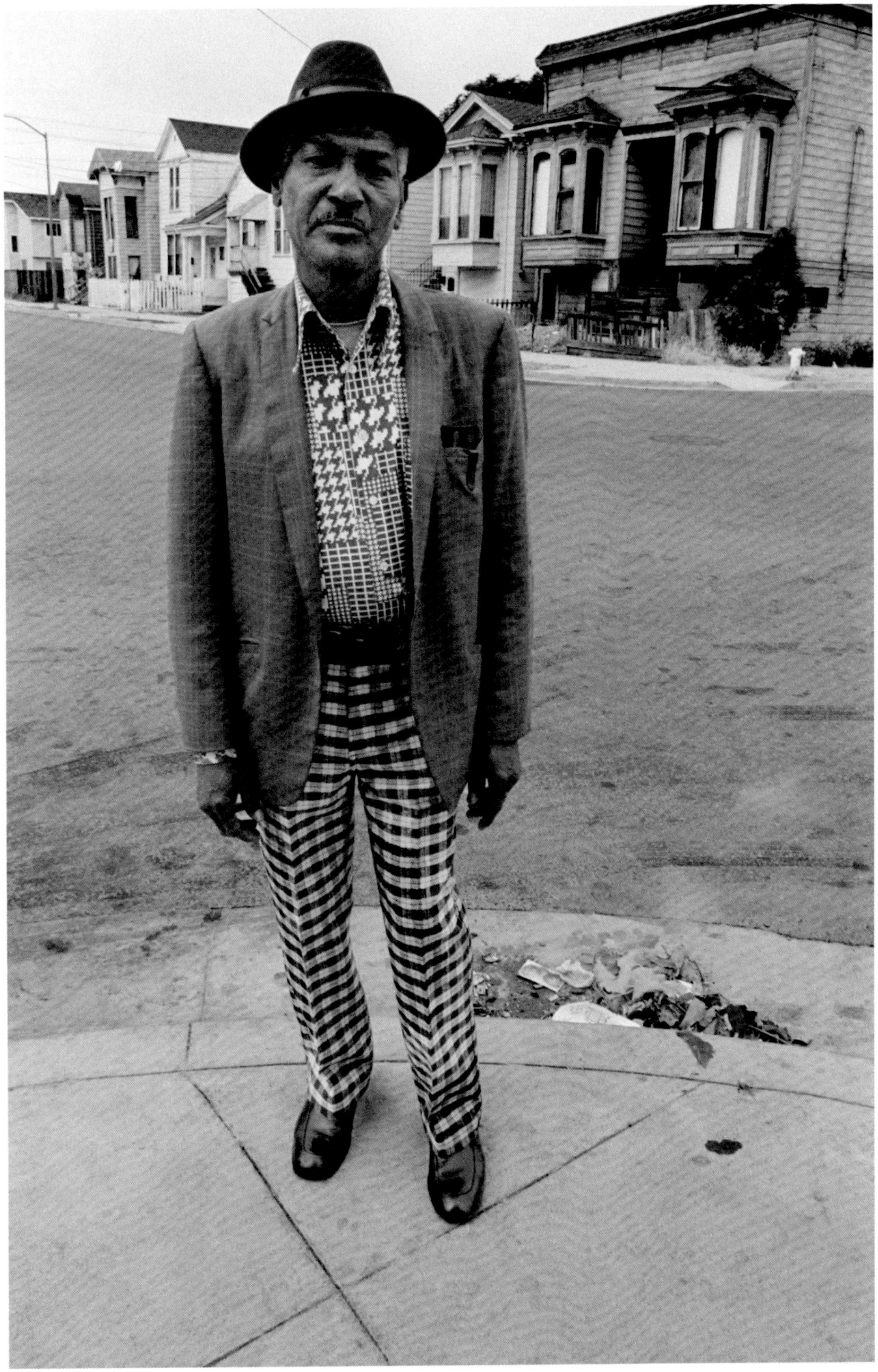

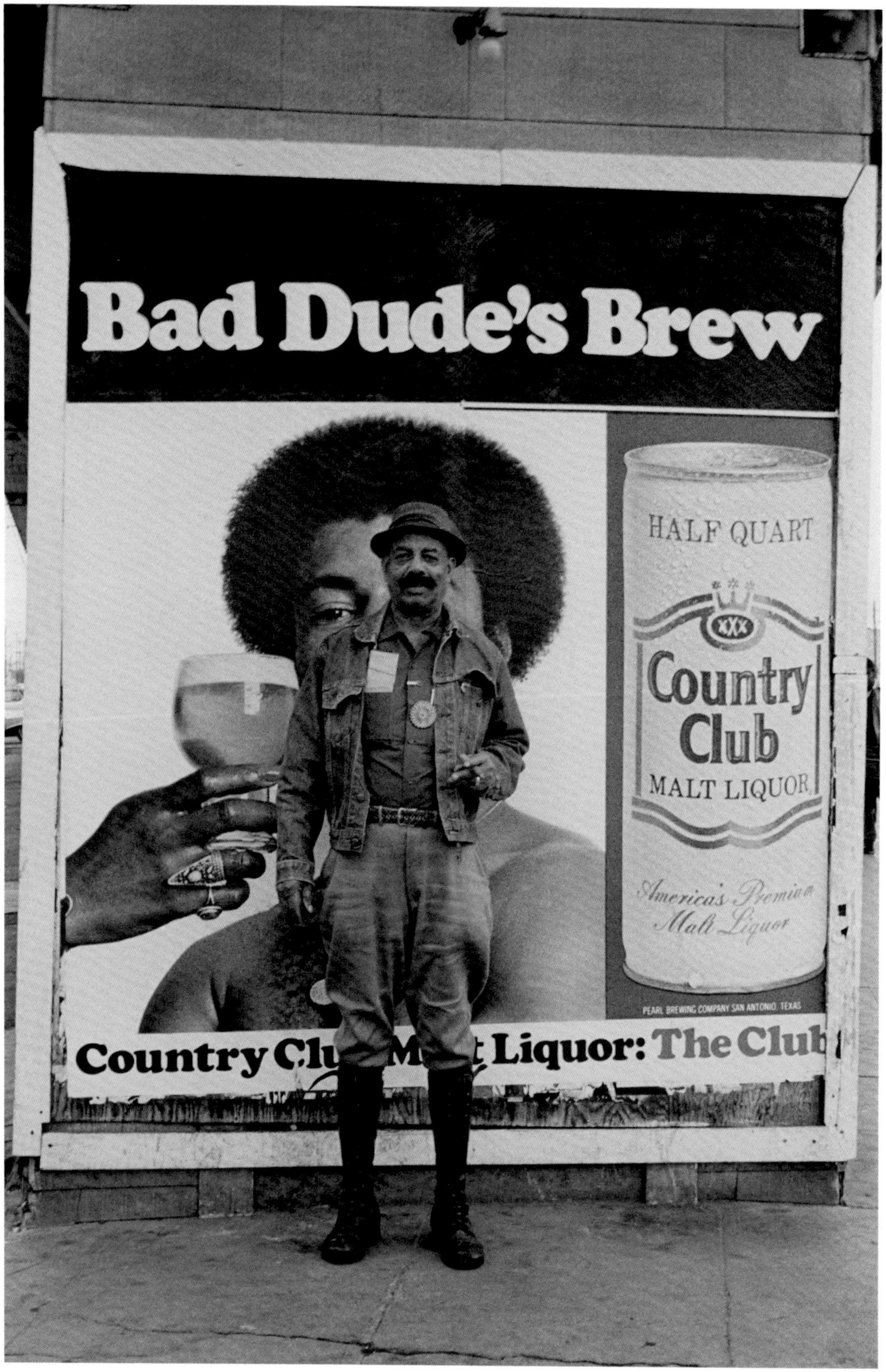
Bad Dude's Brew
HALF QUART
XXX
Country Club
MALT LIQUOR
America's Premium Malt Liquor
PEARL BREWING COMPANY SAN ANTONIO, TEXAS
Country
Liquor: The Club

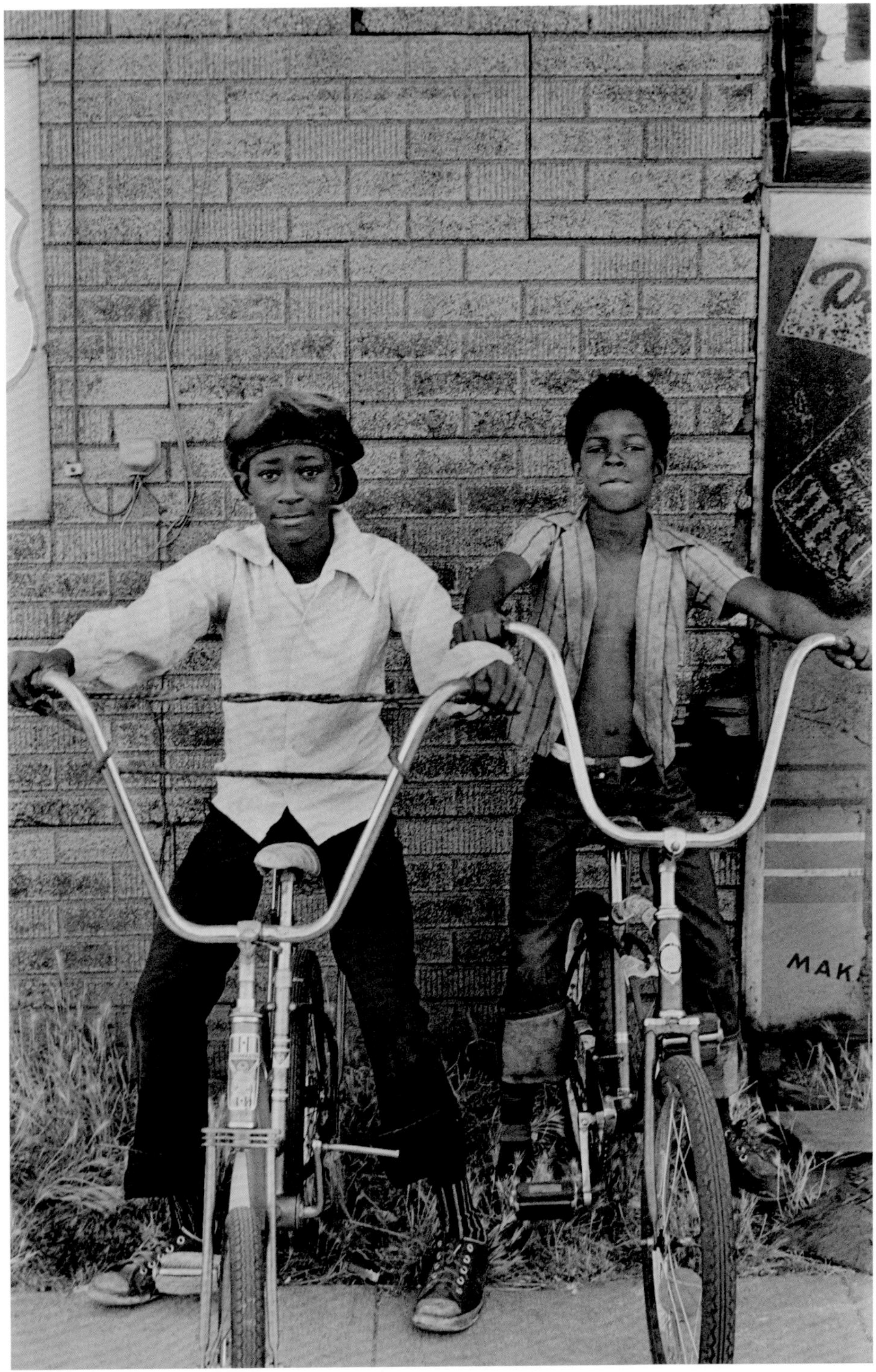

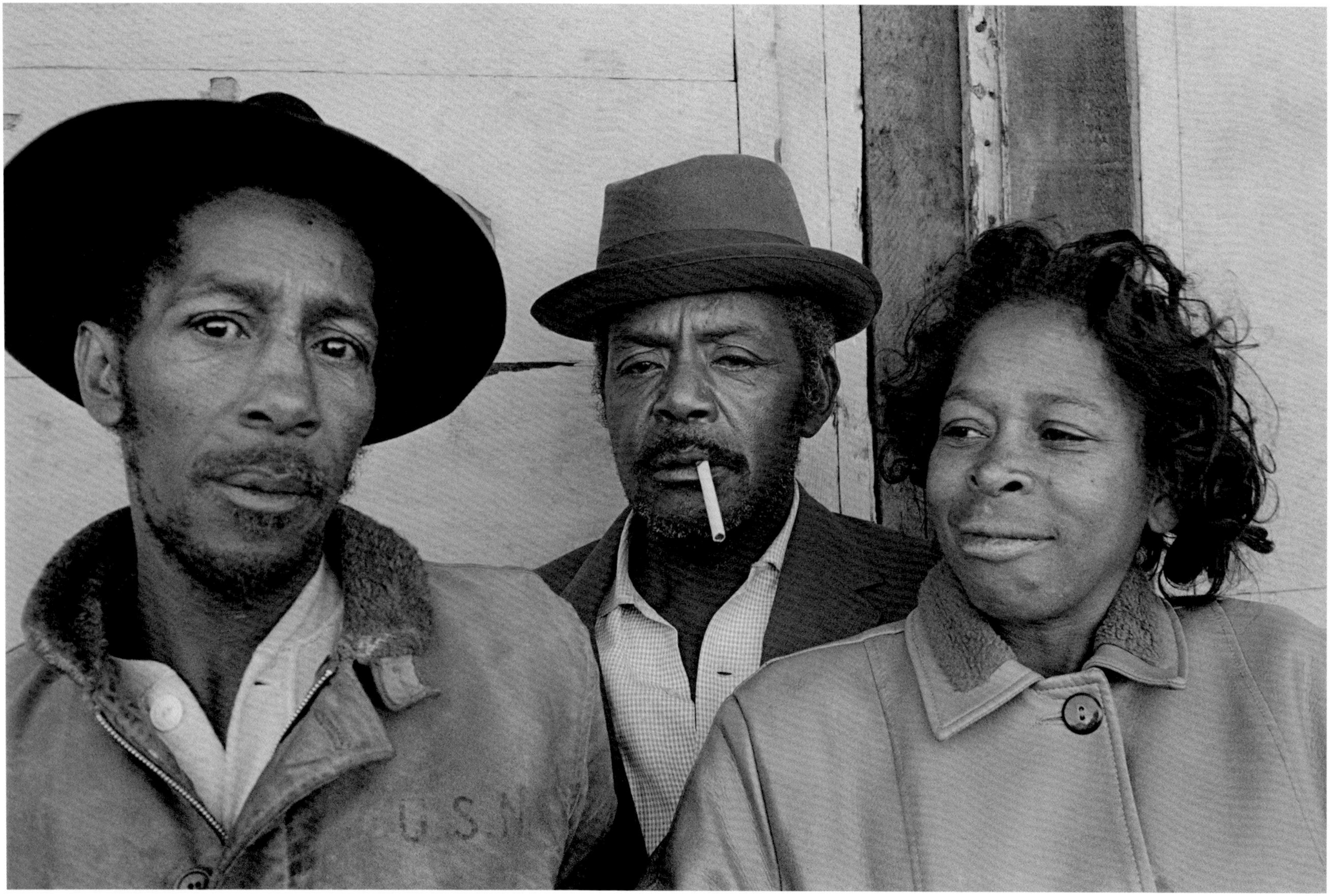
U.S.N

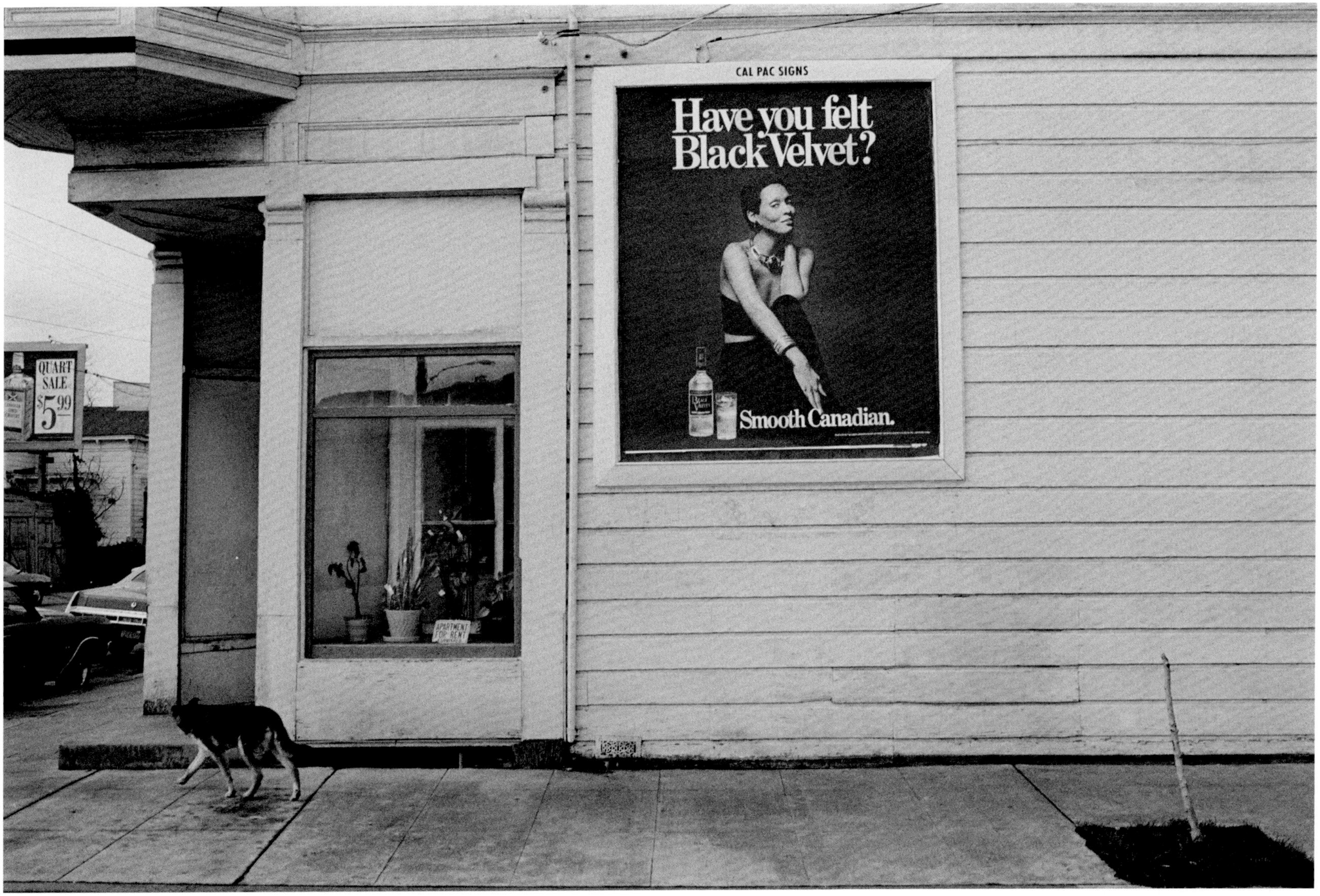
CAL PAC SIGNS
Have you felt Black Velvet?
Smooth Canadian.
QUART SALE
$5.99
APARTMENT FOR RENT

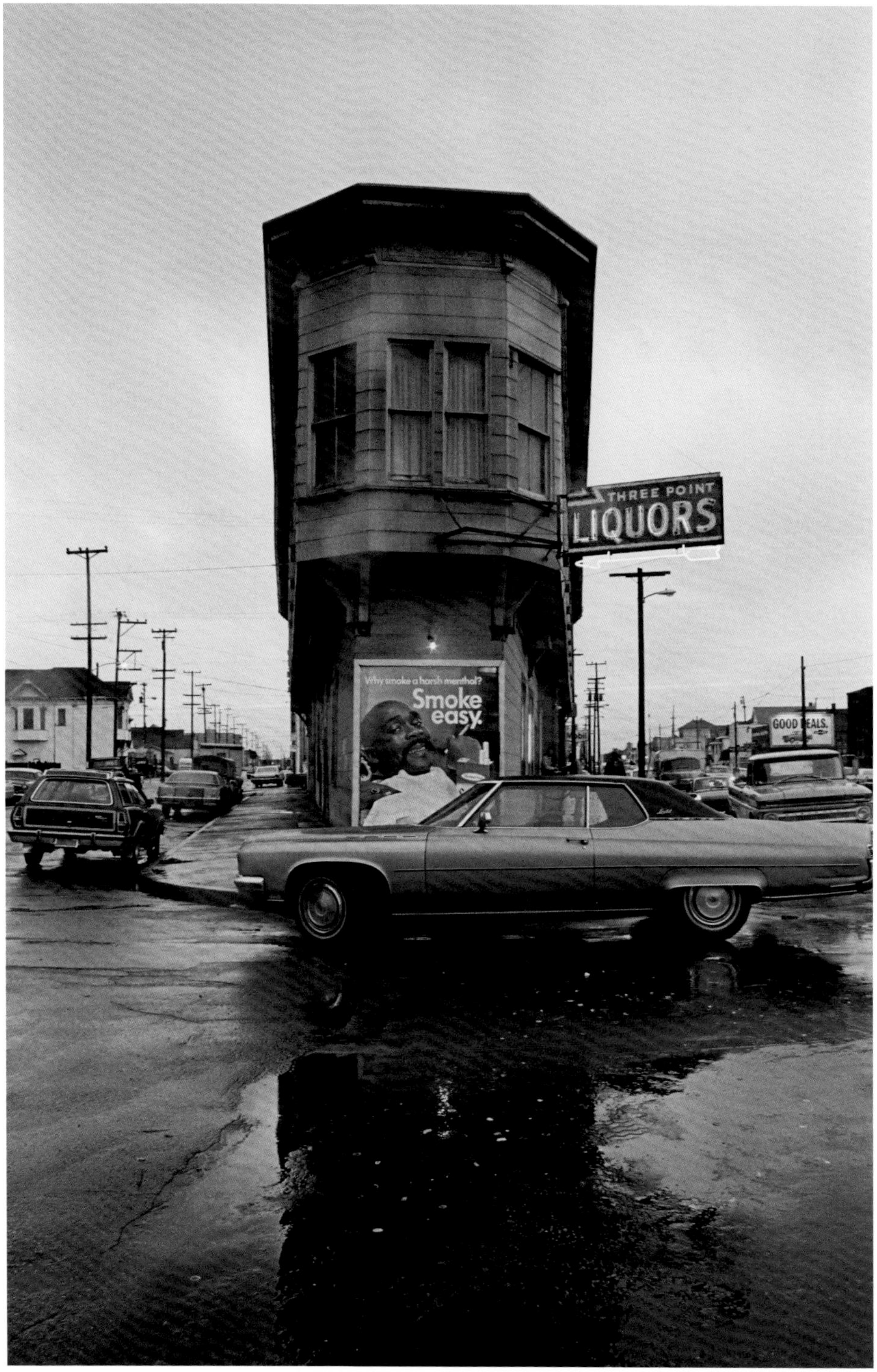
THREE POINT
LIQUORS
Why smoke a harsh menthol?
Smoke
easy.
GOOD DEALS

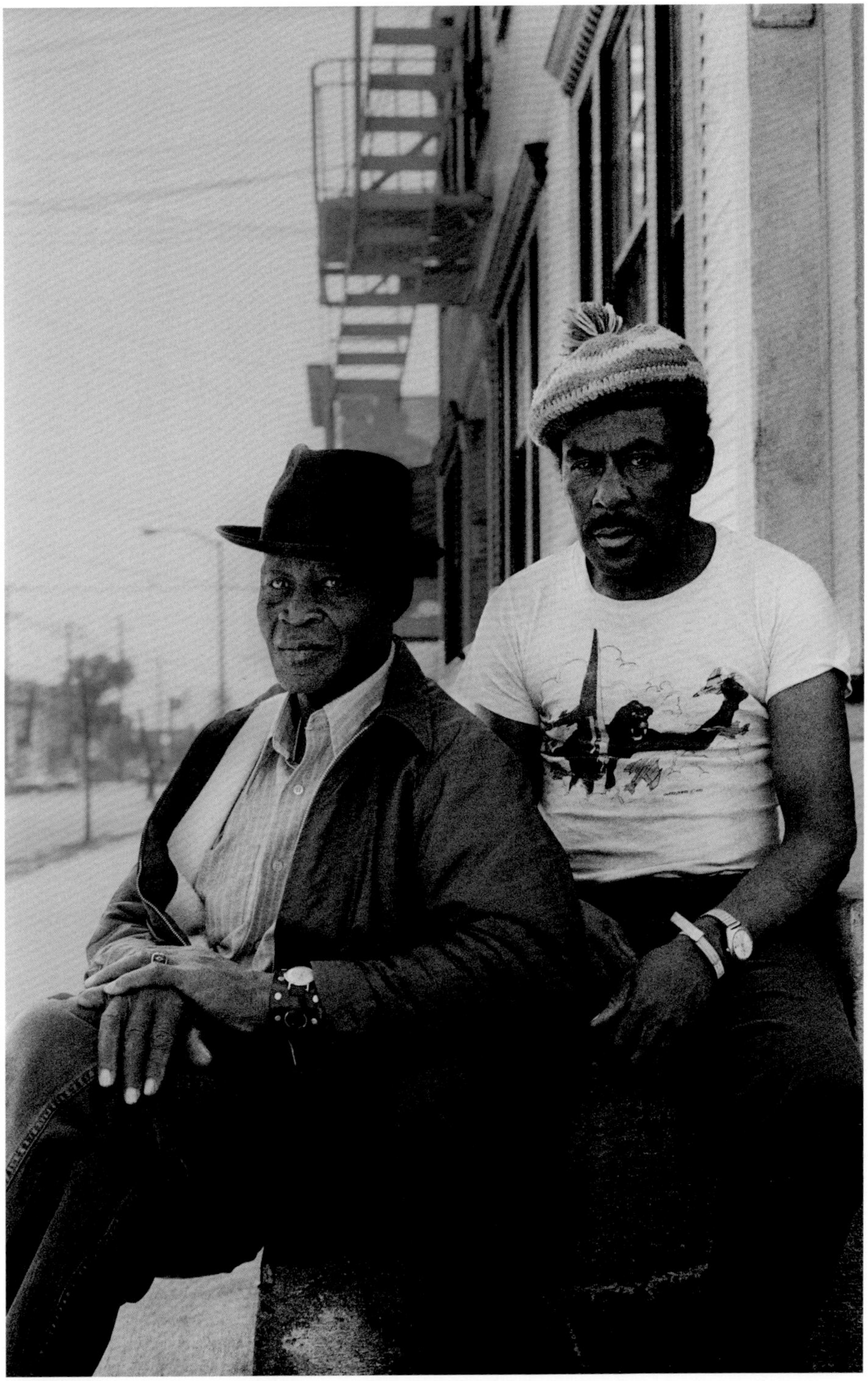

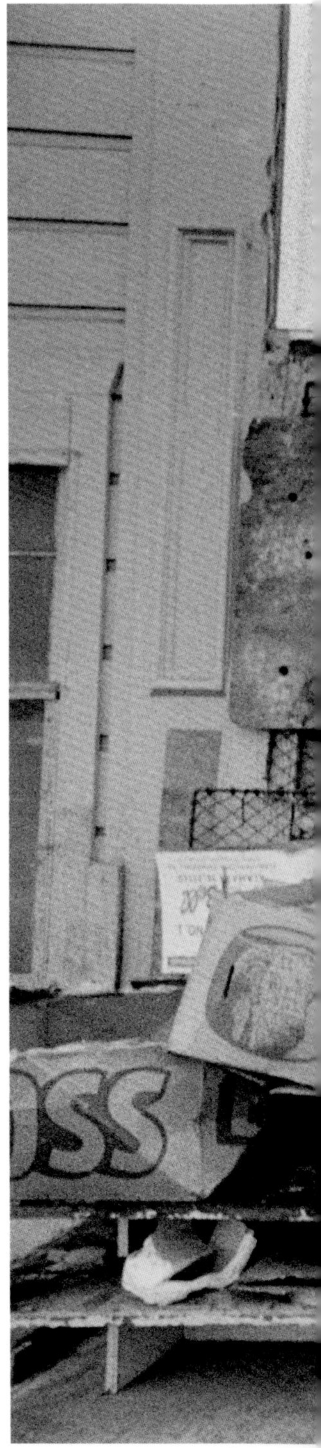

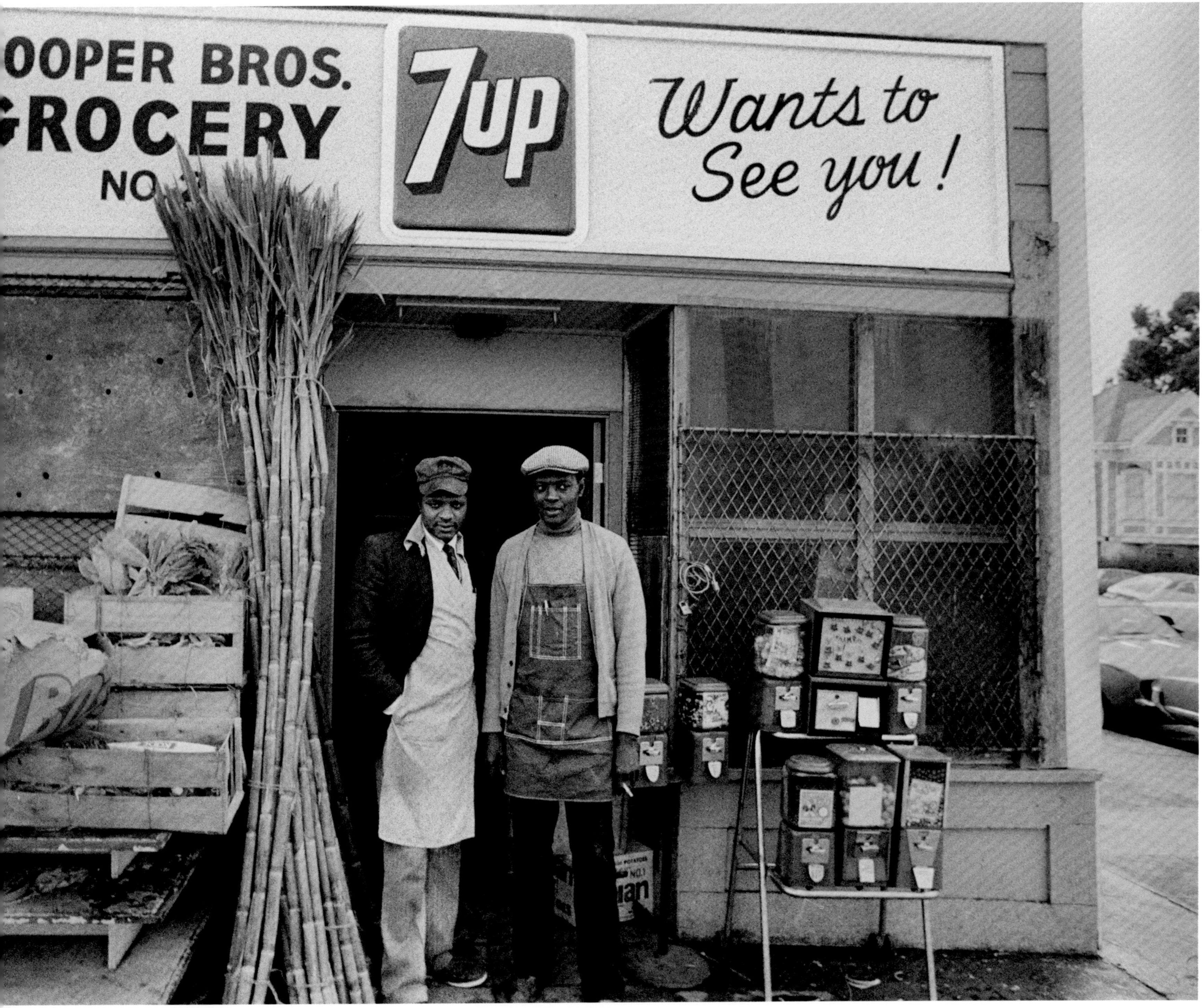
OOPER BROS.
GROCERY
NO
7up
Wants to
See you!

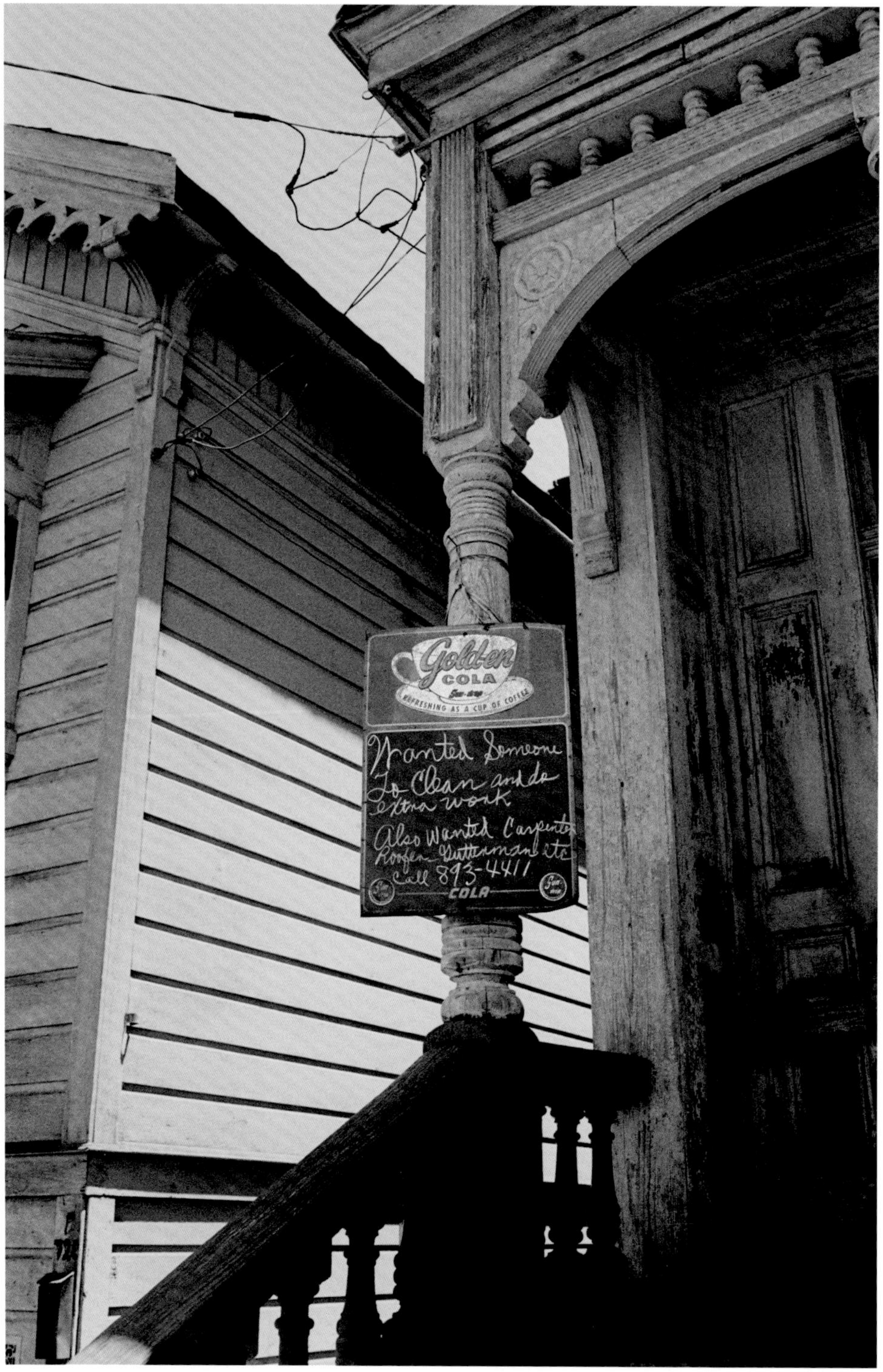
Gold-en
COLA
REFRESHING AS A CUP OF COFFEE
Wanted Someone
To Clean and do
extra work
Also Wanted Carpenter
Roofer Gutterman etc
Call 893-4411
COLA

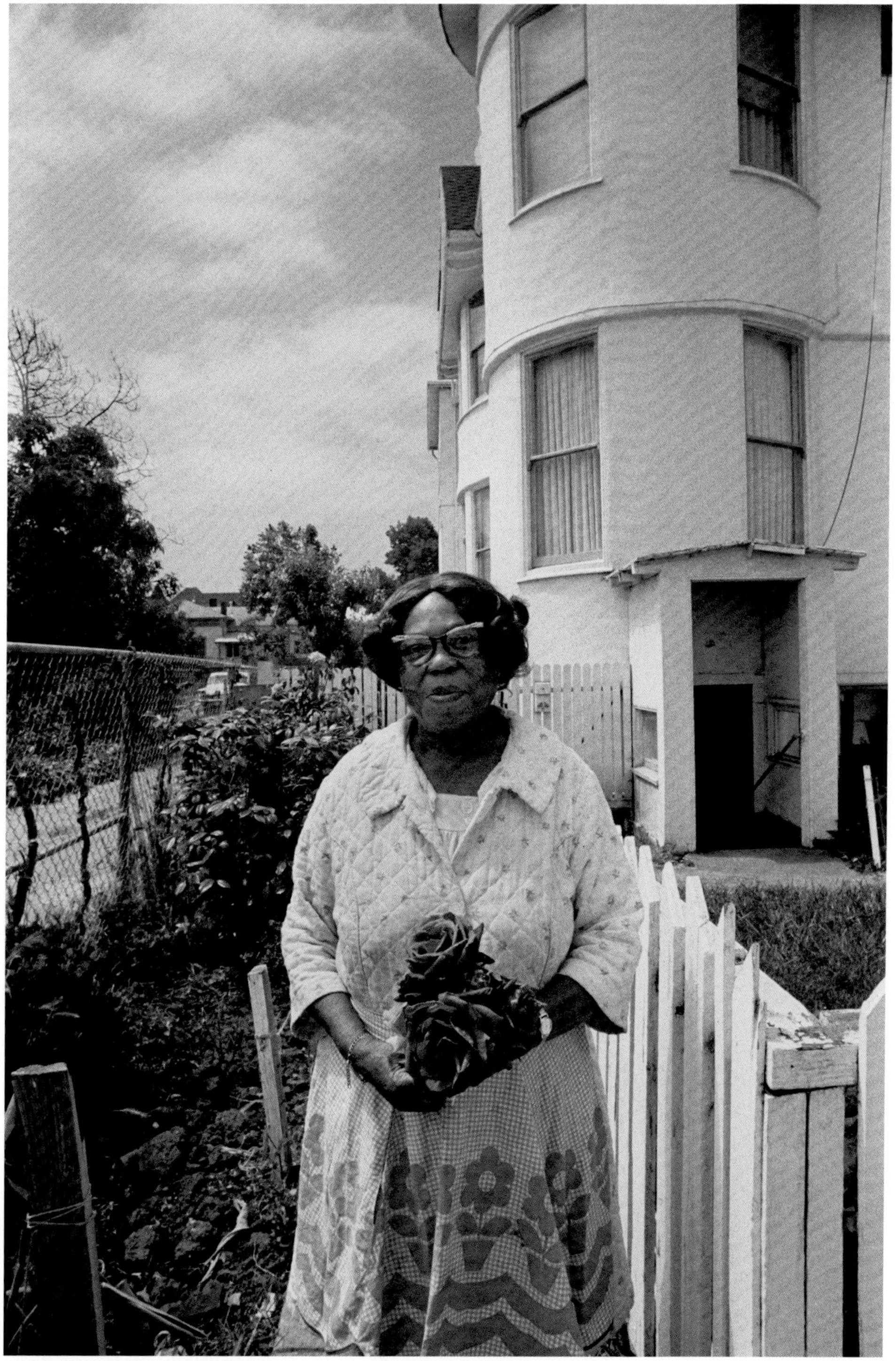

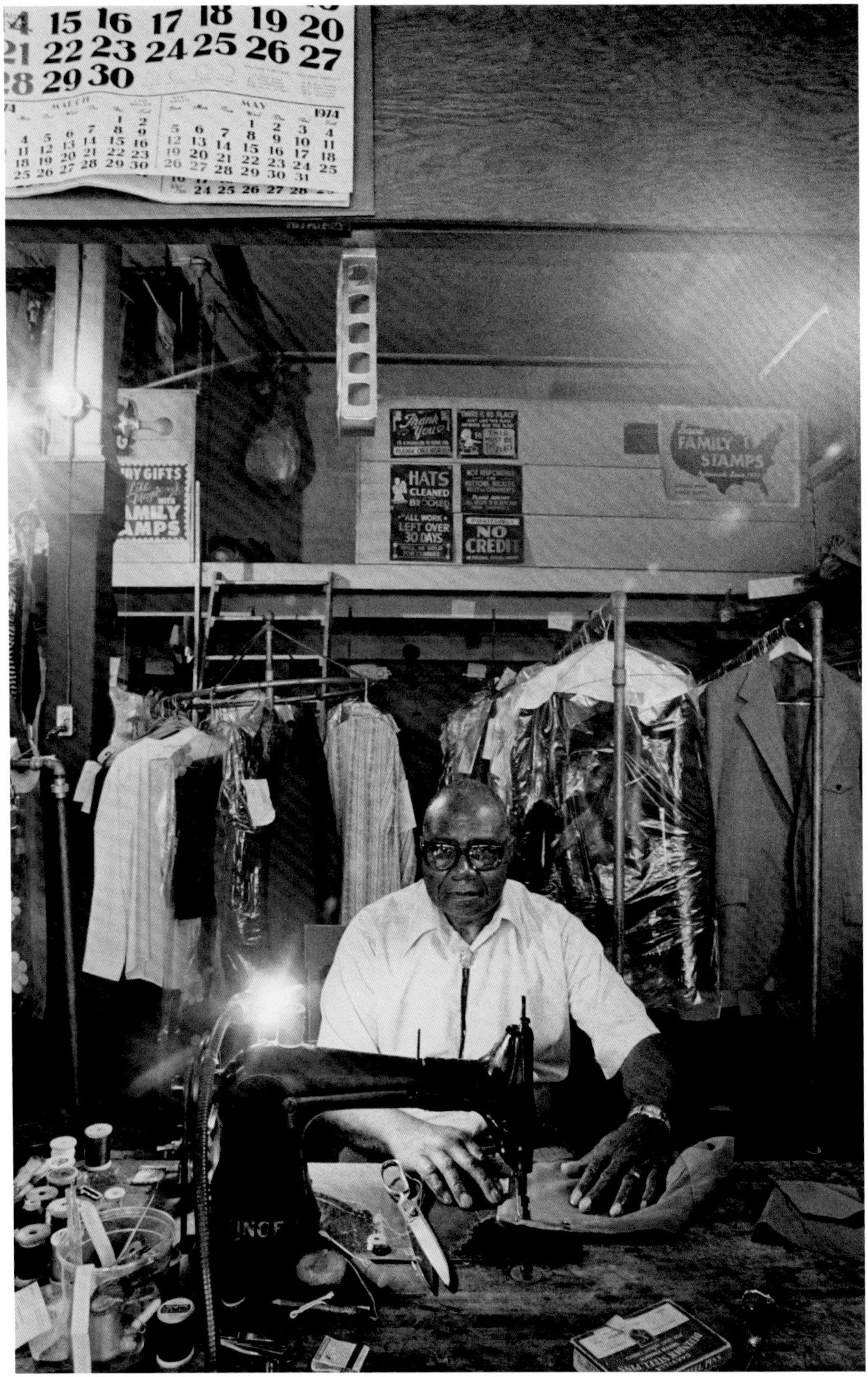
MAY
1974
HATS
CLEANED
ALL WORK
LEFT OVER
30 DAYS
NO
CREDIT
FAMILY
STAMPS

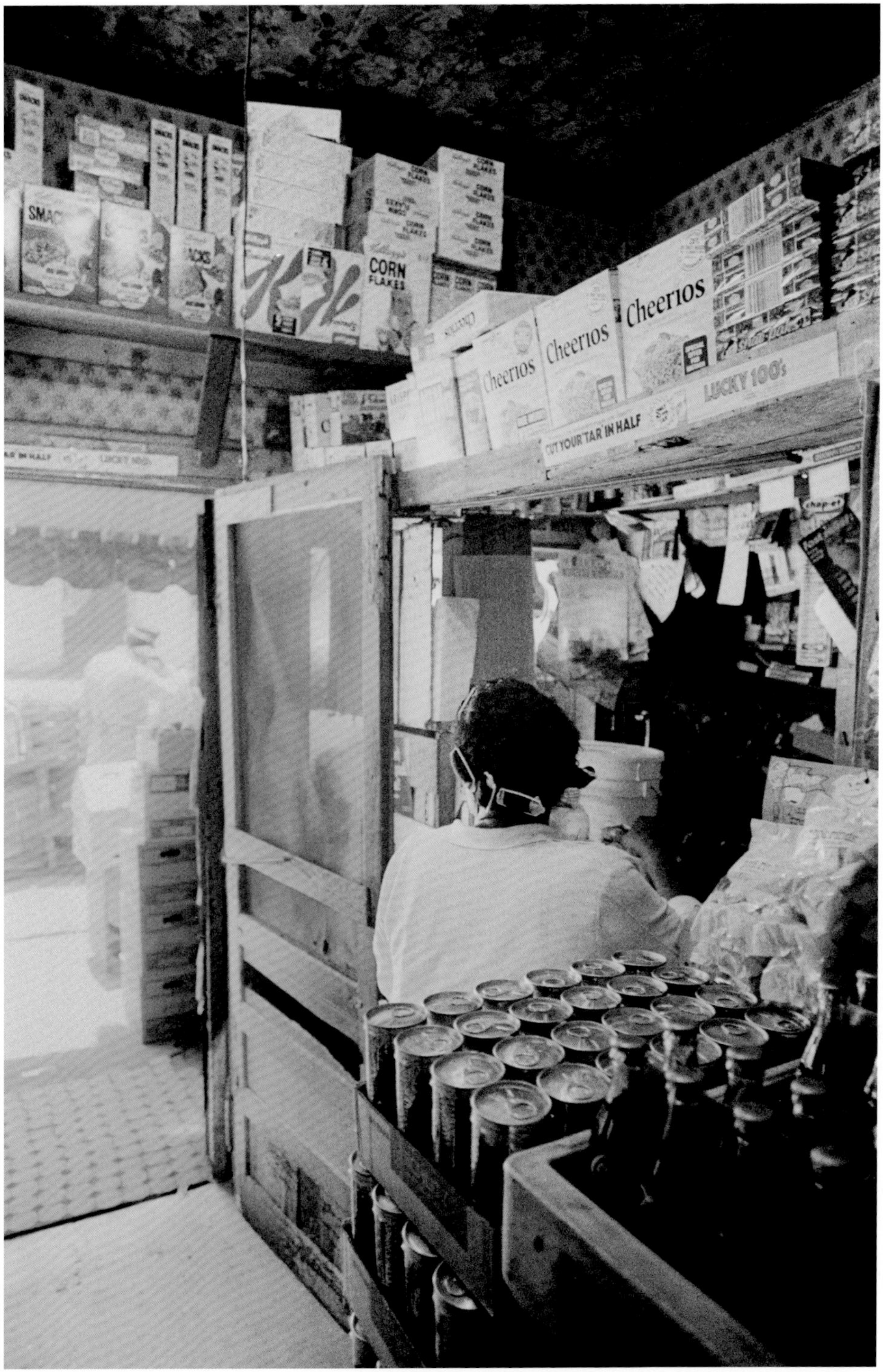
CORN
FLAKES
Cheerios
Cheerios
Cheerios
LUCKY 100's
CUT YOUR 'TAR' IN HALF

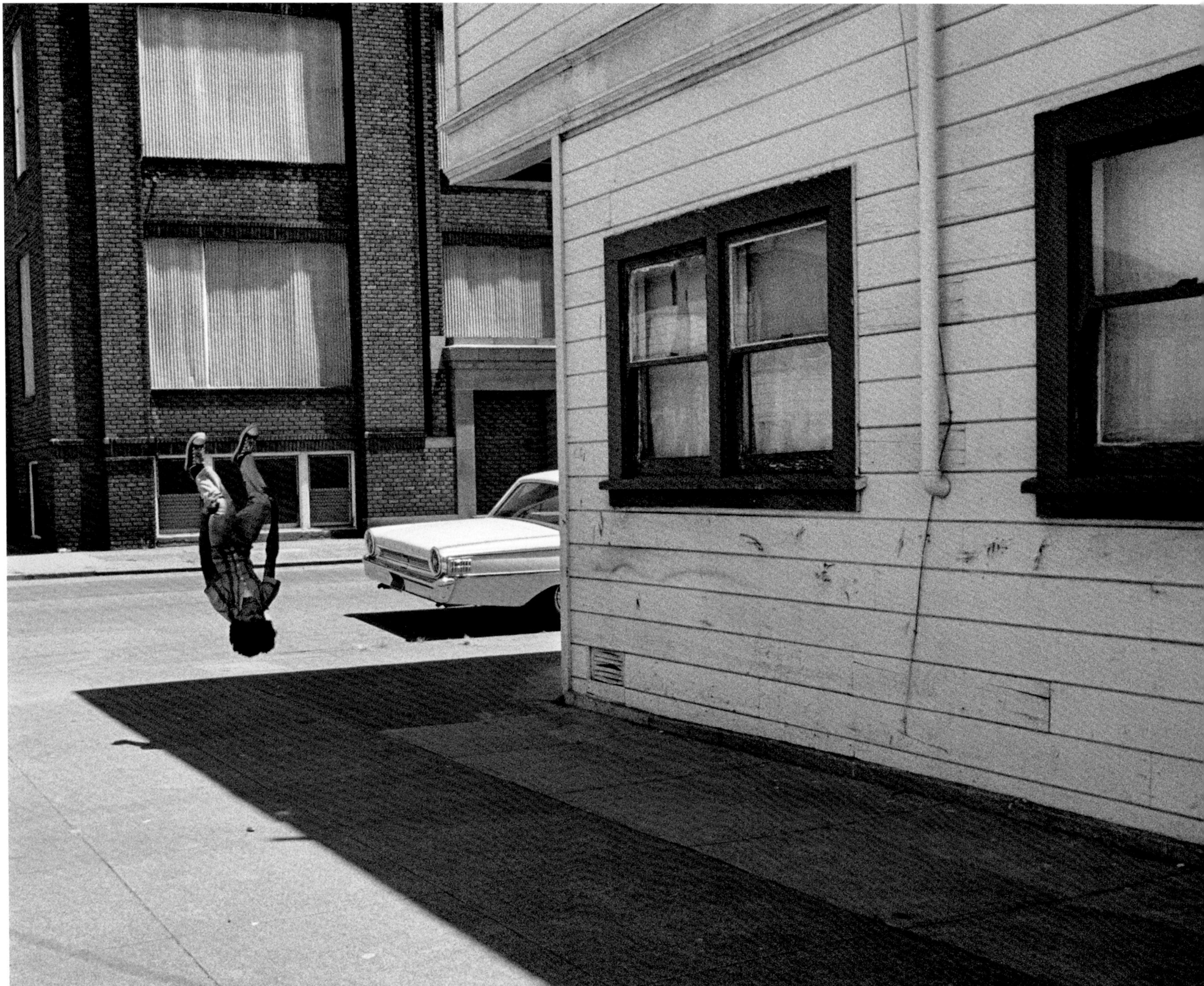

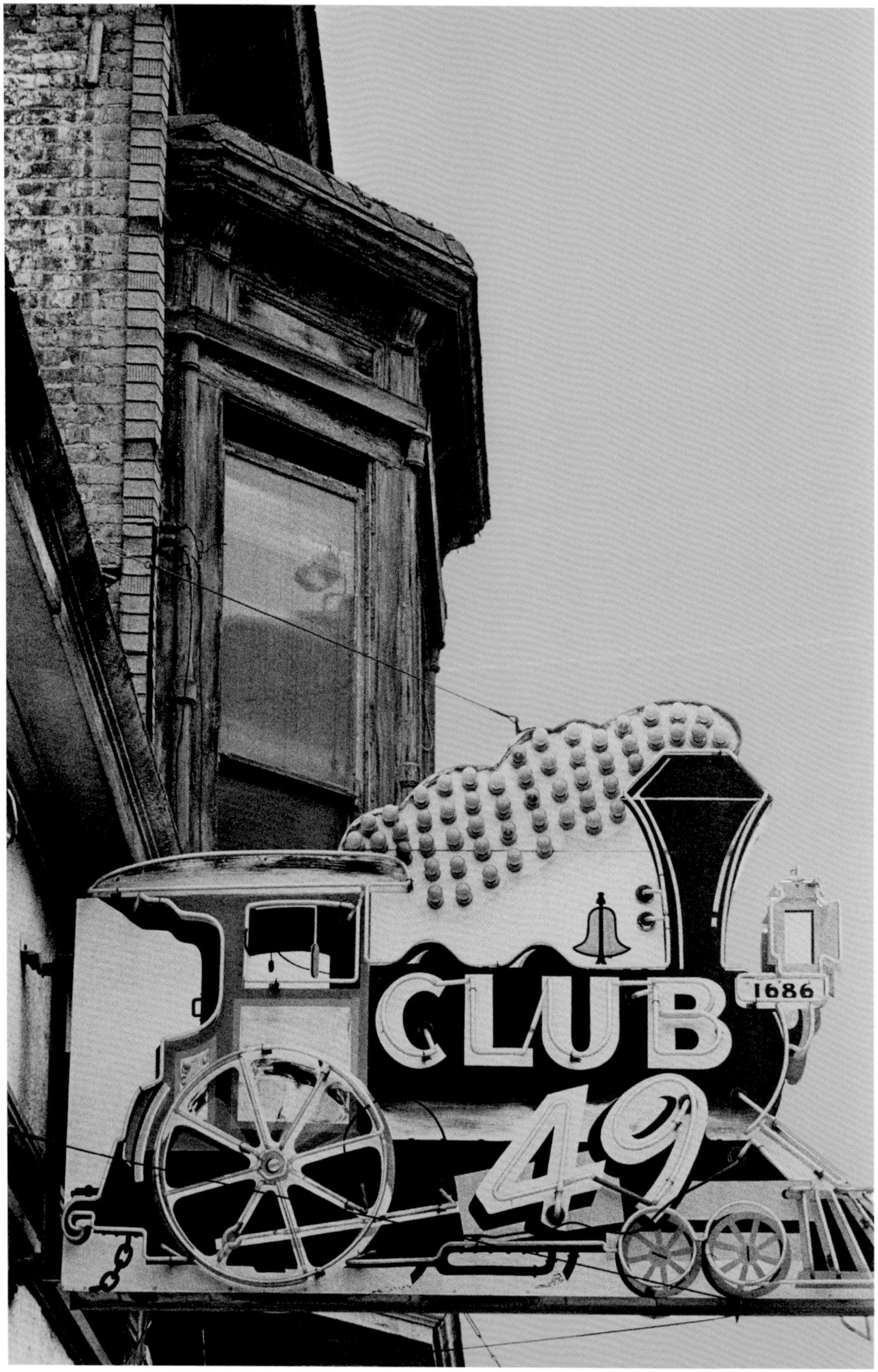
CLUB
49
1686

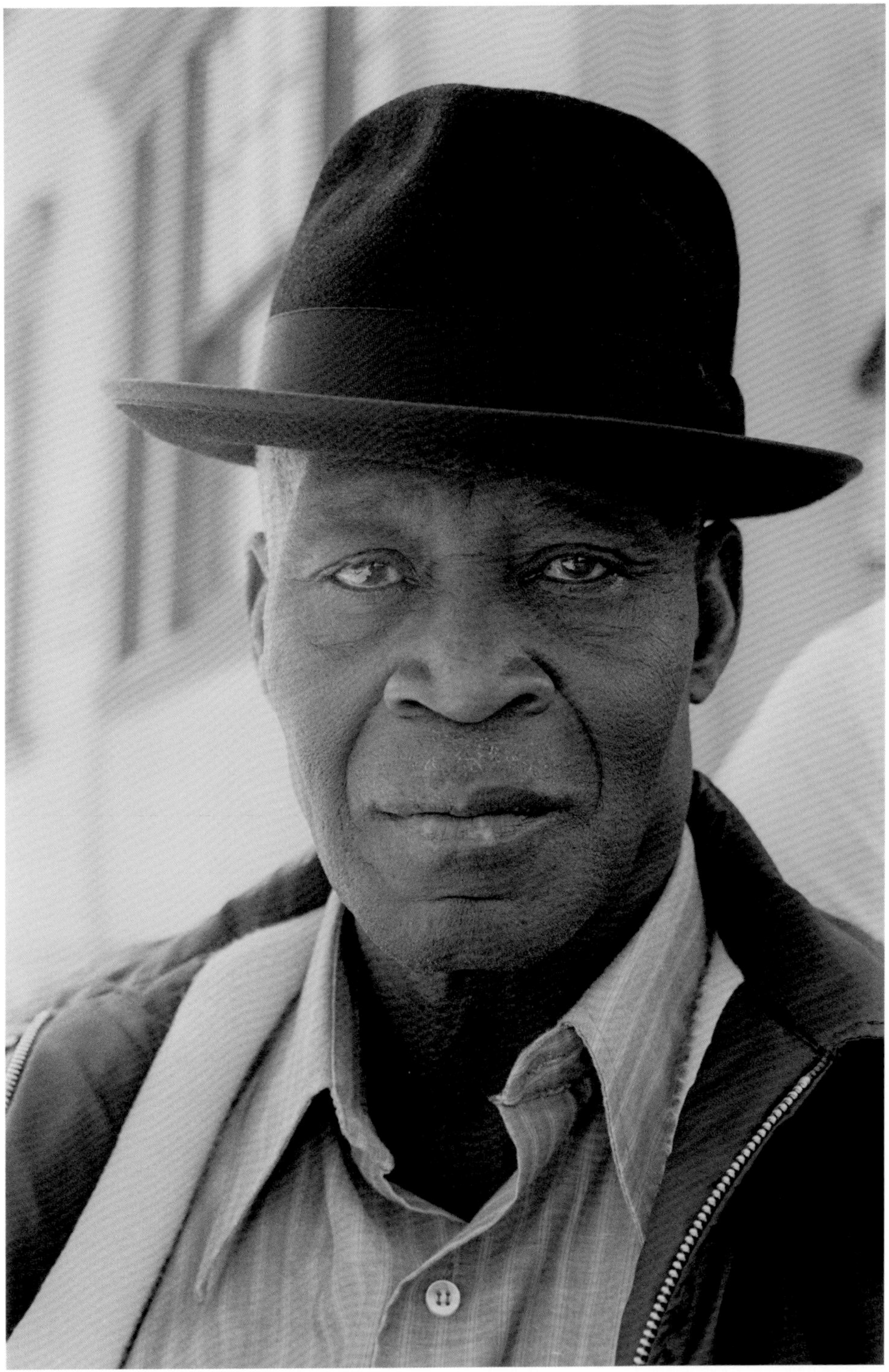

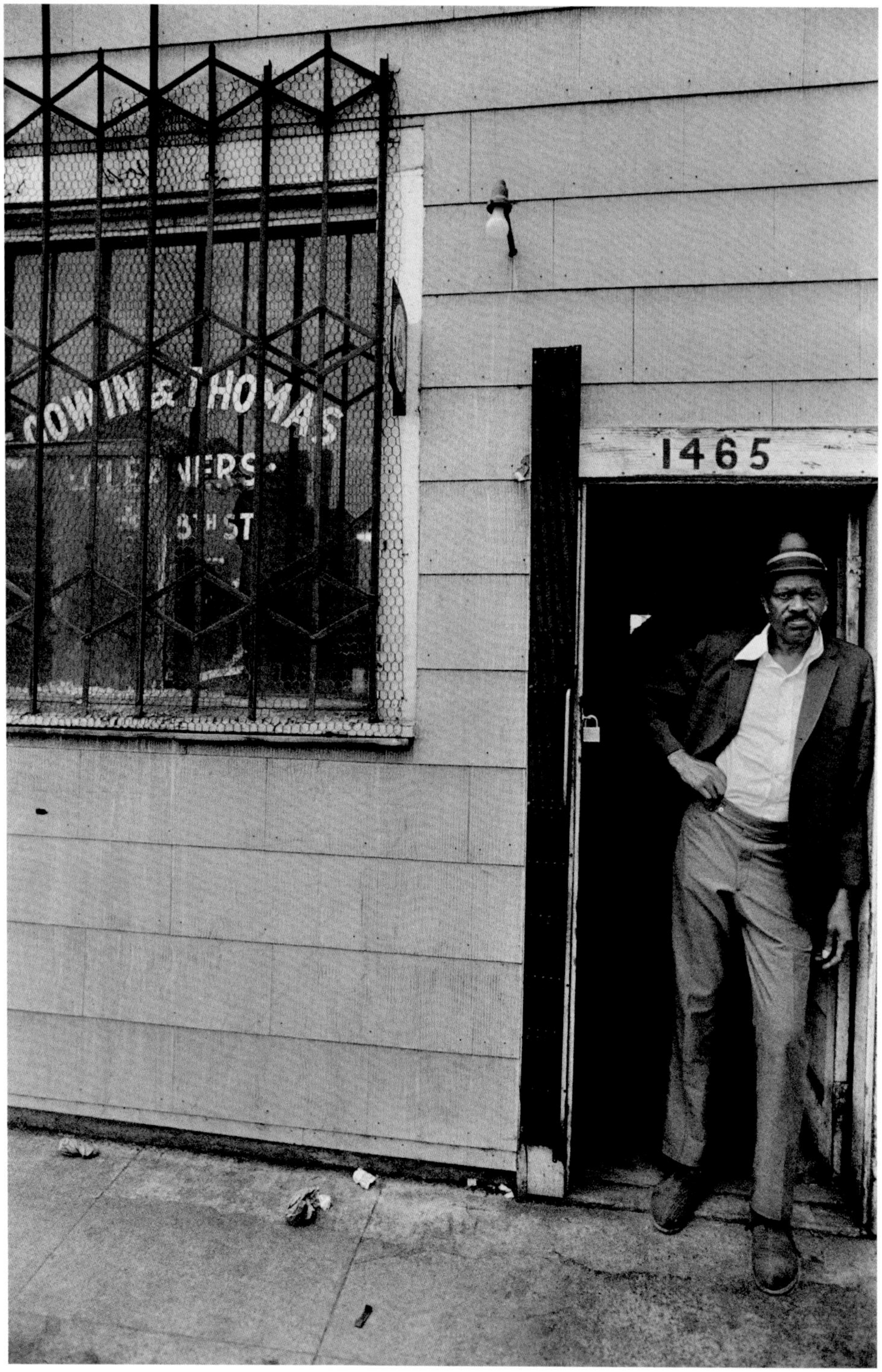
COWIN & THOMAS
1465

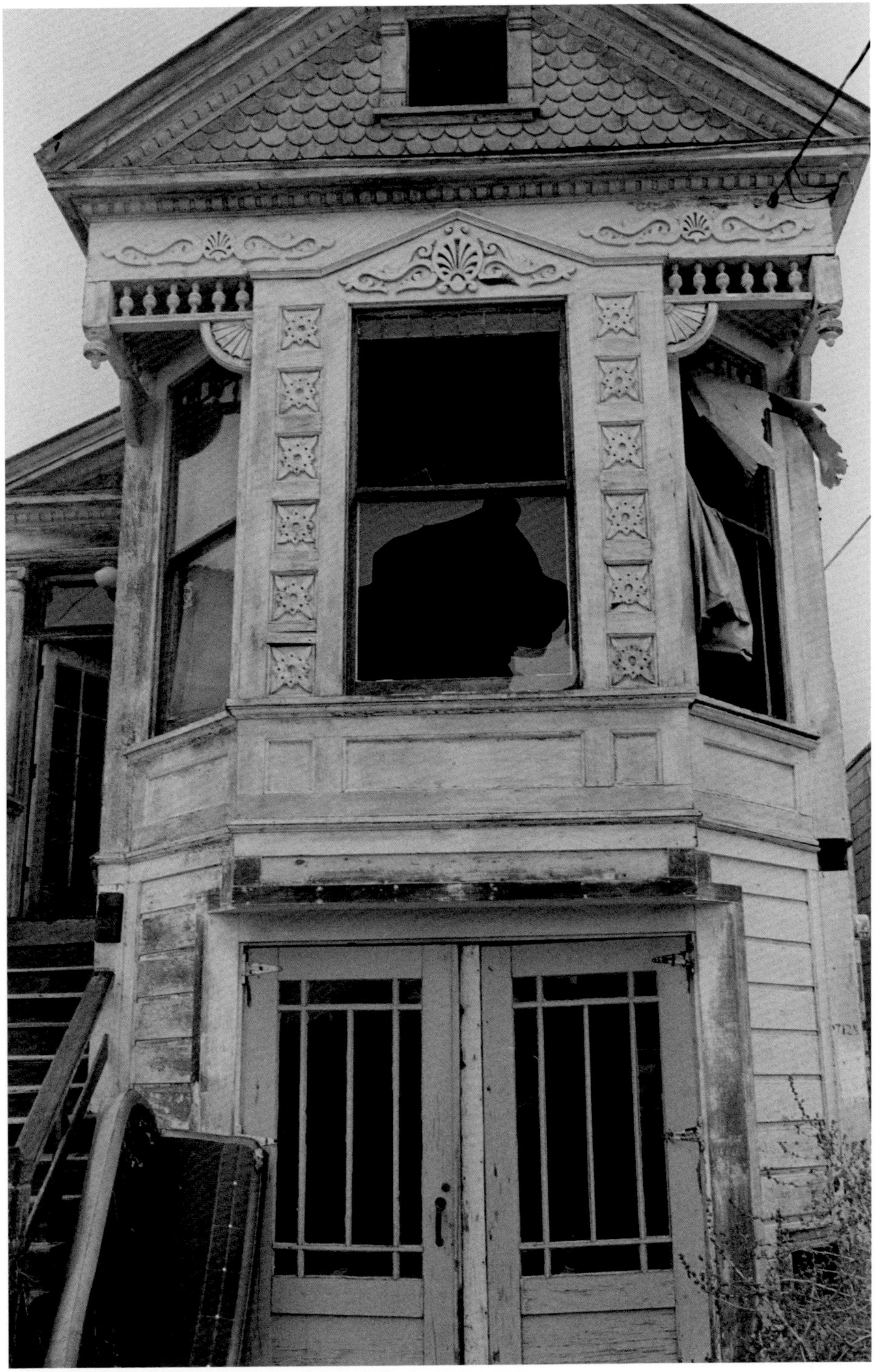

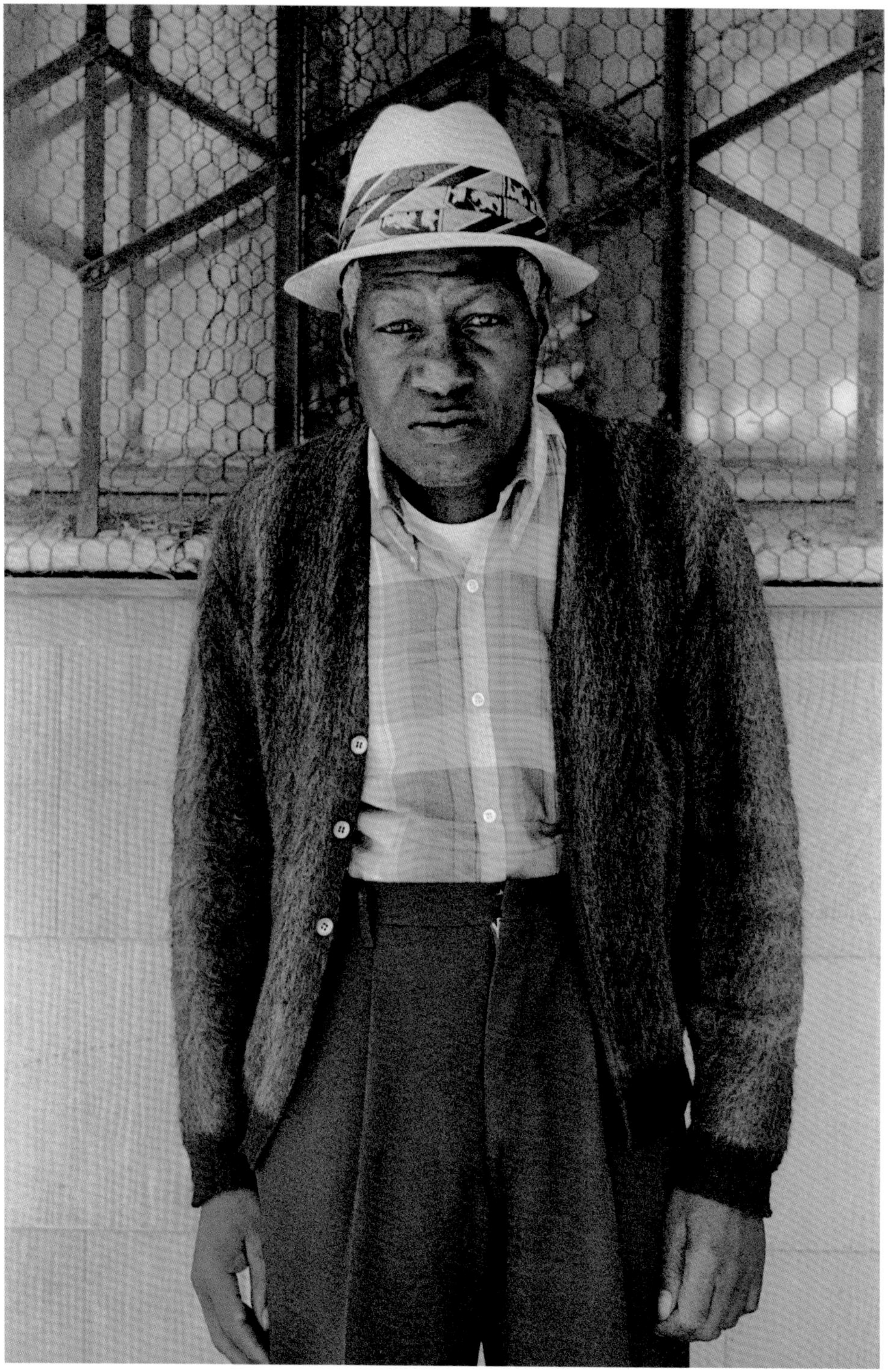

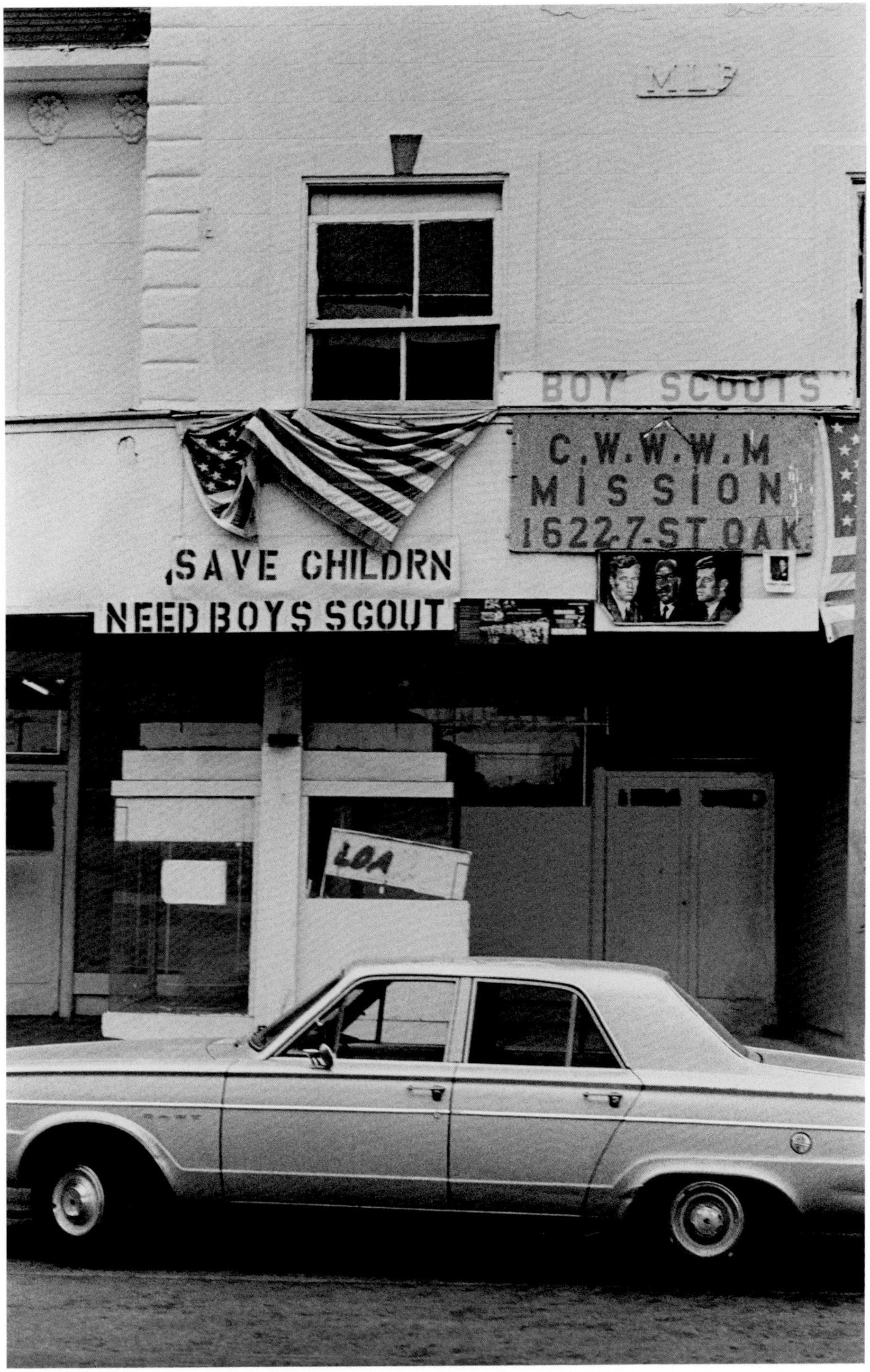
MLF
BOY SCOUTS
C.W.W.W.M
MIS SION
1622-7-ST OAK
SAVE CHILDRN
NEED BOYS SCOUT

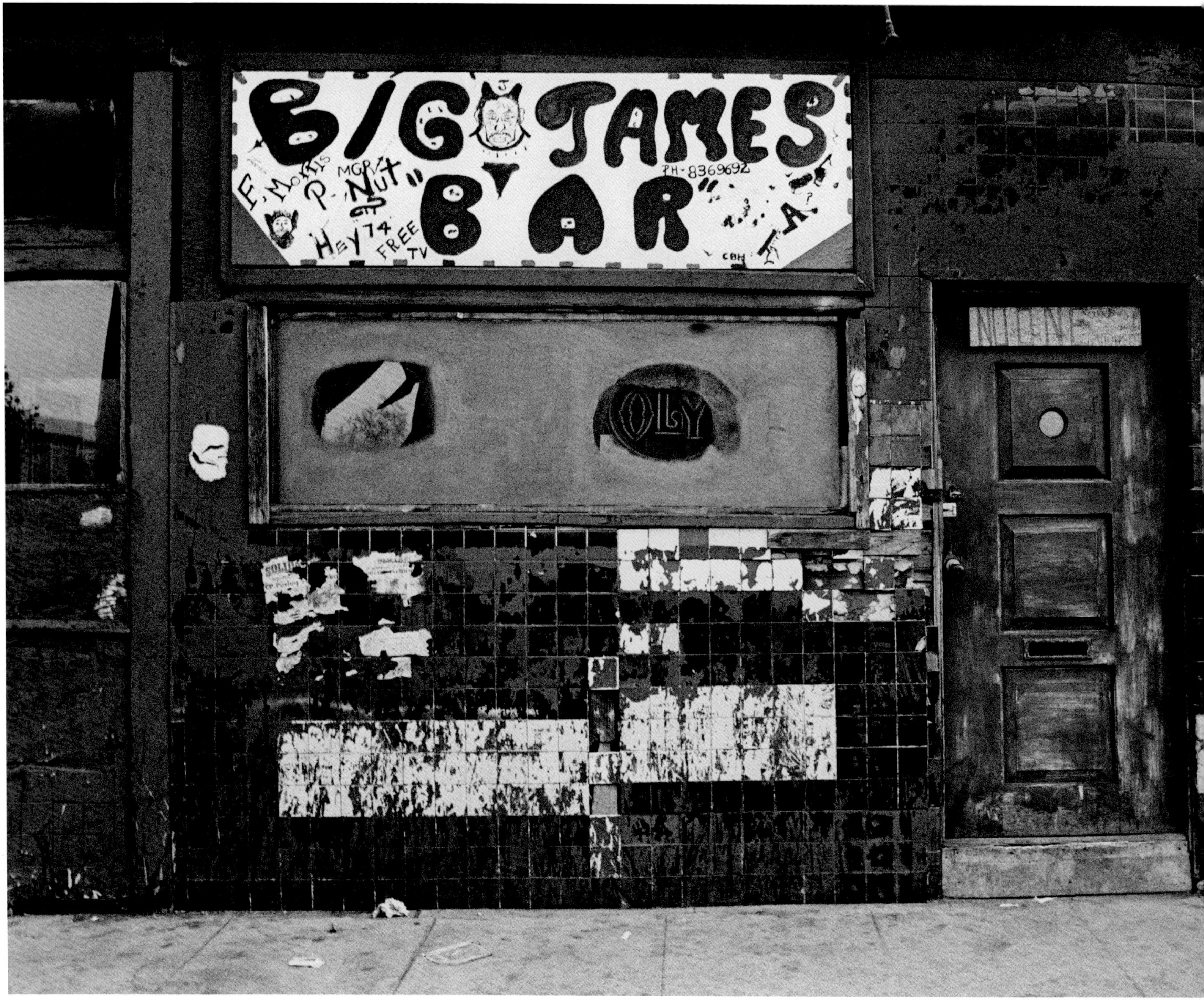
BIG JAMES
"BAR"
PH-8369692
MGR P-NUT
HEY 74
FREE TV
CBH
OLY

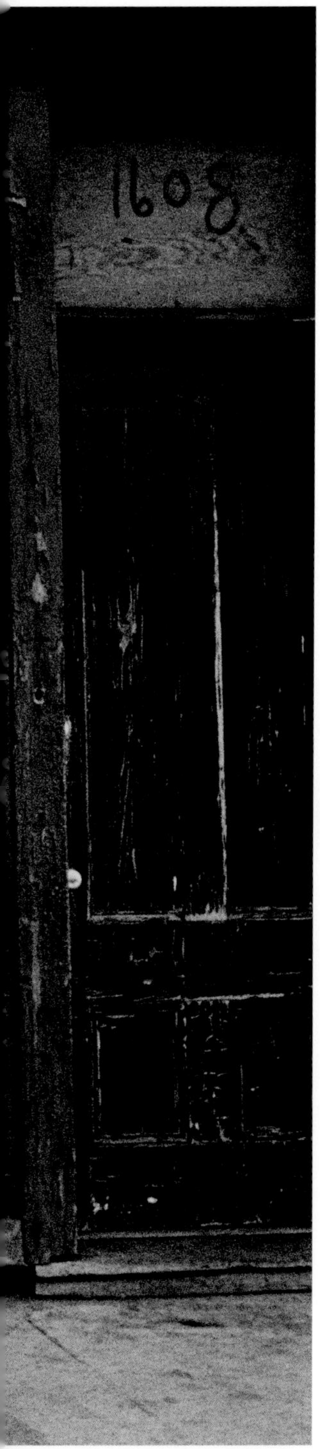
1608

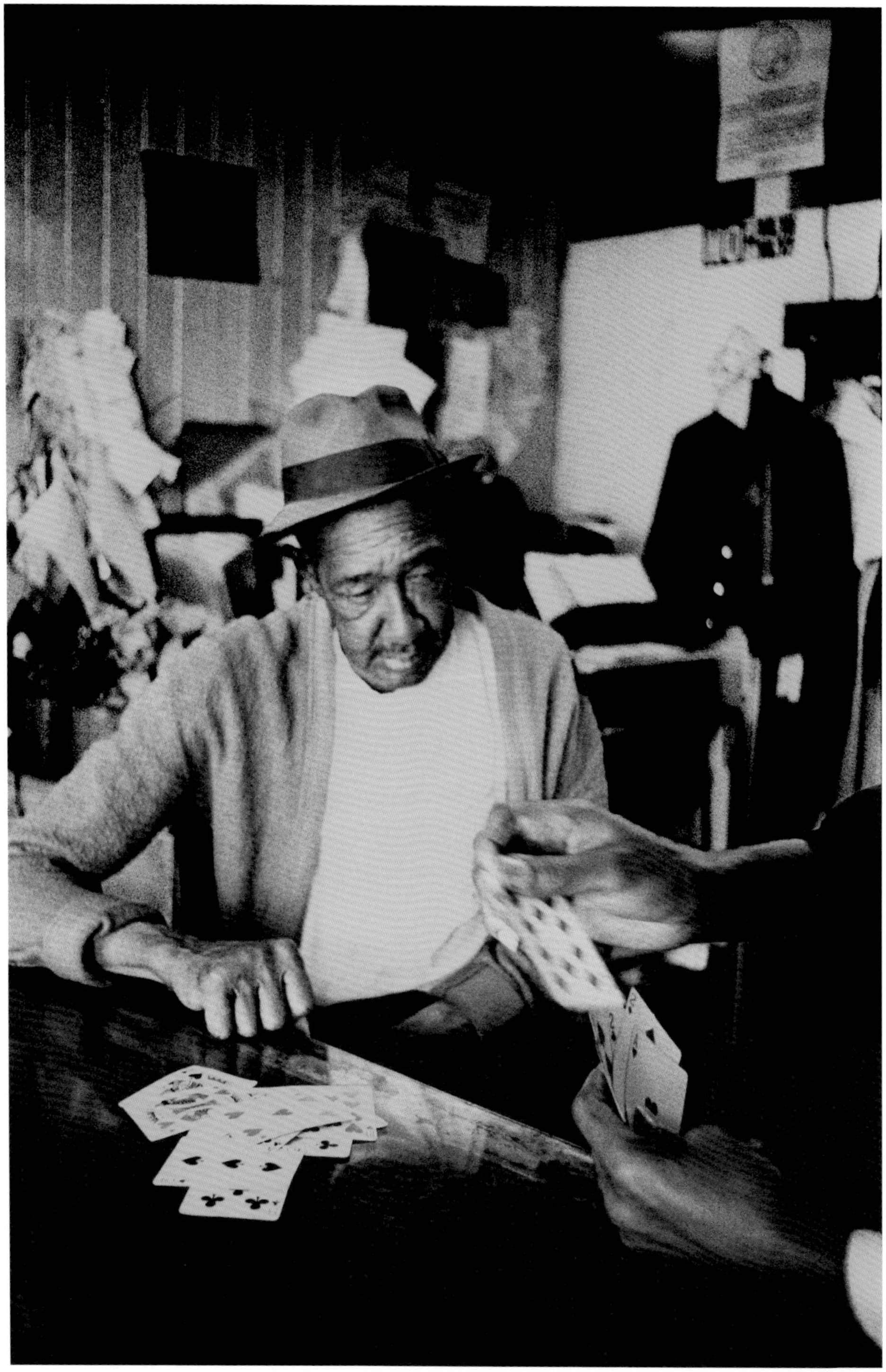

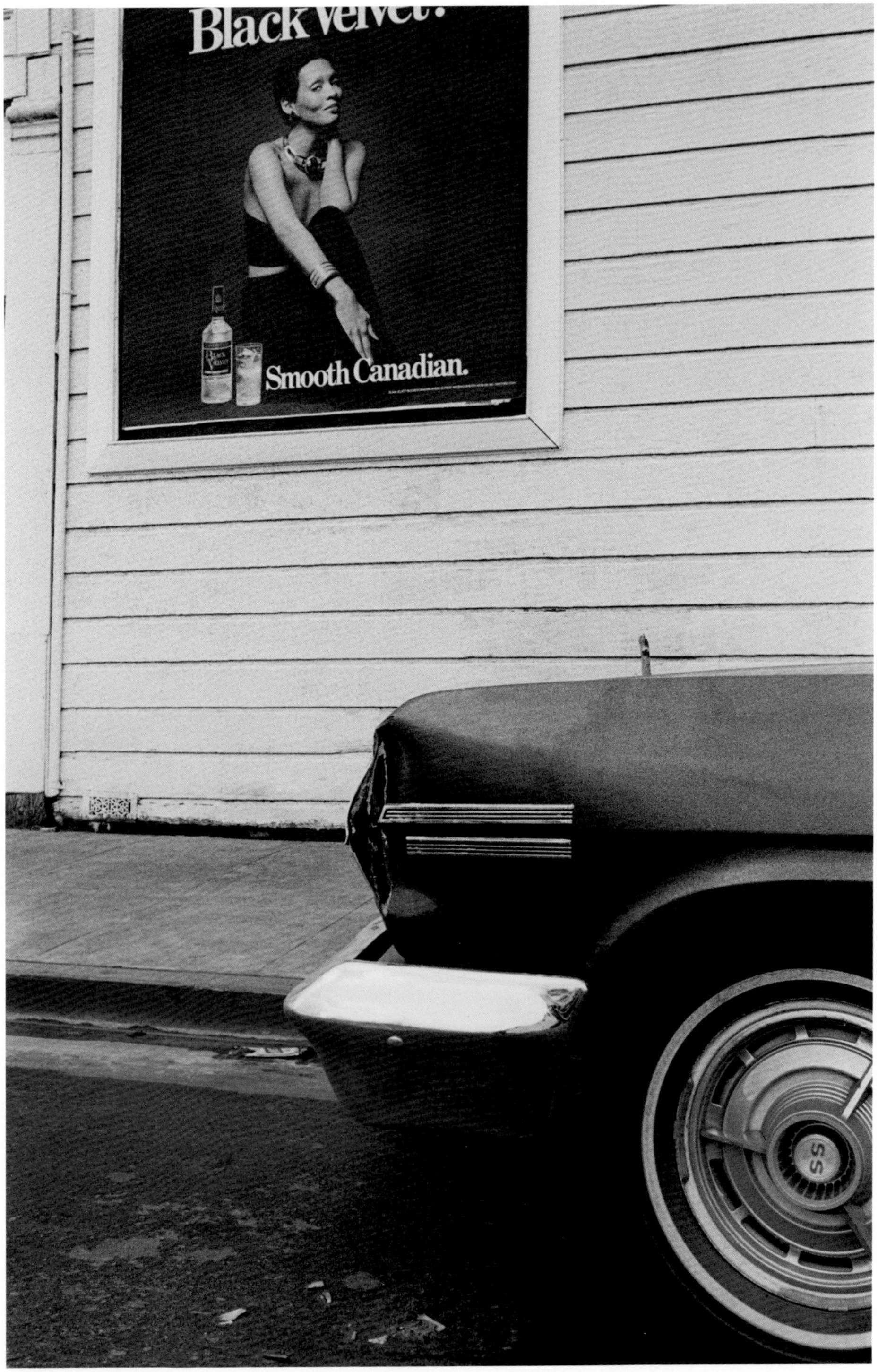
Black Velvet.
Smooth Canadian.
SS

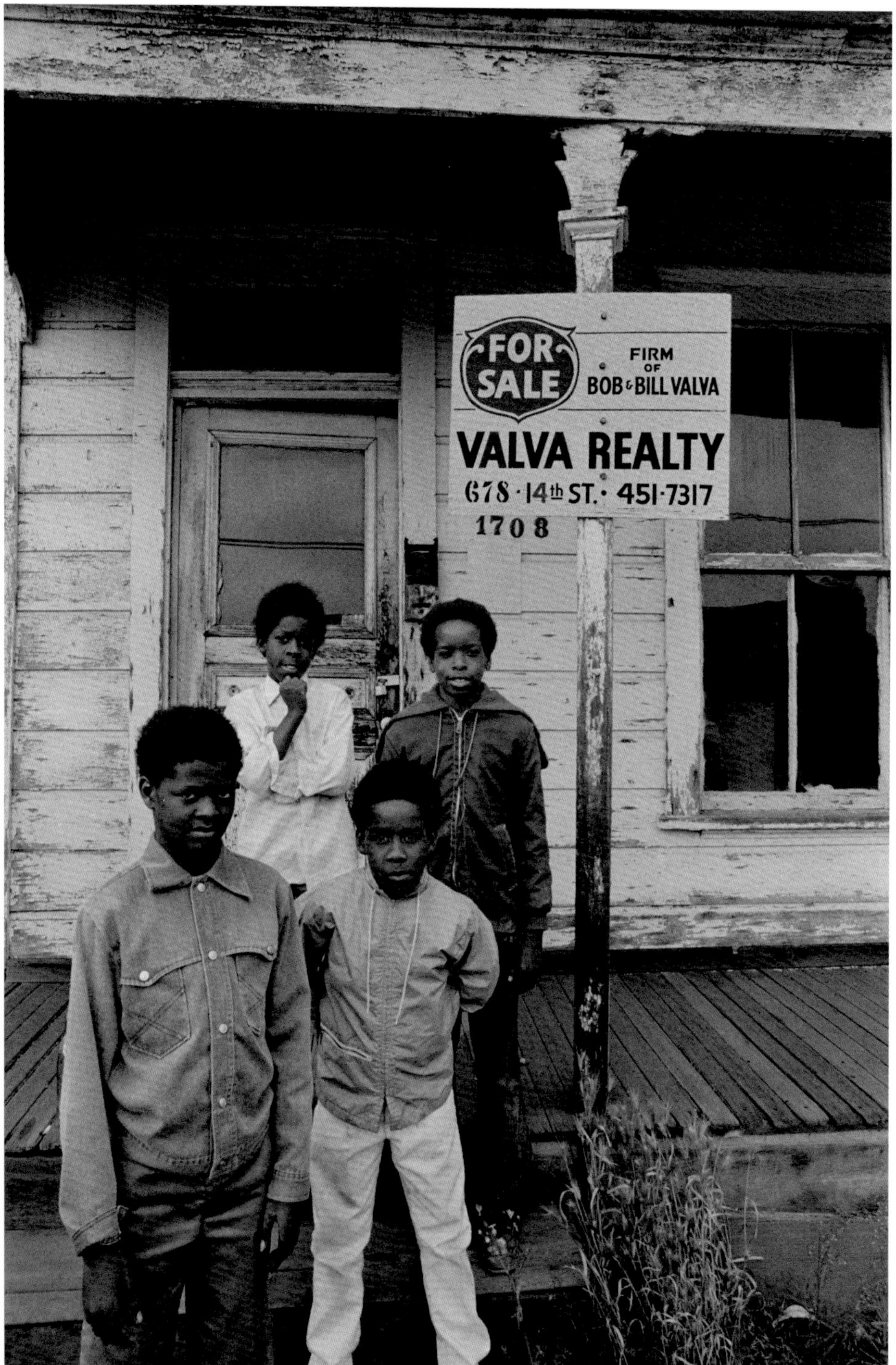
FOR SALE
FIRM OF BOB & BILL VALVA
VALVA REALTY
678 · 14th ST. · 451-7317
1708

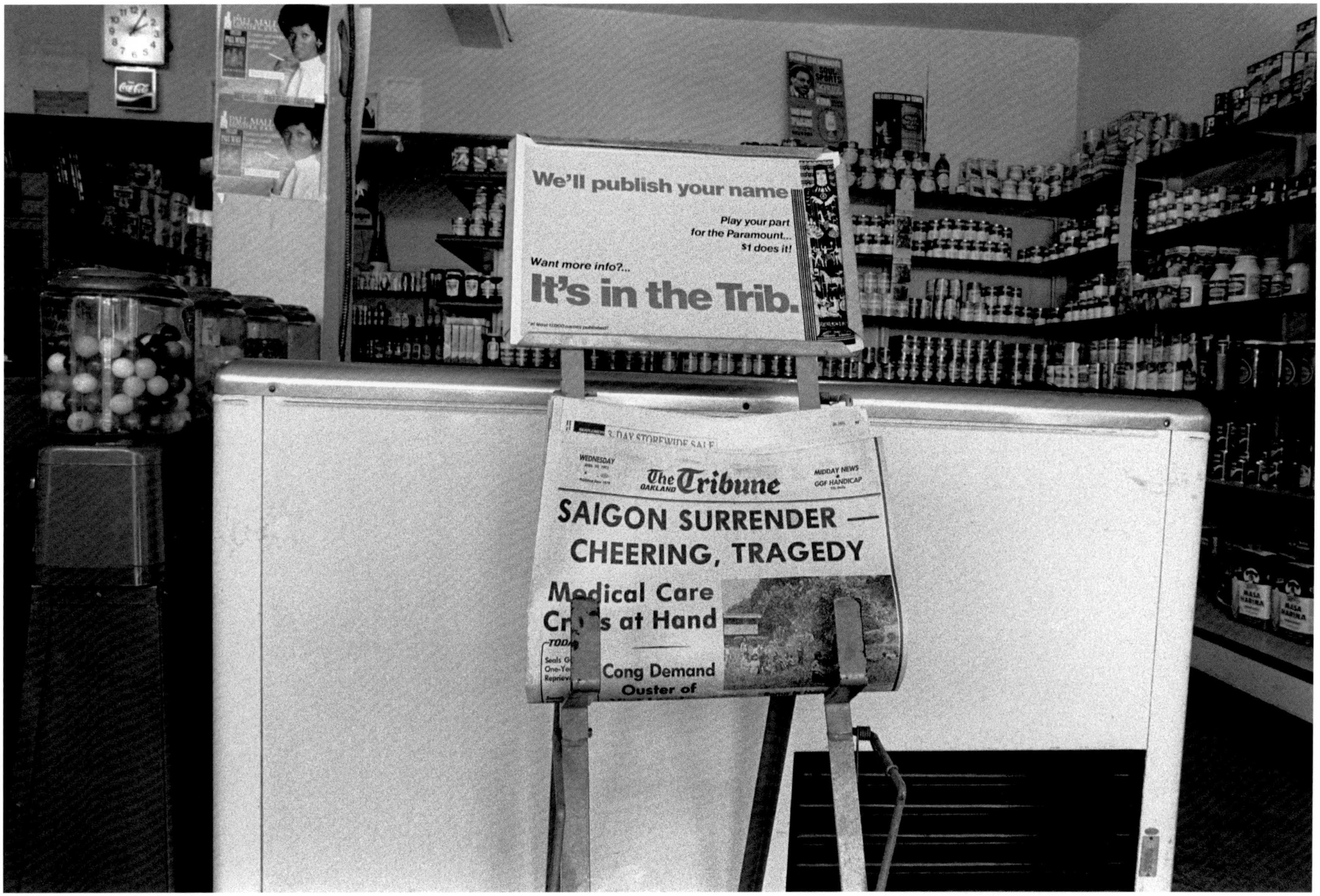
We'll publish your name
Play your part
for the Paramount...
$1 does it!
Want more info?...
It's in the Trib.
3-DAY STOREWIDE SALE
WEDNESDAY
The OAKLAND Tribune
MIDDAY NEWS
GGF HANDICAP
SAIGON SURRENDER —
CHEERING, TRAGEDY
Cong Demand
Ouster of

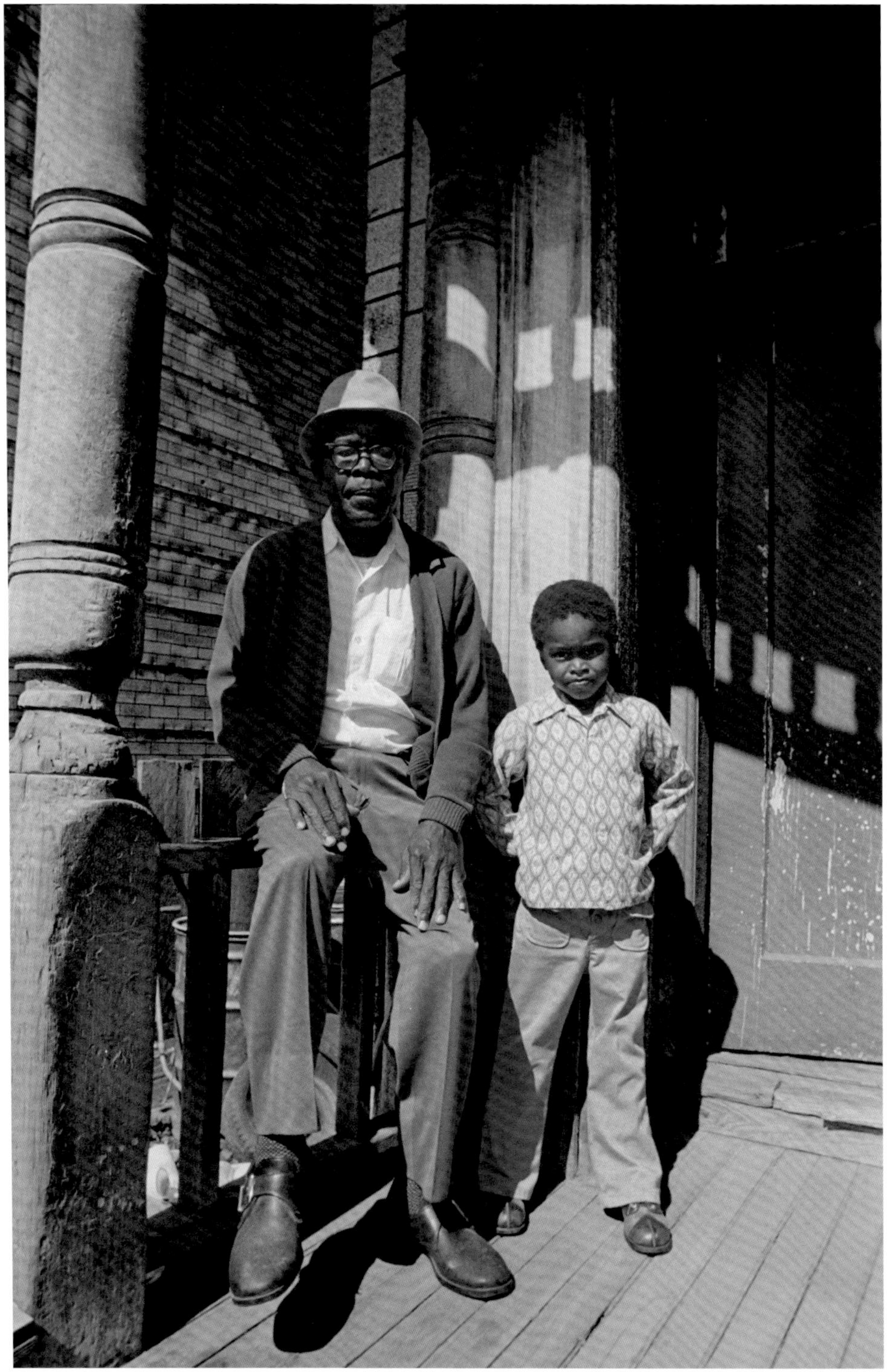

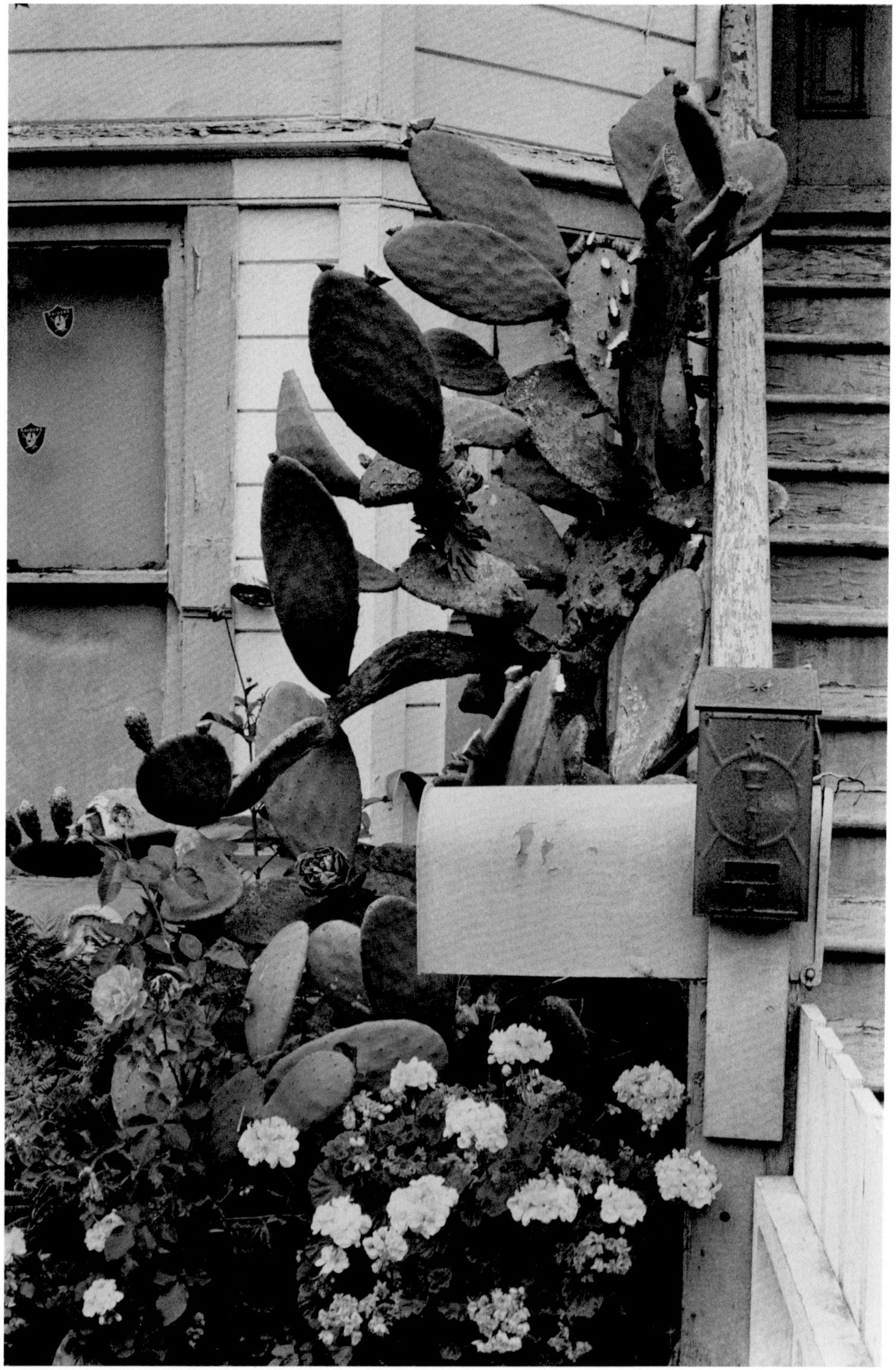

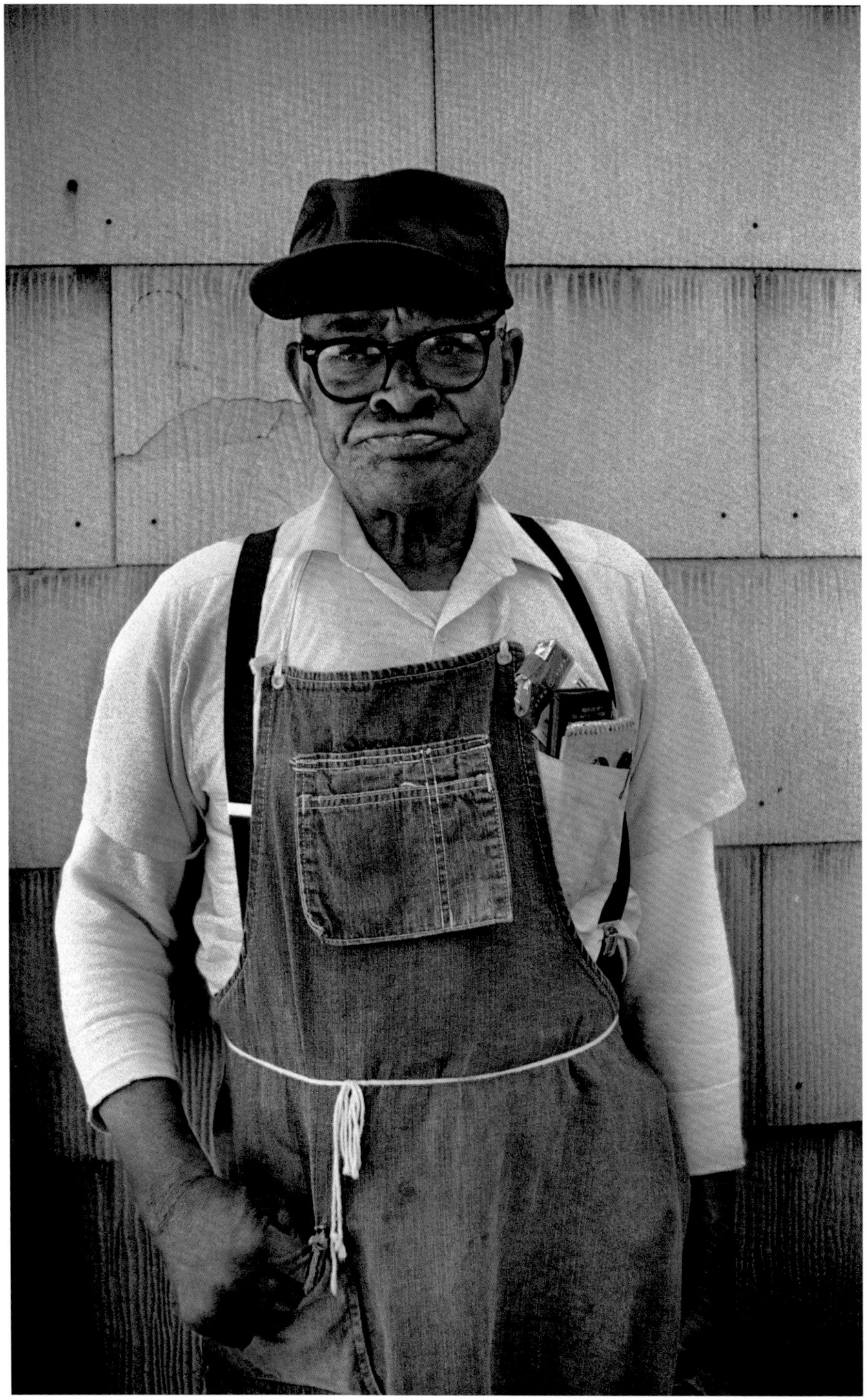

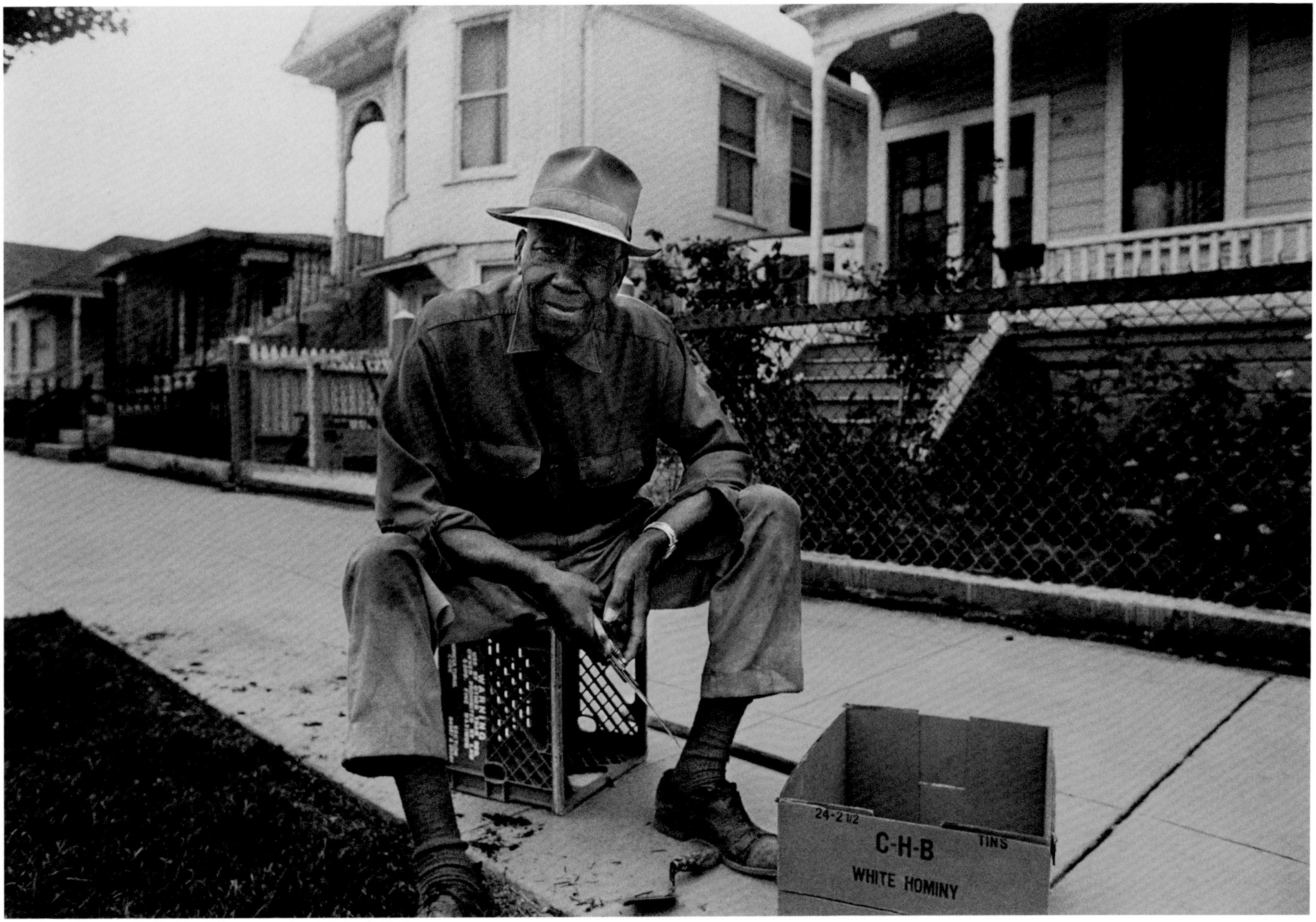
24-2 1/2
C-H-B
TINS
WHITE HOMINY

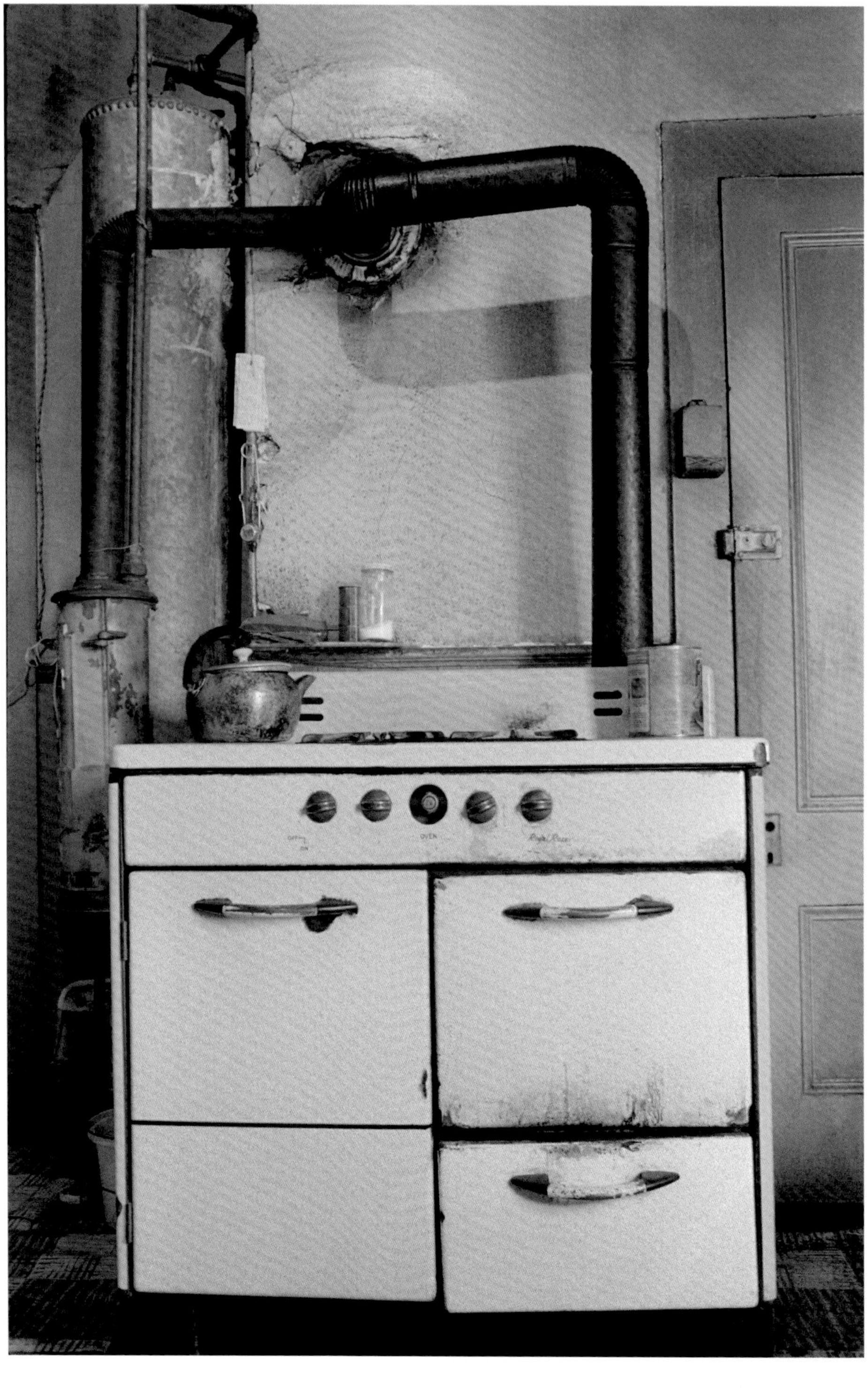

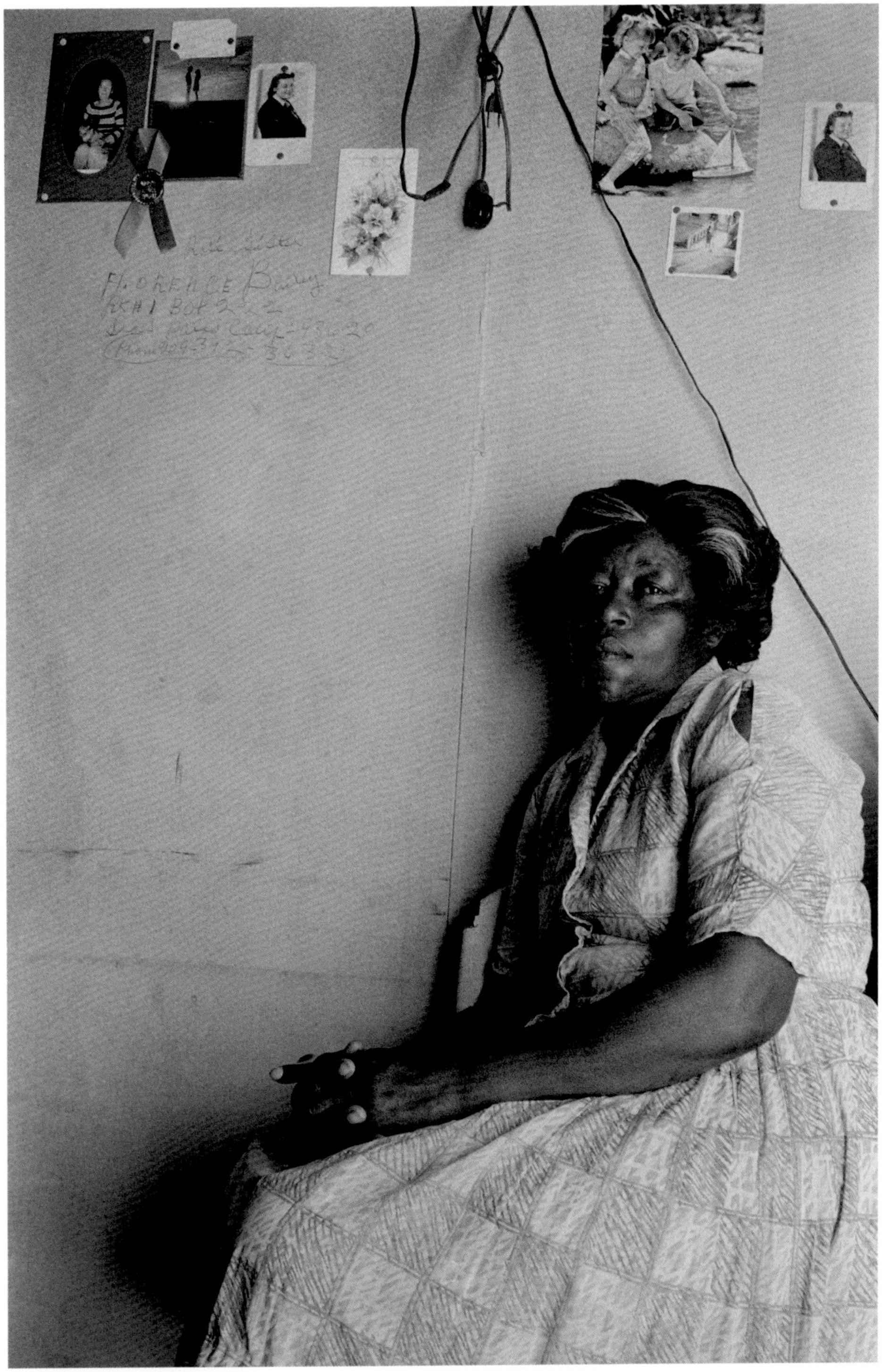

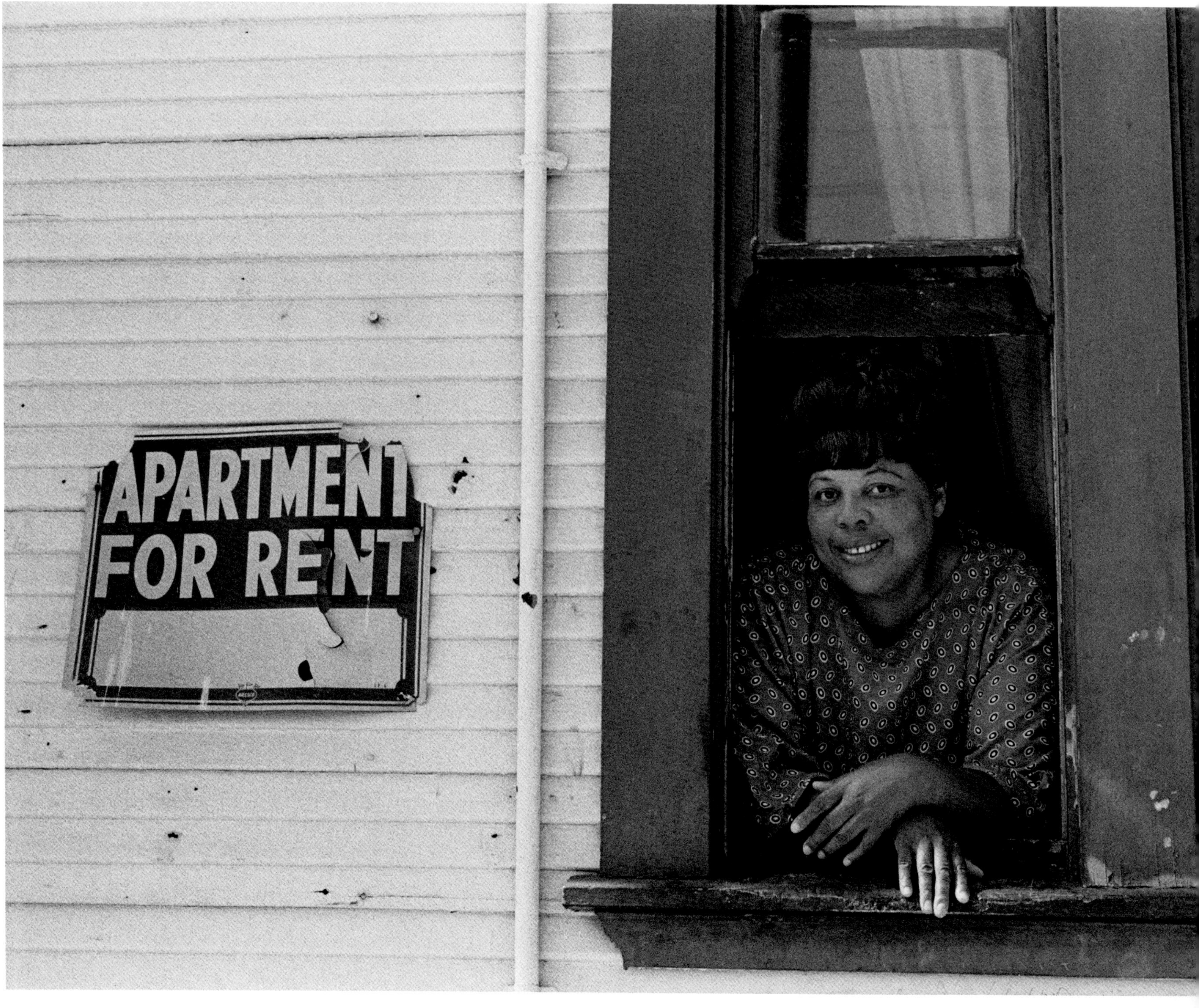
APARTMENT
FOR RENT

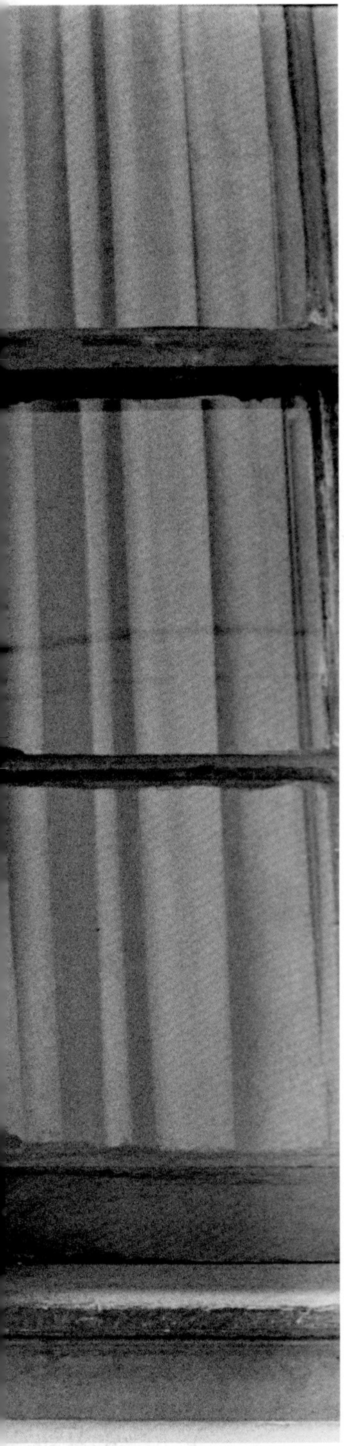

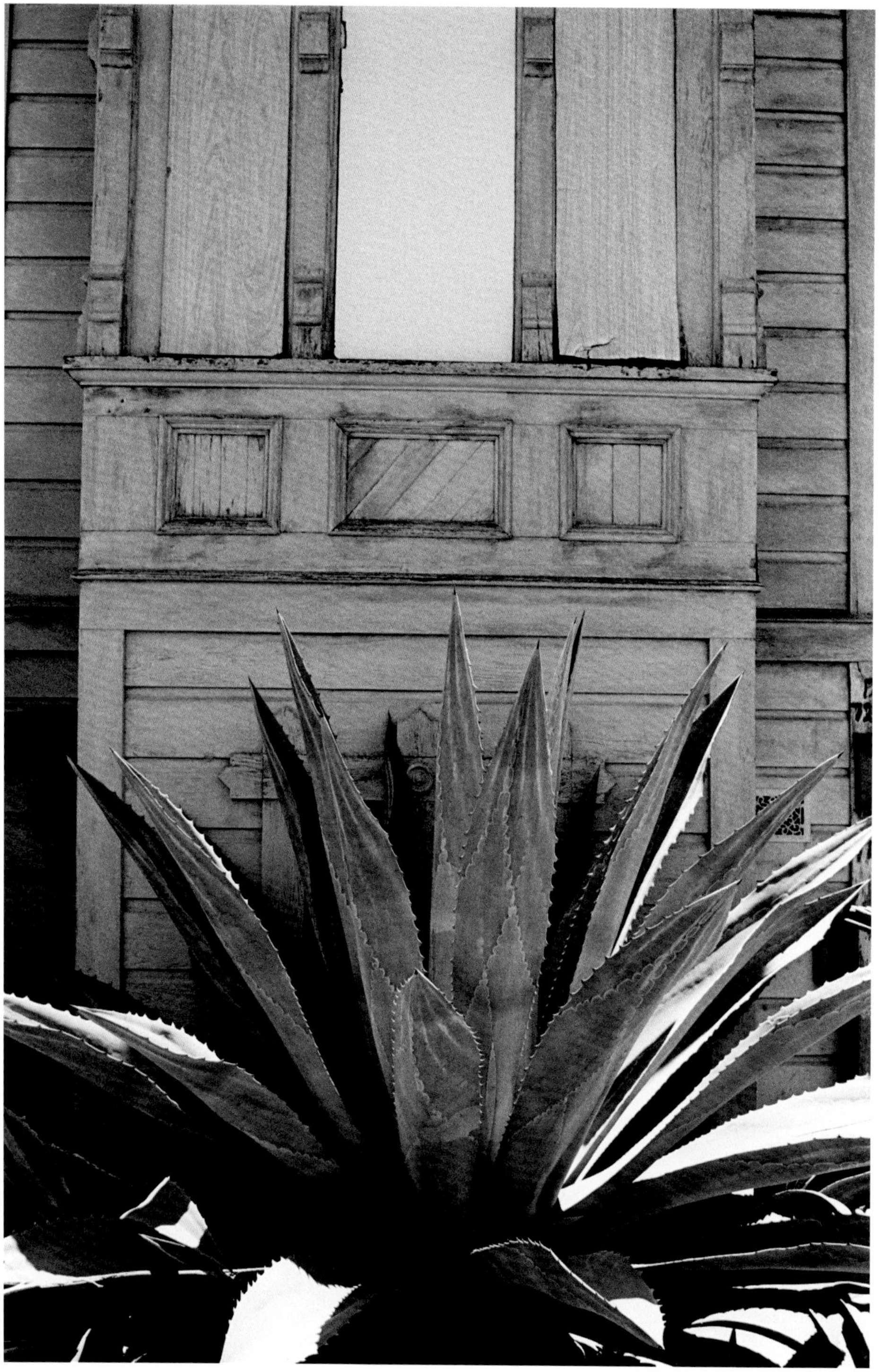

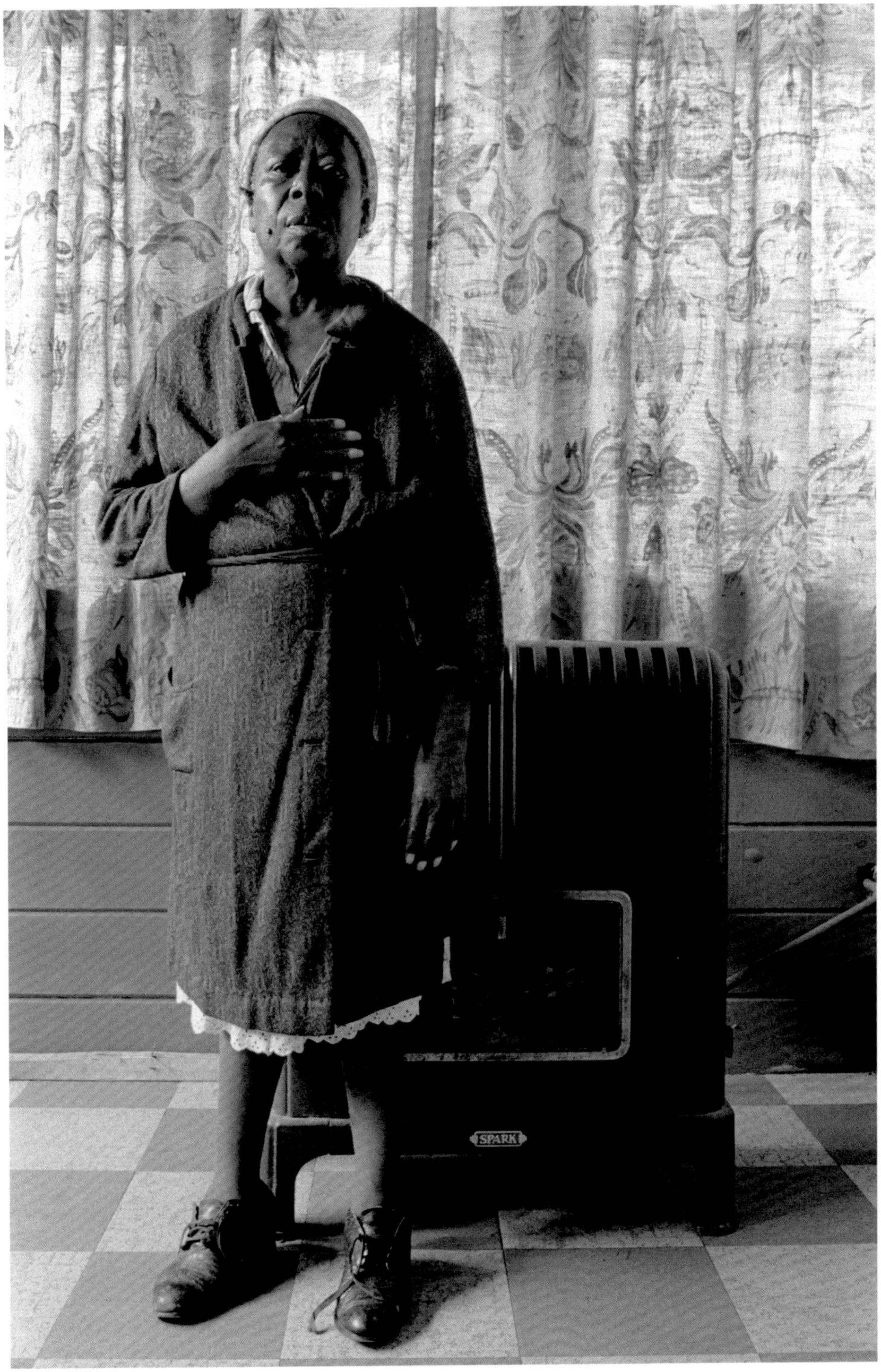
SPARK

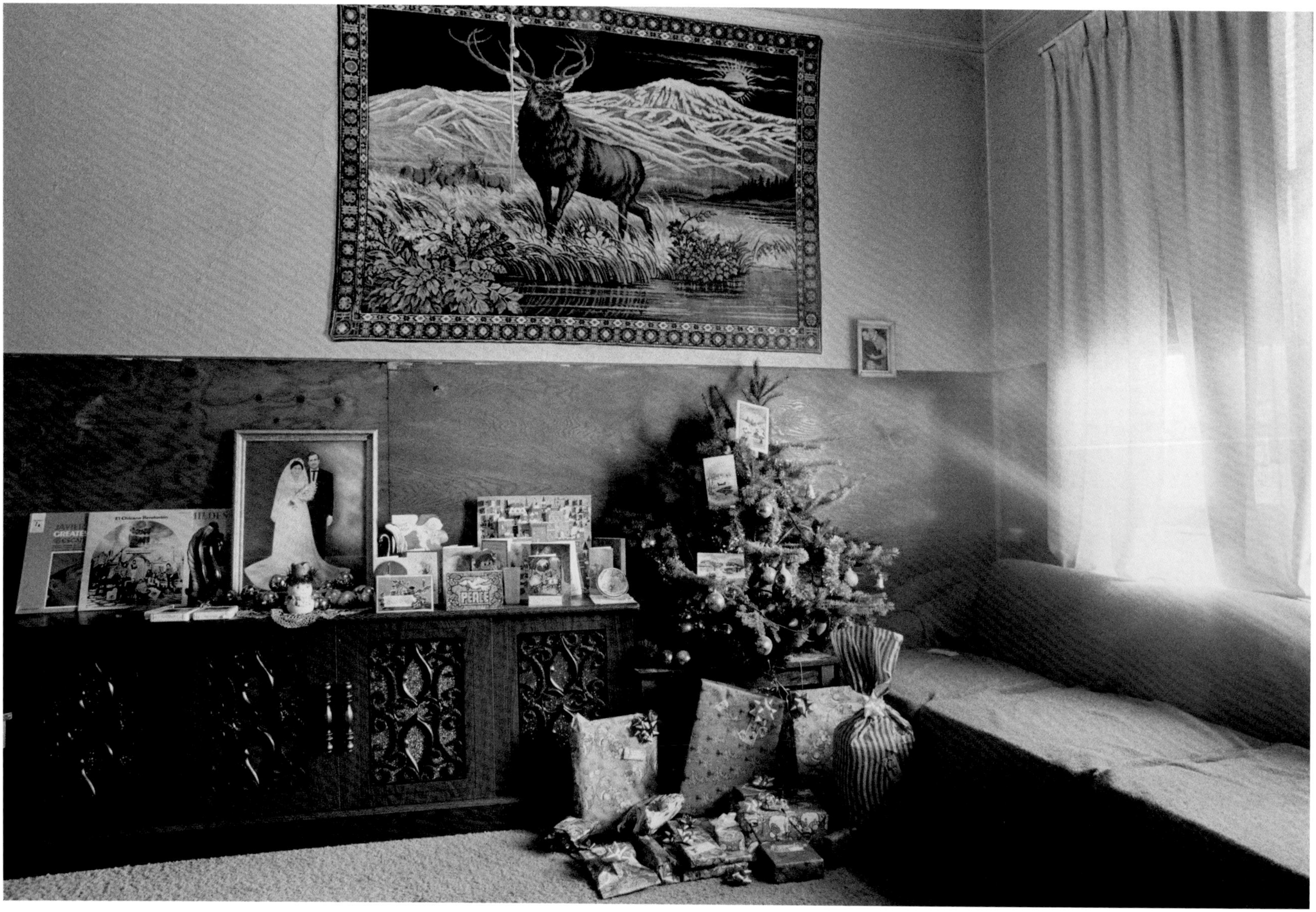

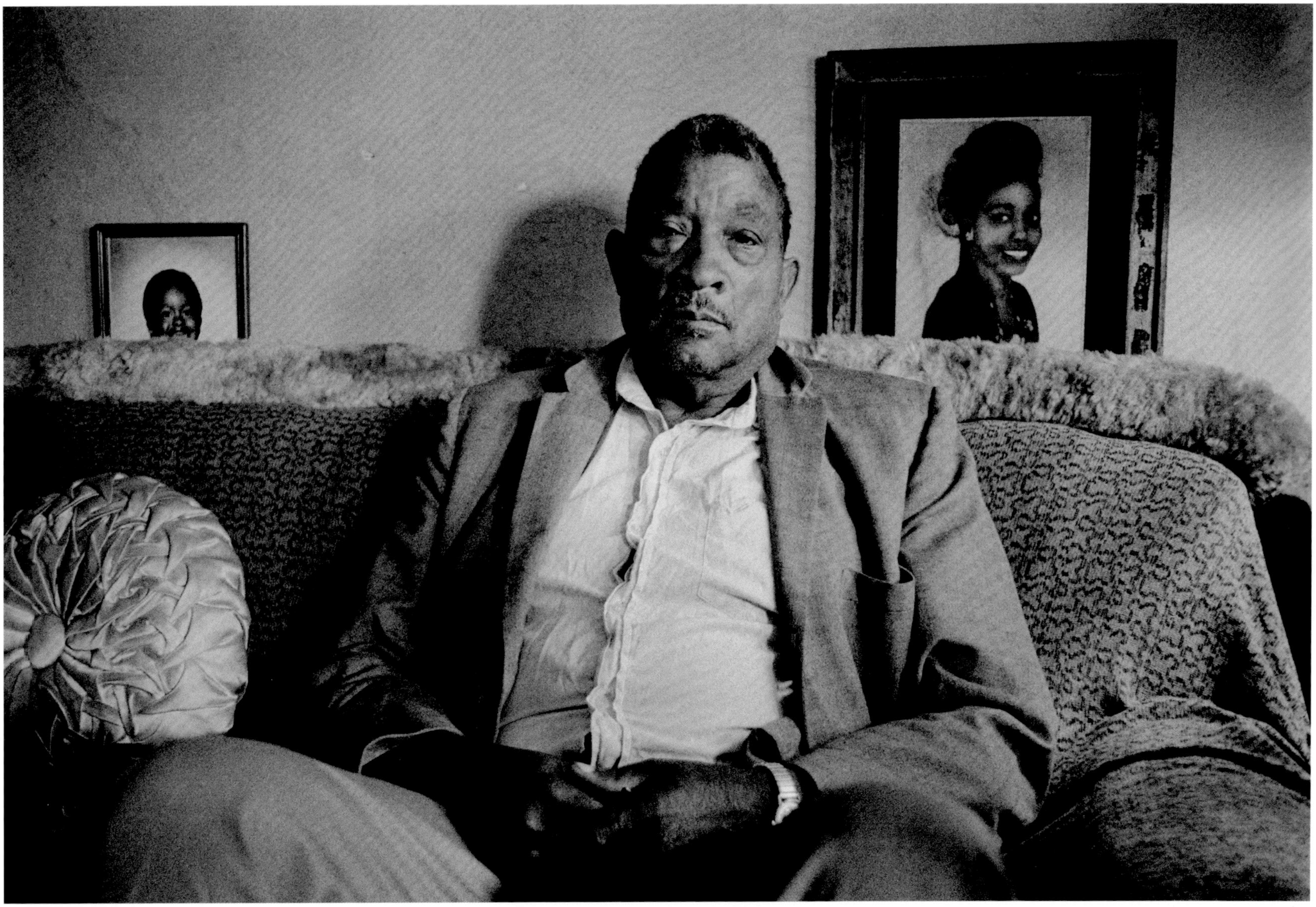

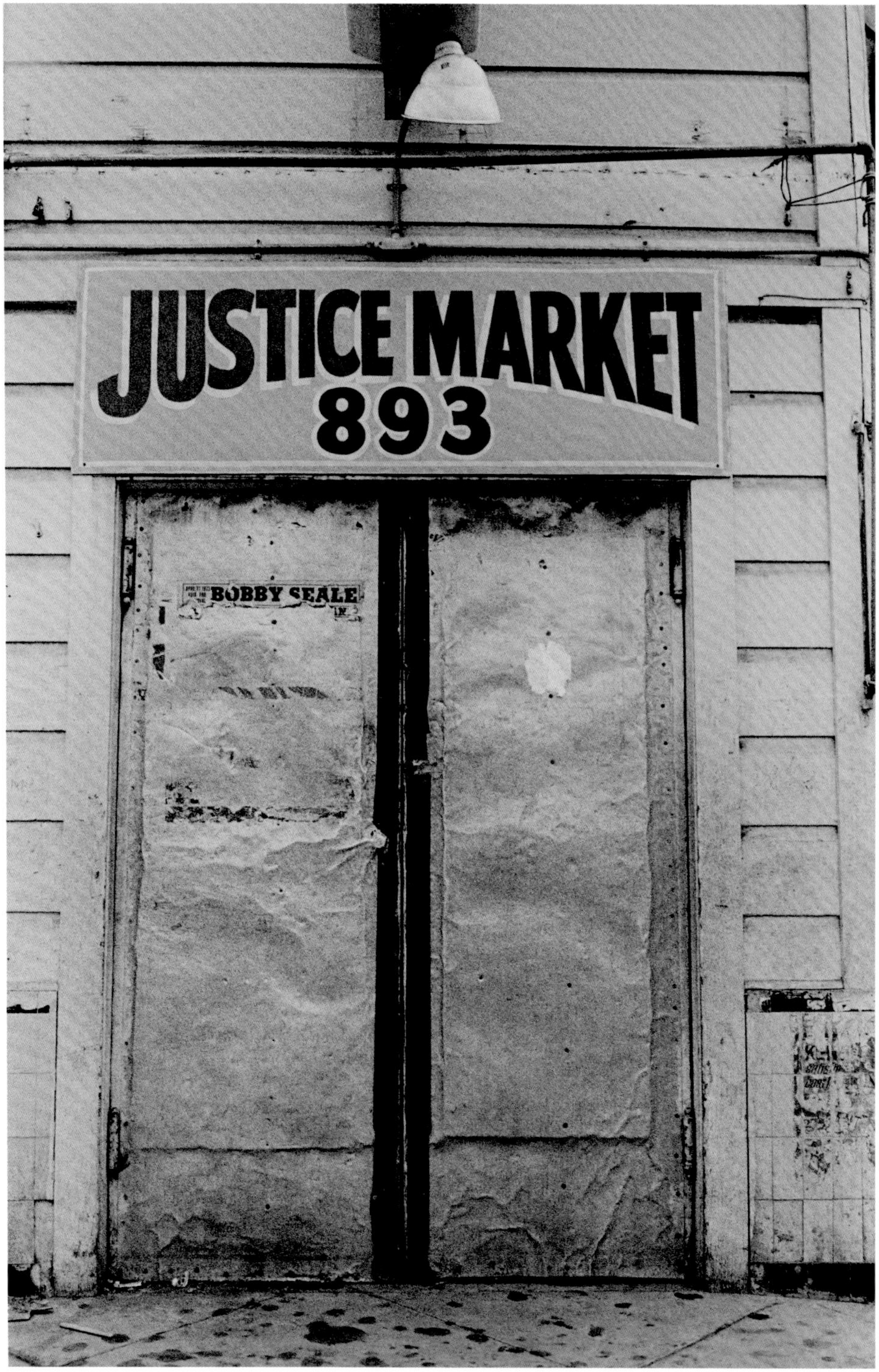
JUSTICE MARKET
893
BOBBY SEALE

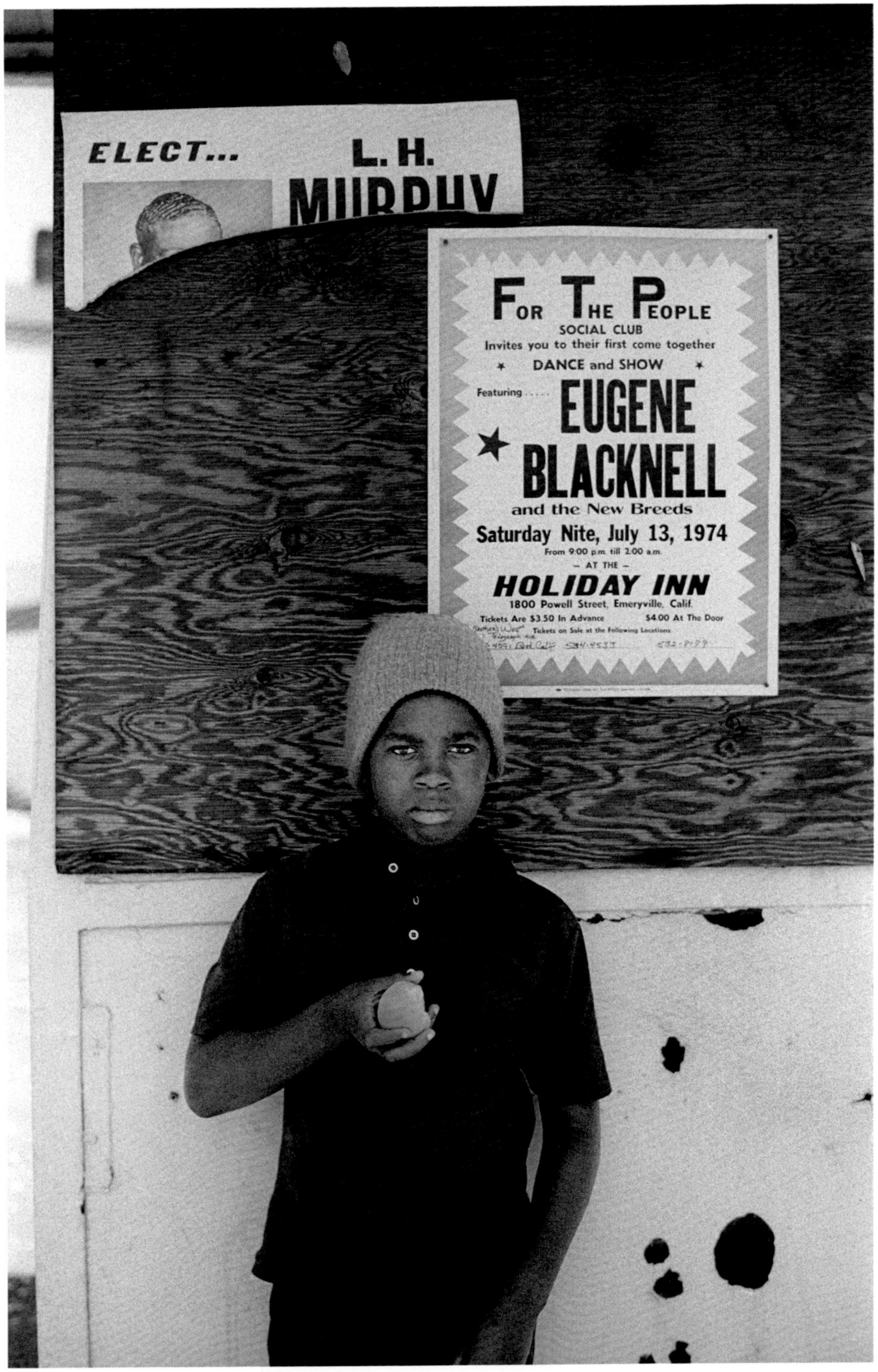
ELECT...
L. H.
For The People
SOCIAL CLUB
Invites you to their first come together
DANCE and SHOW
Featuring.....
EUGENE
BLACKNELL
and the New Breeds
Saturday Nite, July 13, 1974
From 9:00 p.m. till 2:00 a.m.
– AT THE –
HOLIDAY INN
1800 Powell Street, Emeryville, Calif.
Tickets Are $3.50 In Advance
$4.00 At The Door
Tickets on Sale at the Following Locations

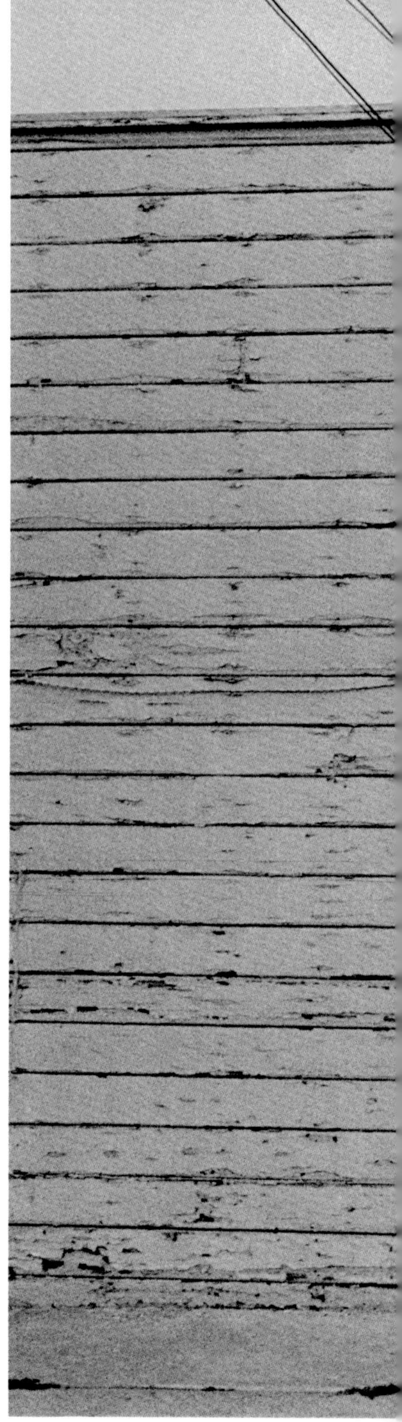

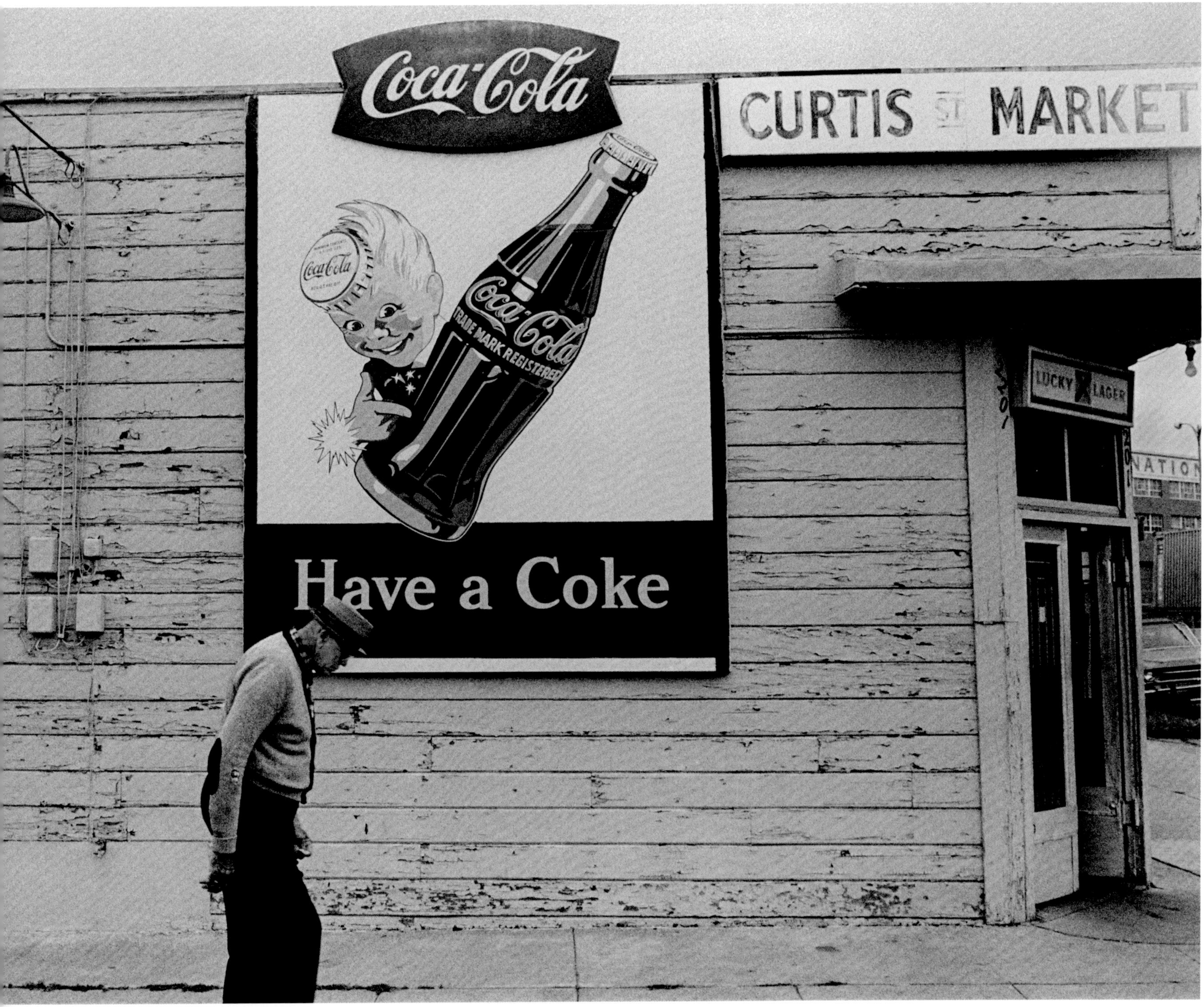
Coca-Cola
CURTIS ST MARKET
Coca-Cola
Coca-Cola
TRADE MARK REGISTERED
Have a Coke
LUCKY LAGER
201
NATION

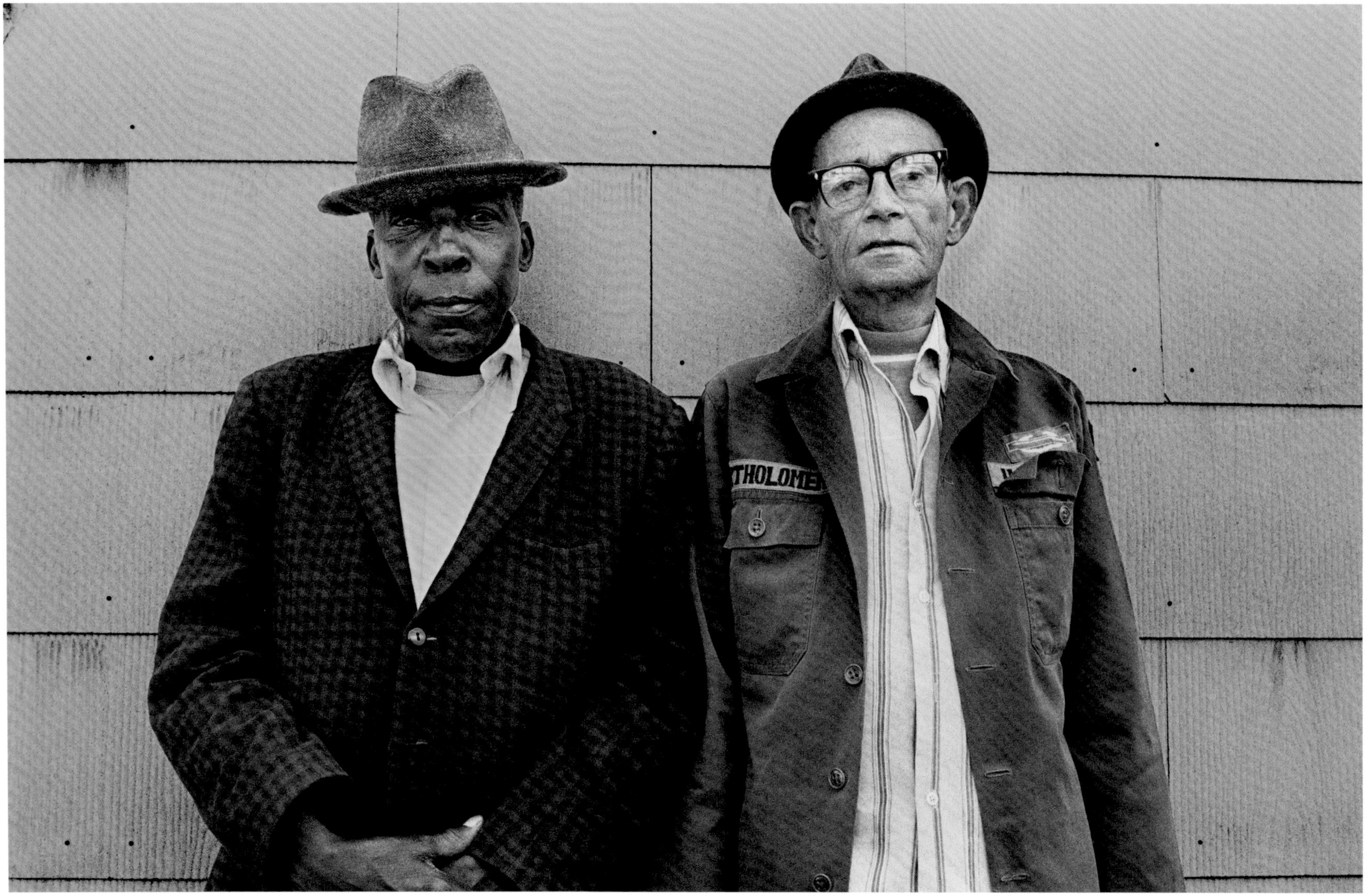

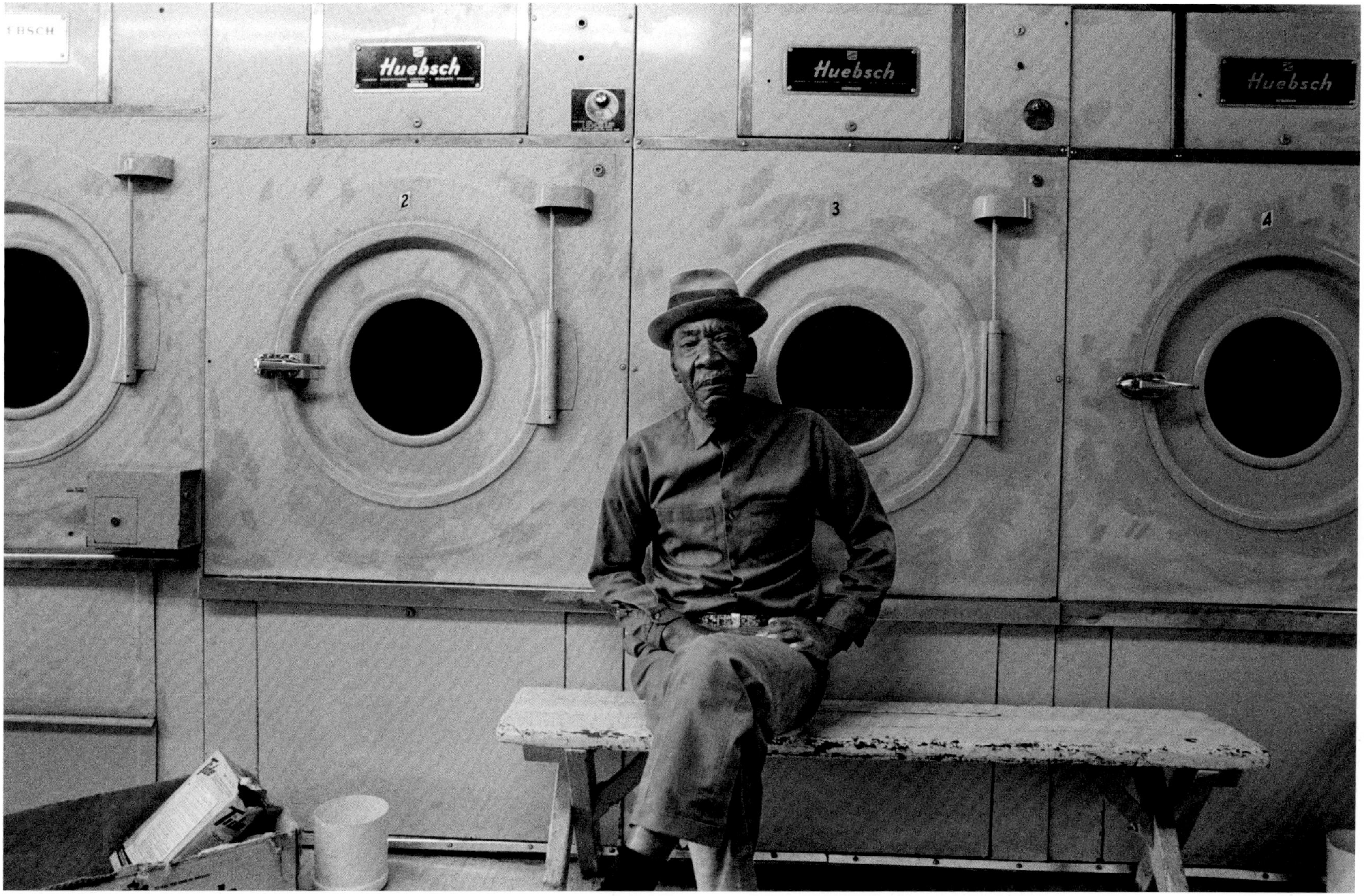
Huebsch
Huebsch
Huebsch
2
3
4

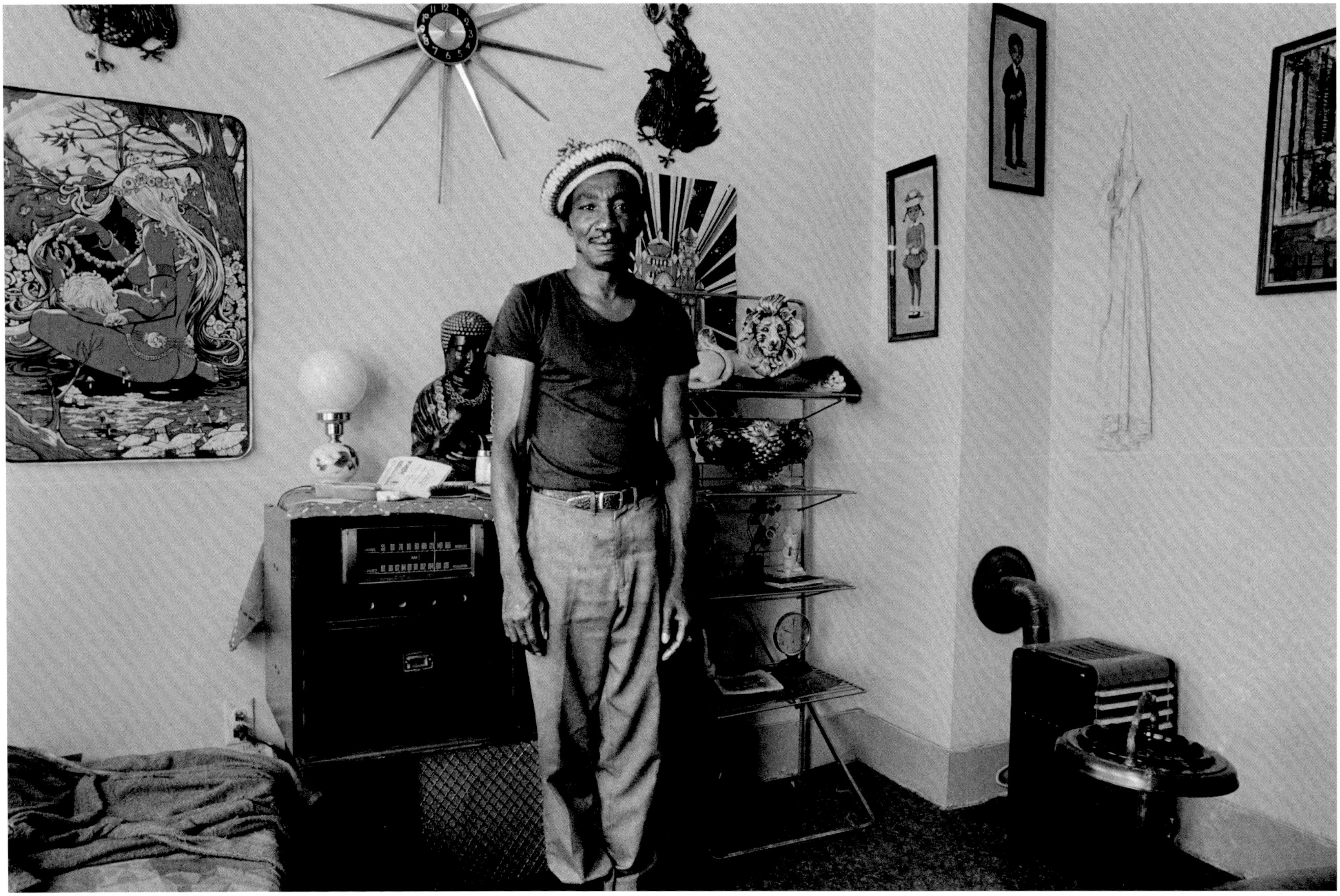

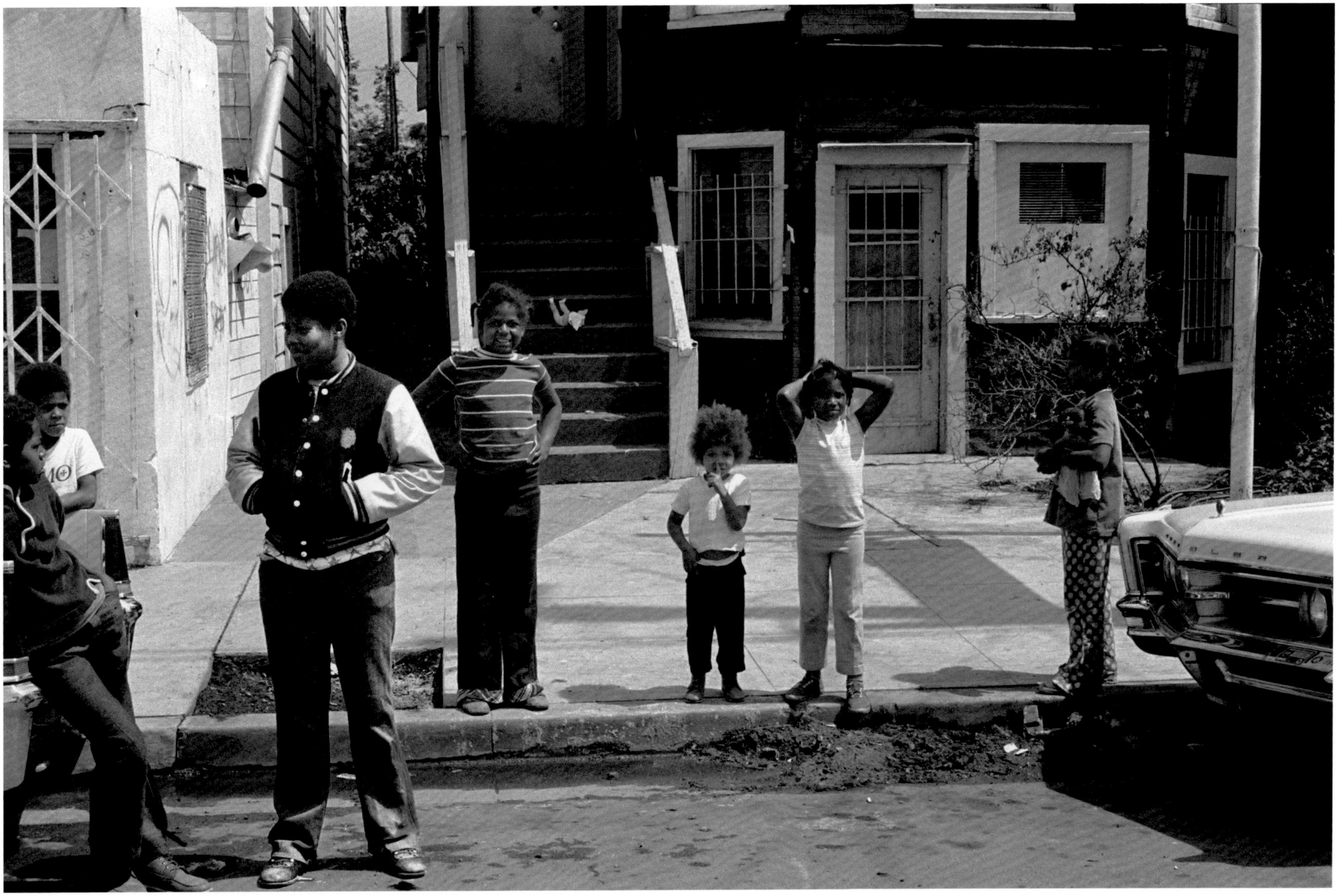

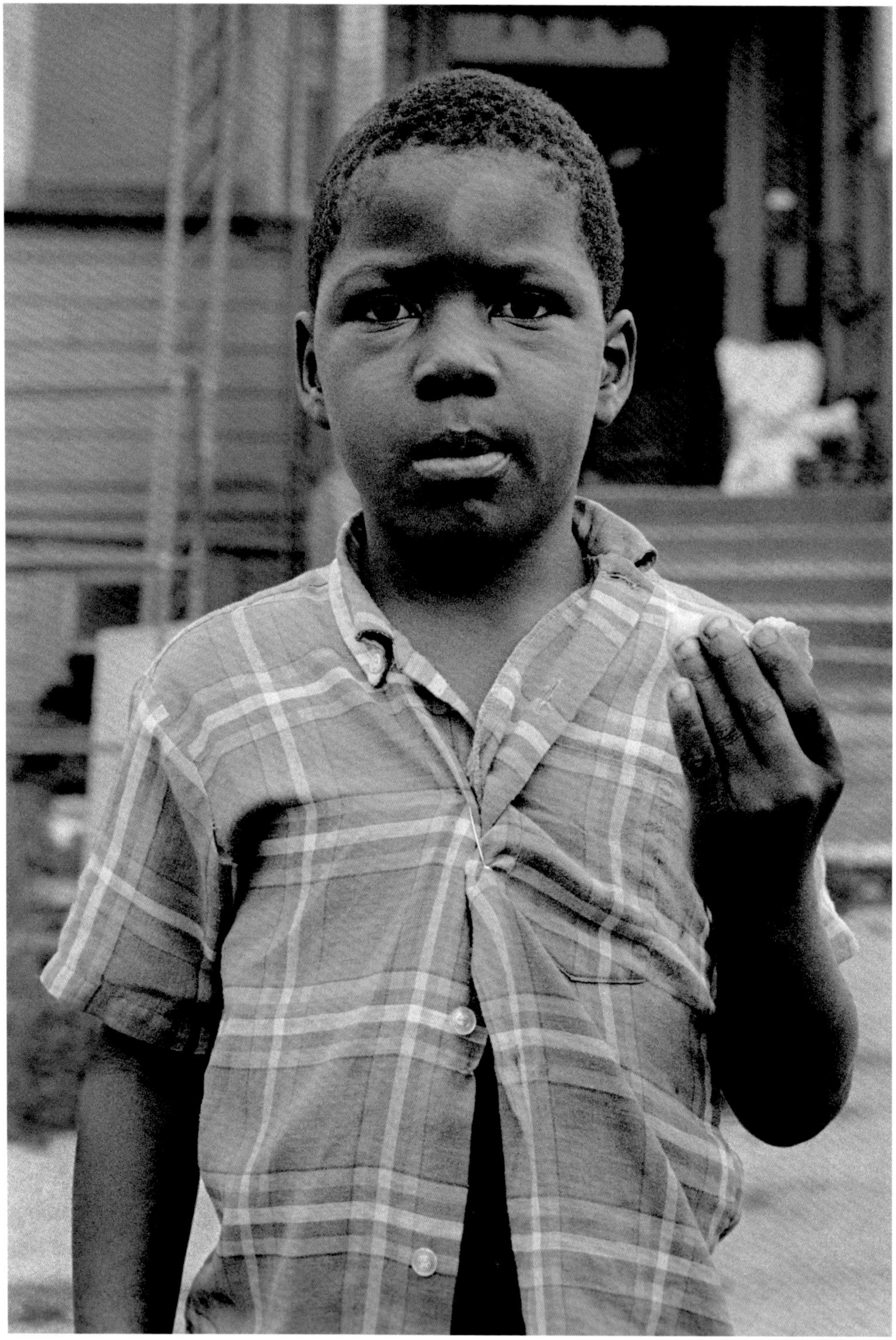

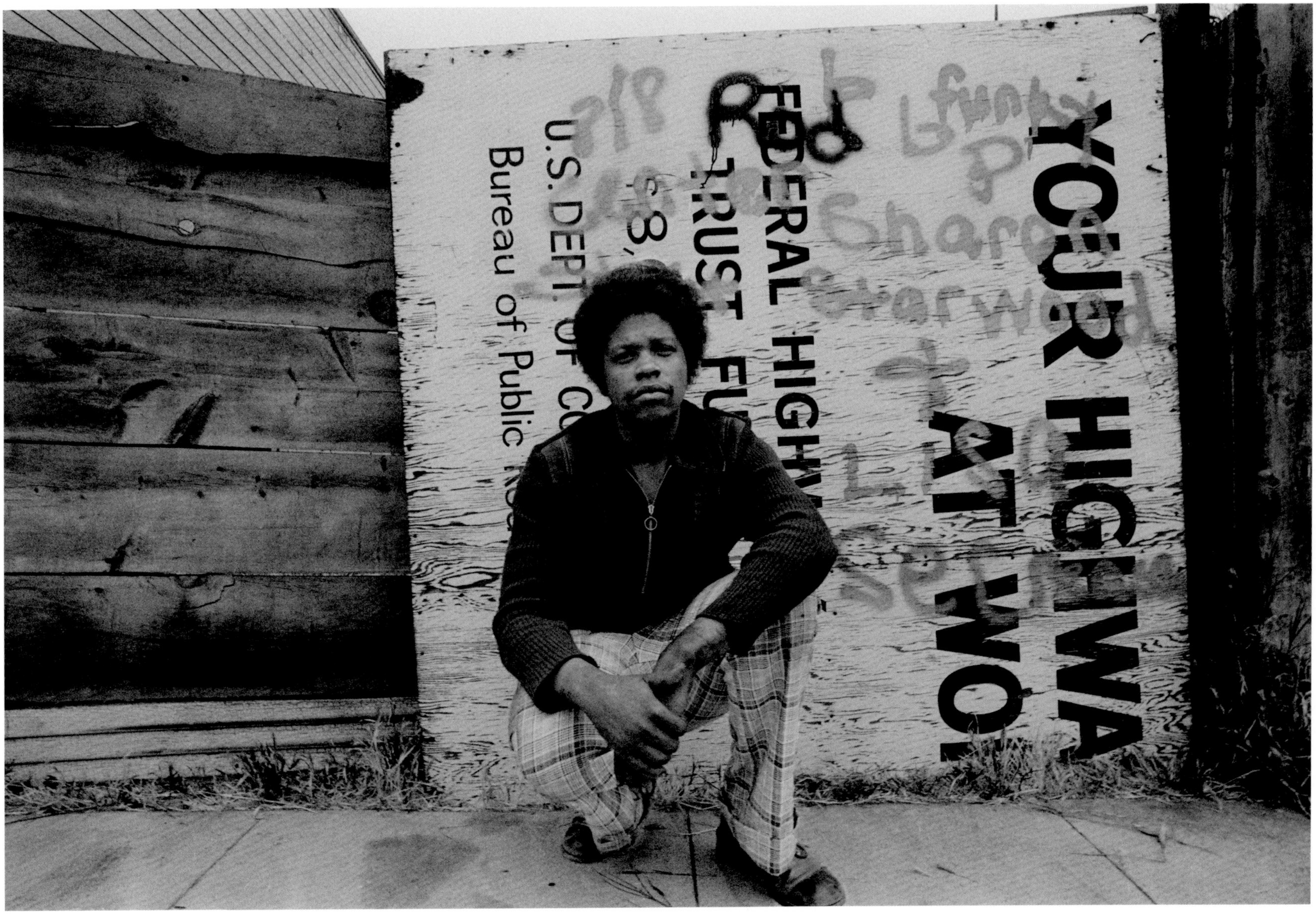
YOUR HIGHWA
AT WO
FEDERAL HIGH
Bureau of Public

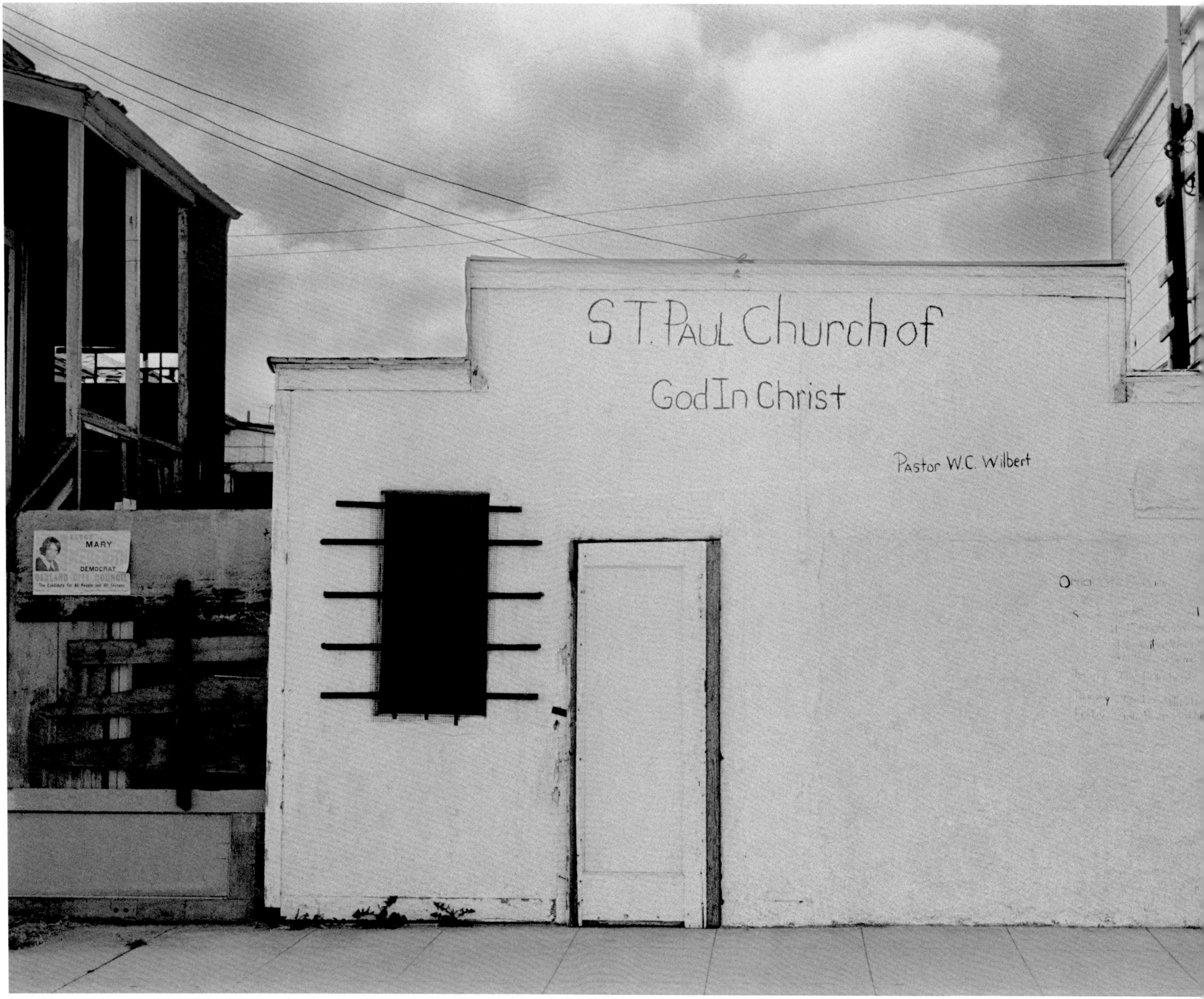
S T. PAUL Church of
God In Christ
Pastor W.C. Wilbert
MARY
DEMOCRAT

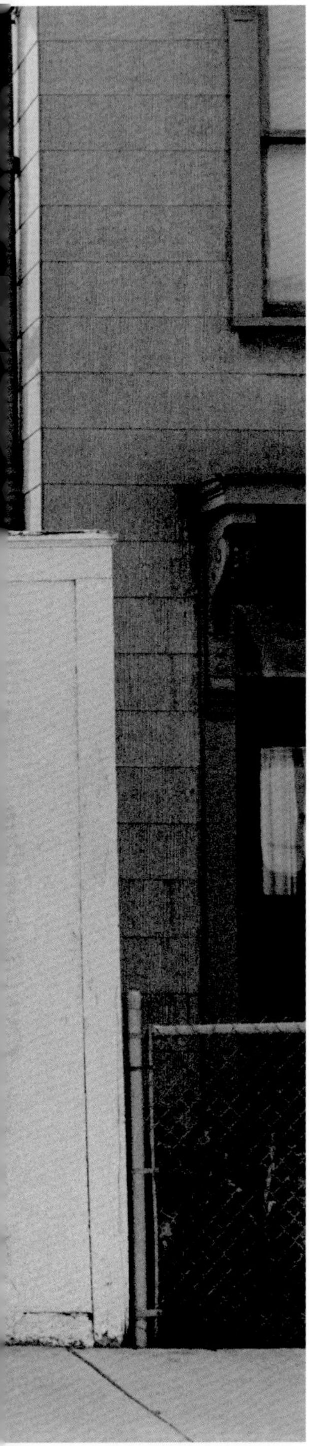

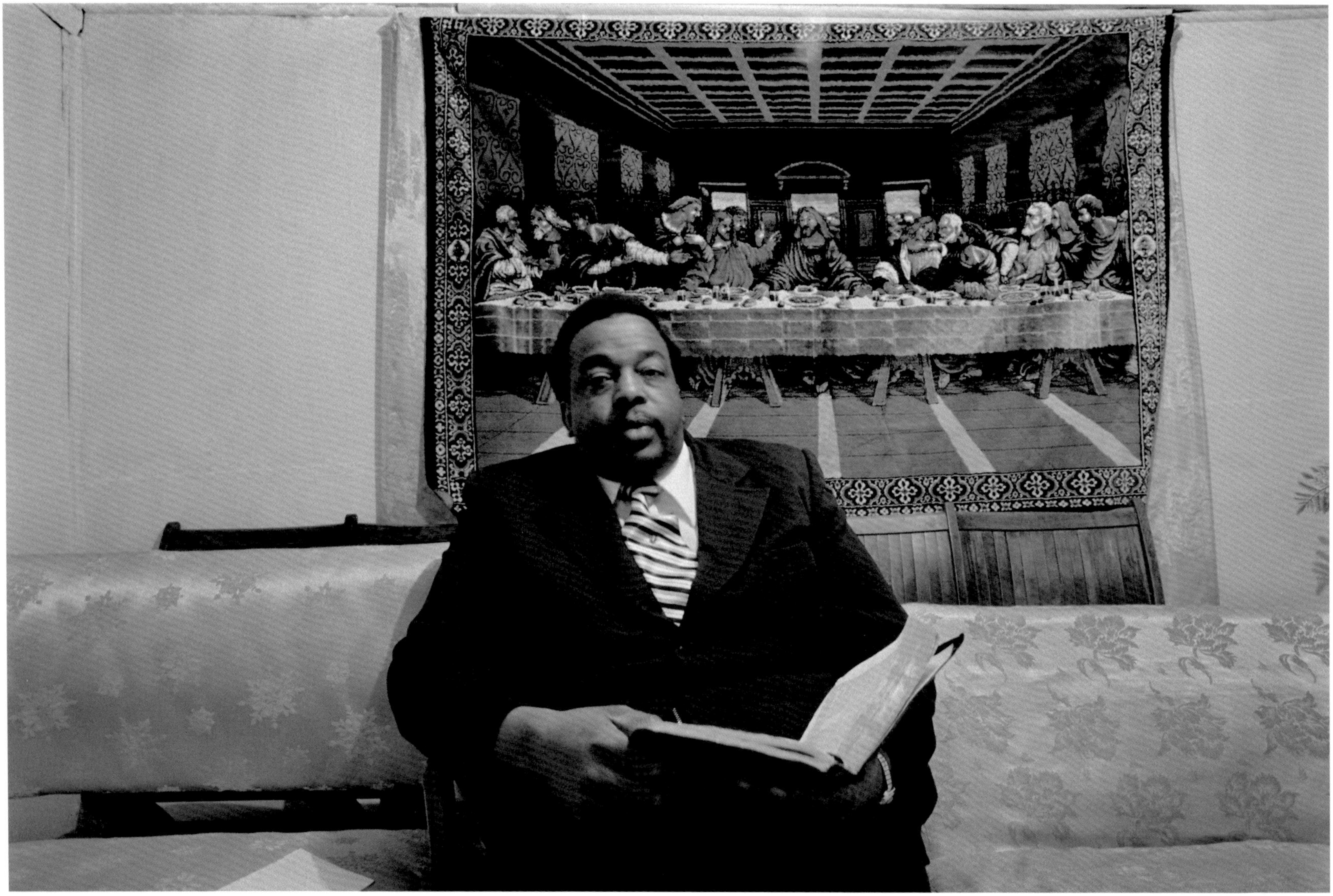

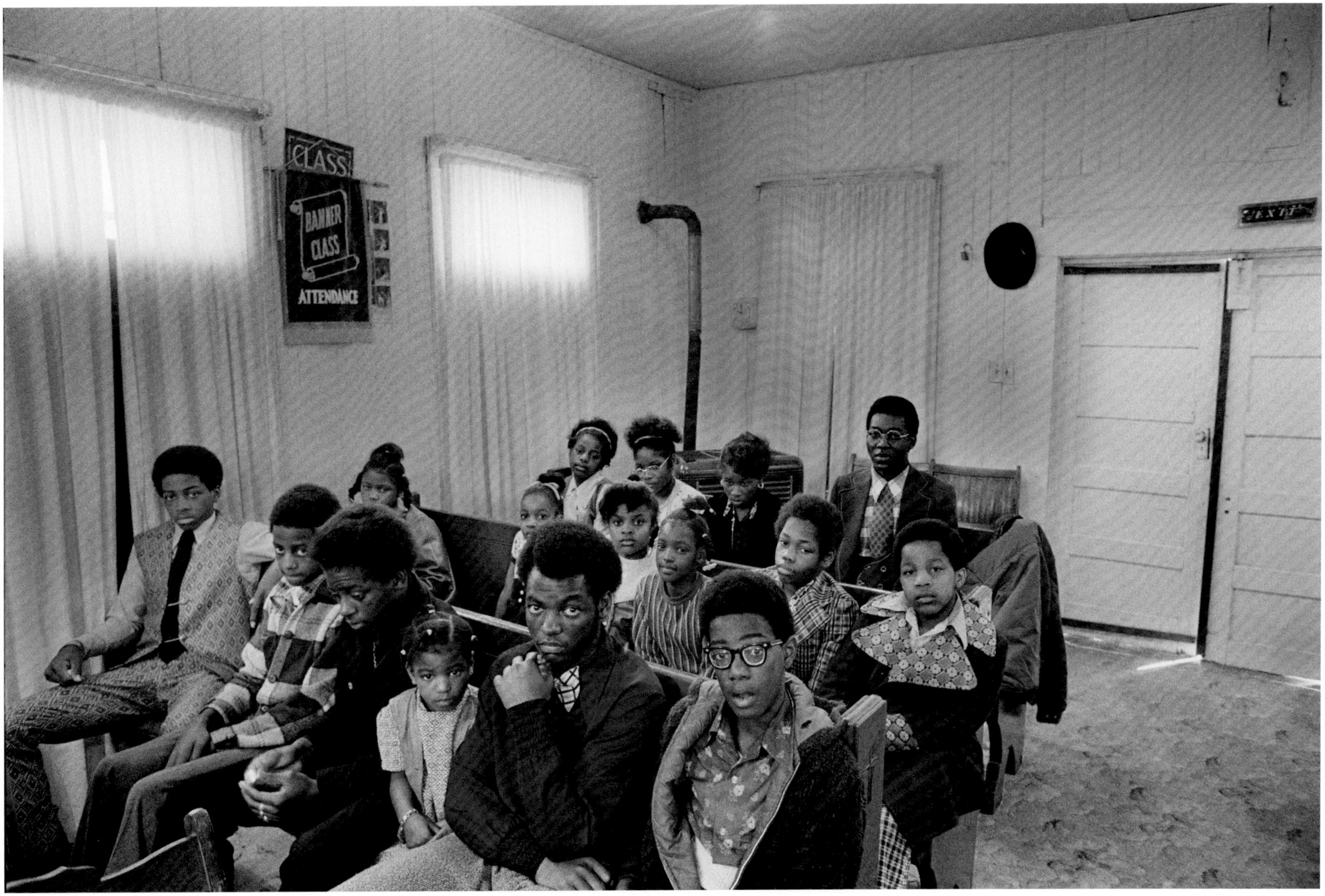
CLASS
BANNER
CLASS
ATTENDANCE

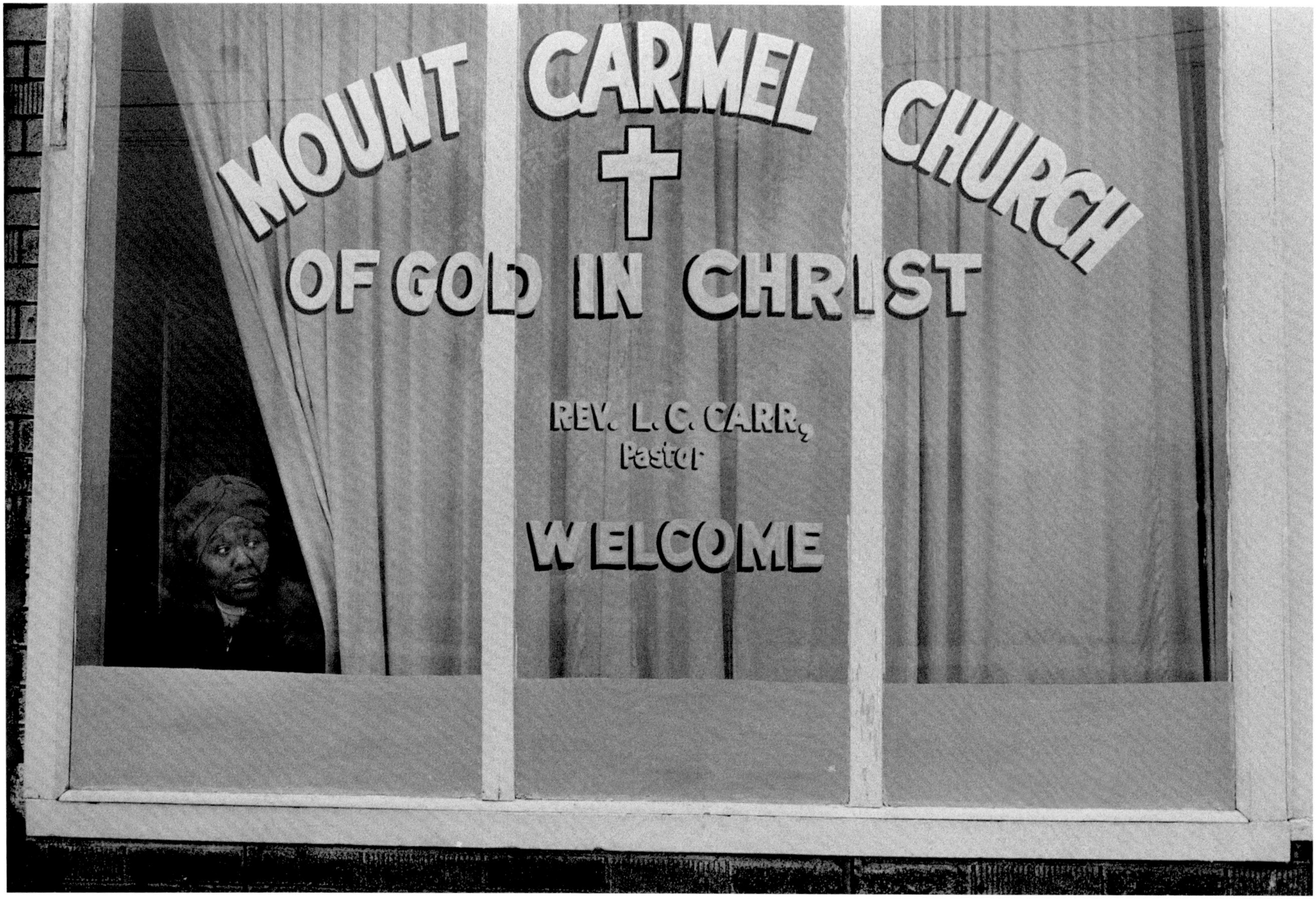
MOUNT CARMEL CHURCH
OF GOD IN CHRIST
REV. L. C. CARR,
Pastor
WELCOME

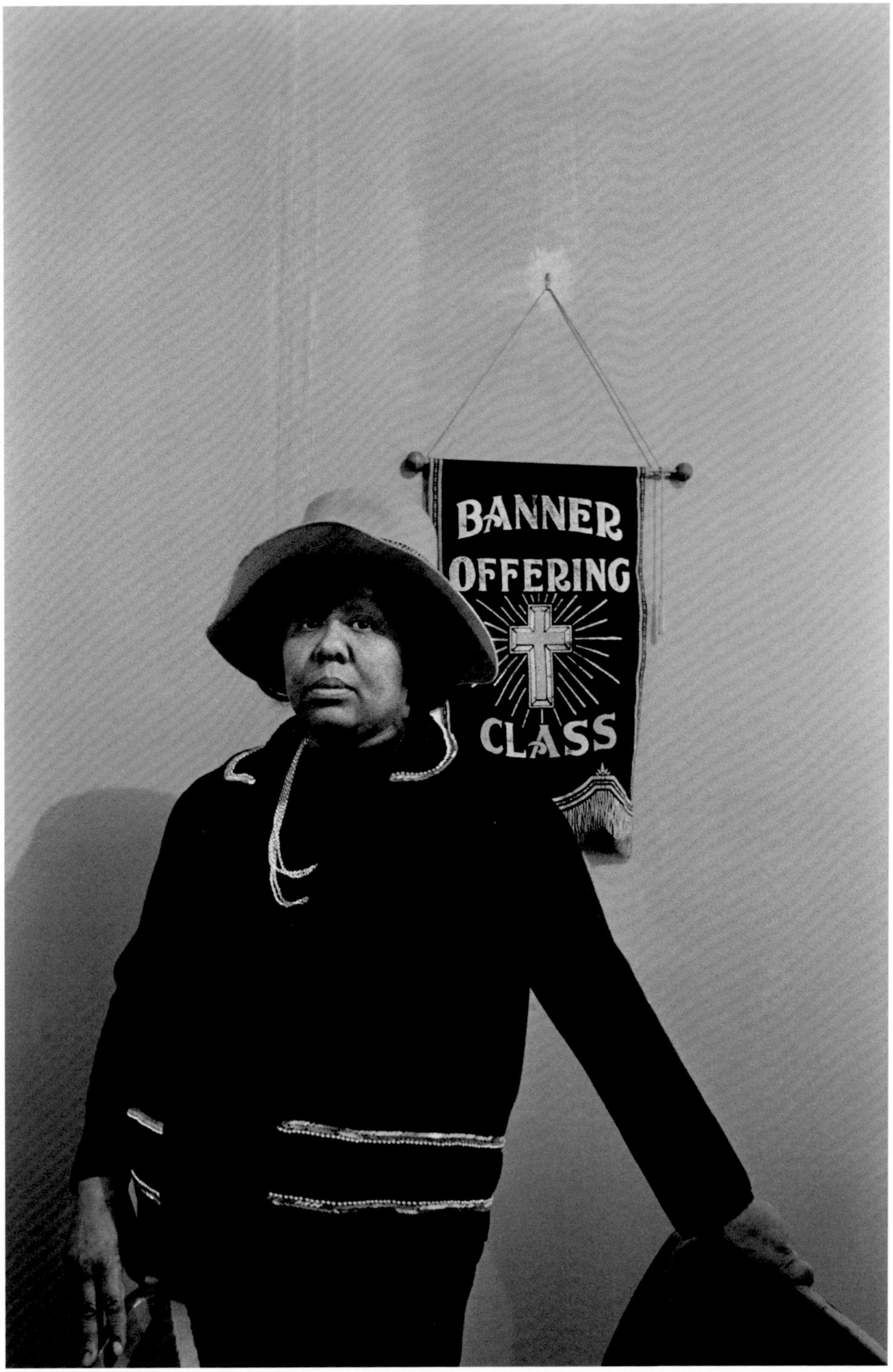
BANNER
OFFERING
CLASS

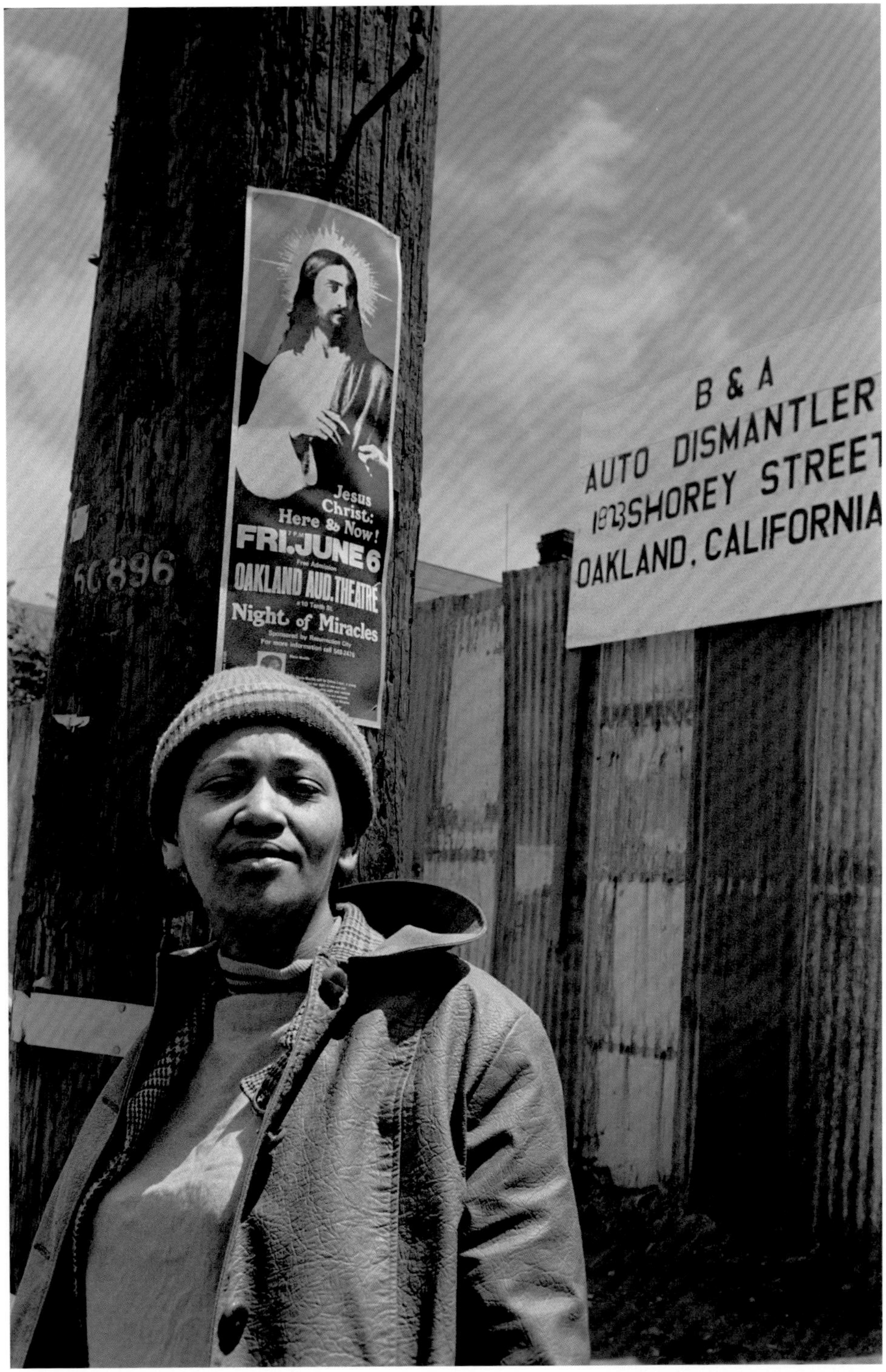
Jesus
Christ:
Here & Now!
FRI. JUNE 6
OAKLAND AUD. THEATRE
Night of Miracles
B & A
AUTO DISMANTLER
SHOREY STREET
OAKLAND, CALIFORNIA

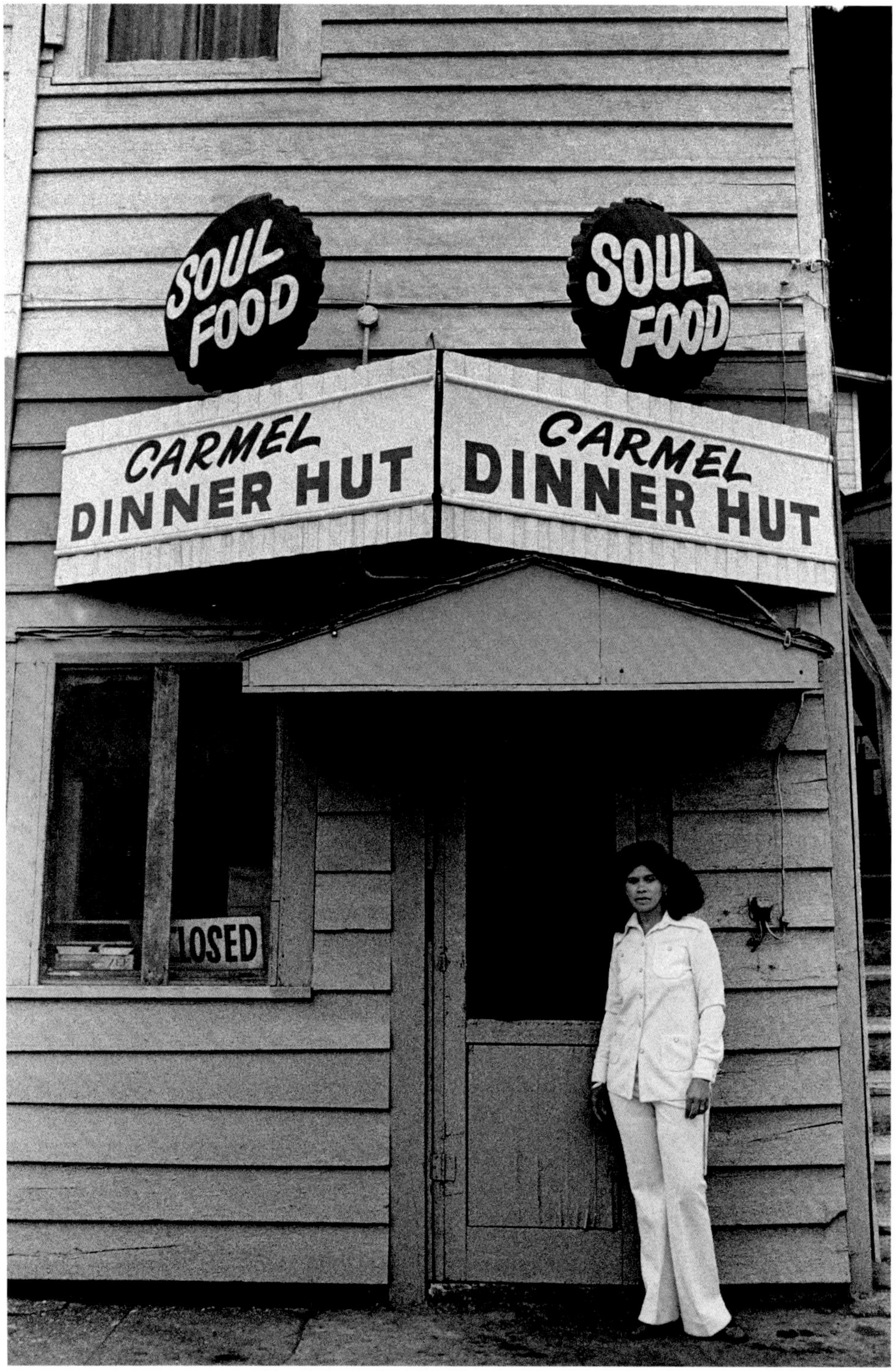
SOUL FOOD
SOUL FOOD
CARMEL DINNER HUT
CARMEL DINNER HUT
LOSED

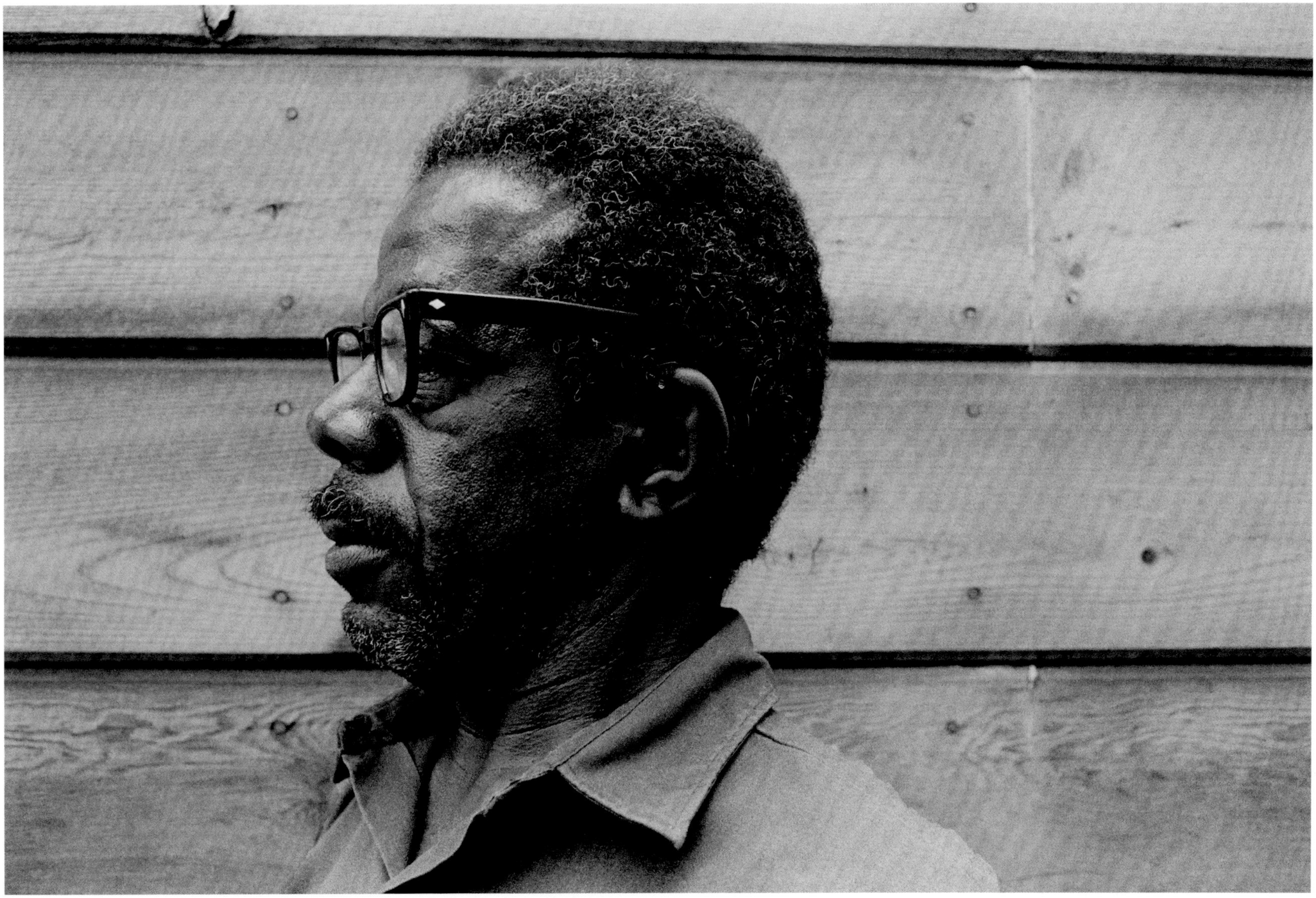

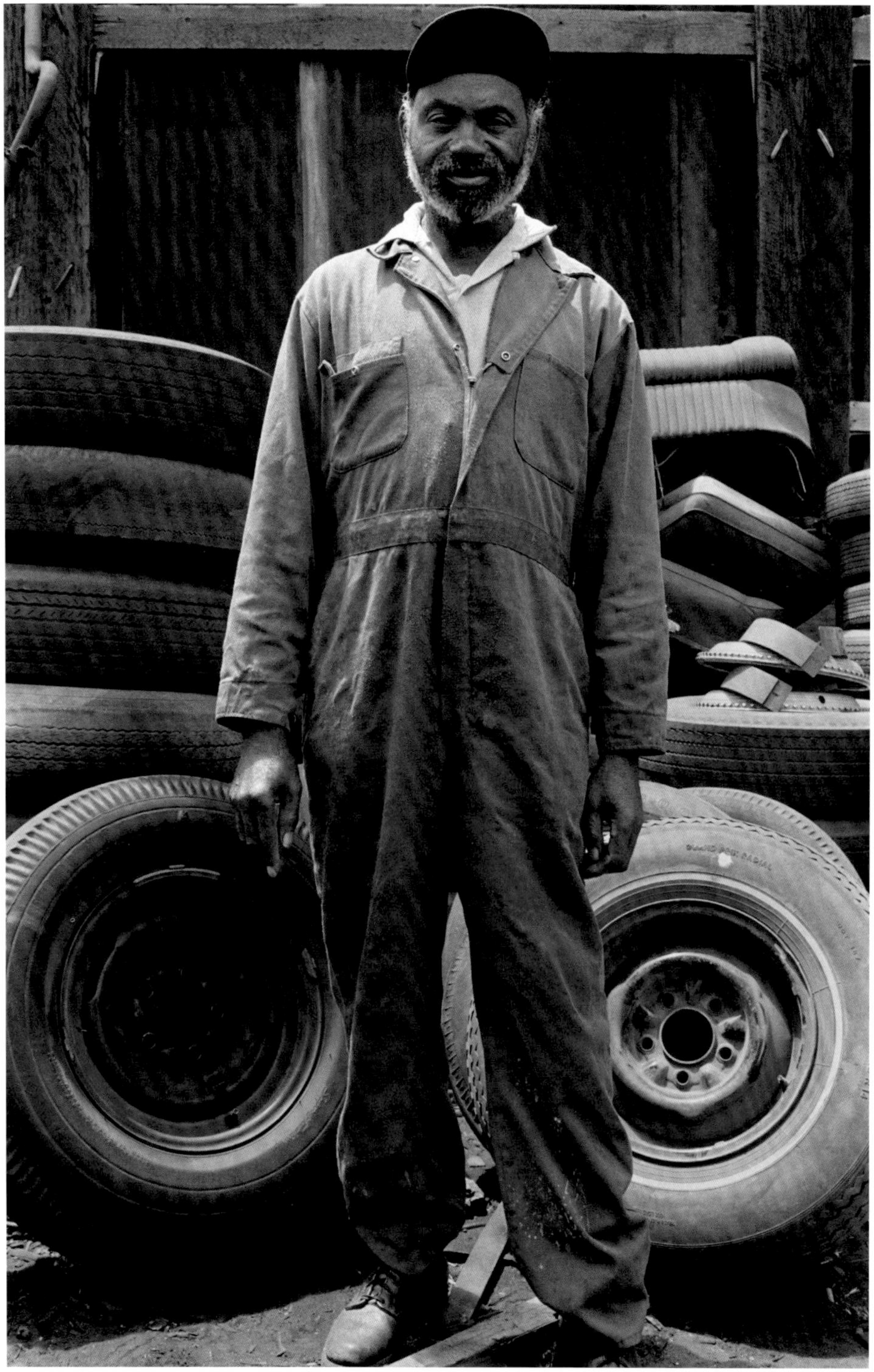

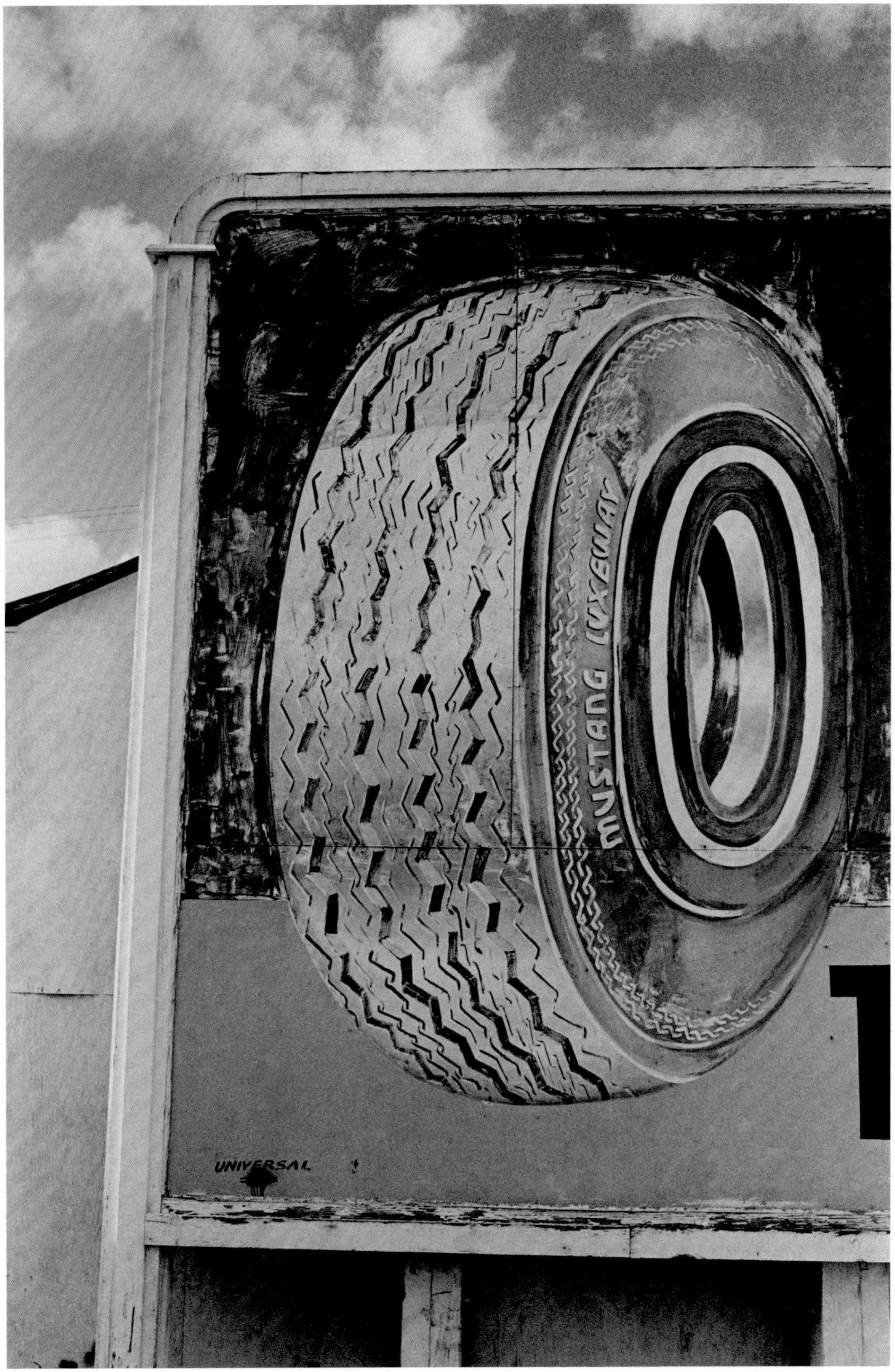
MUSTANG LUXEWAY
UNIVERSAL

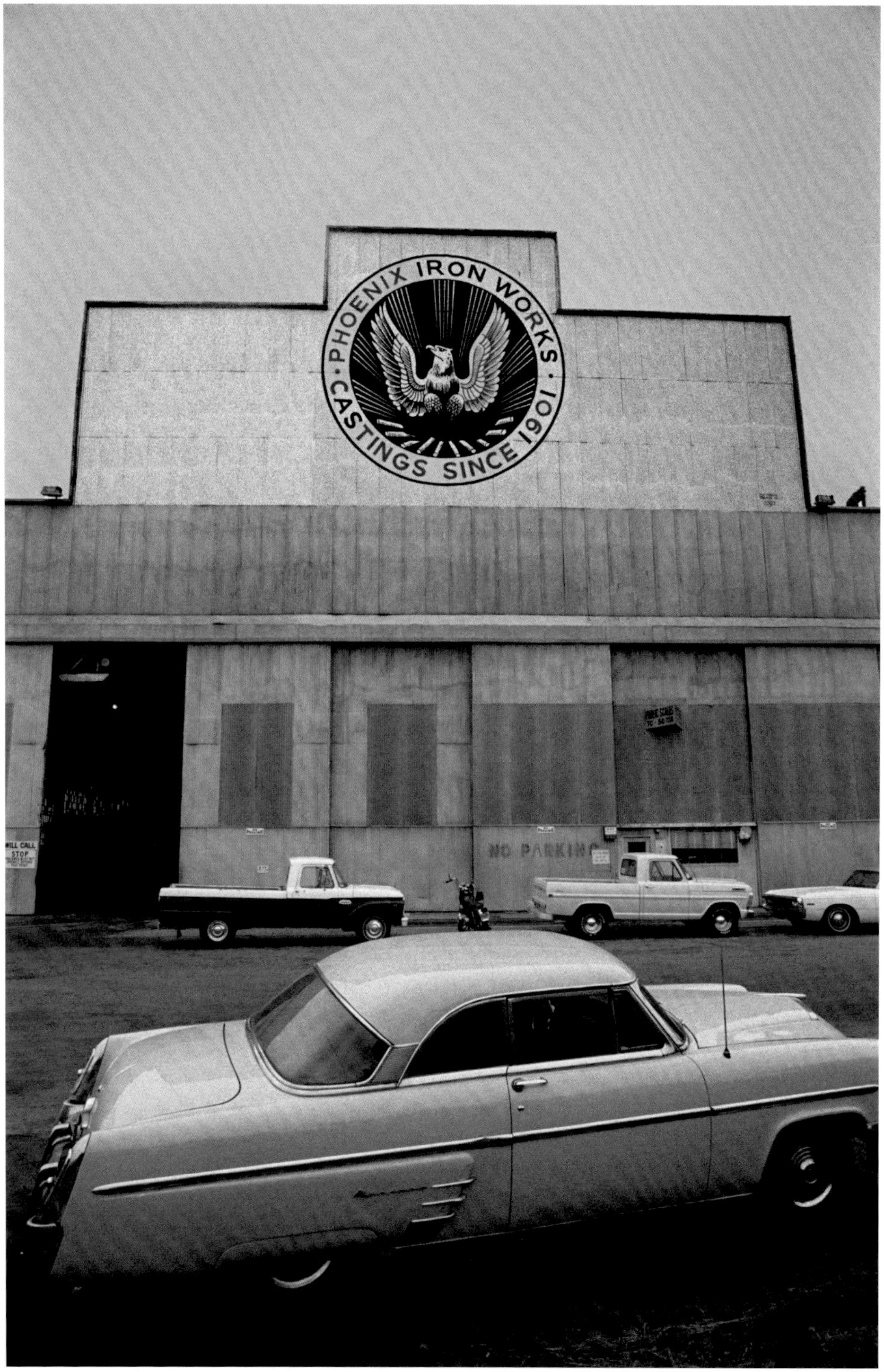
PHOENIX IRON WORKS
CASTINGS SINCE 1901

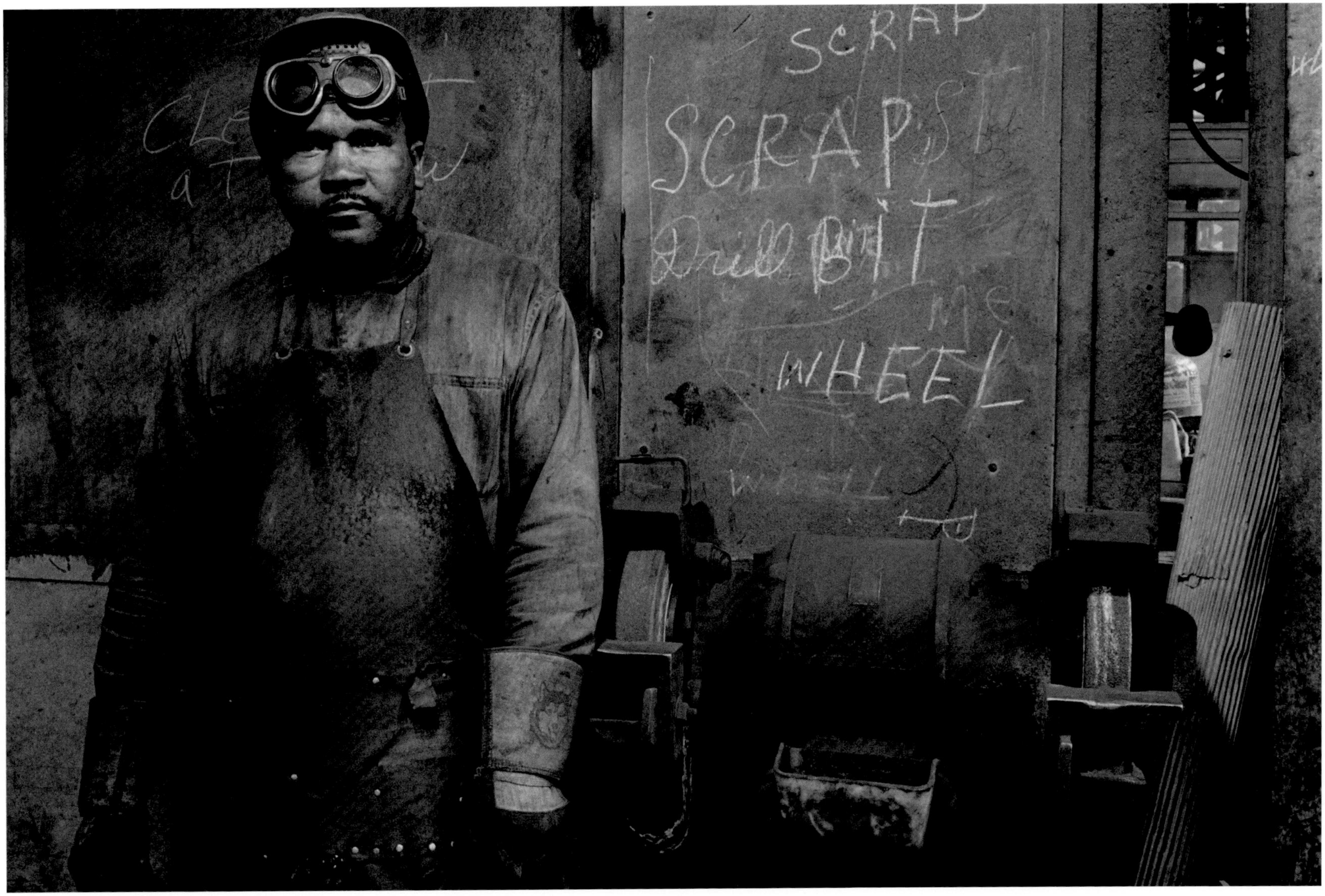
SCRAP
SCRAP
Drill BIT
WHEEL

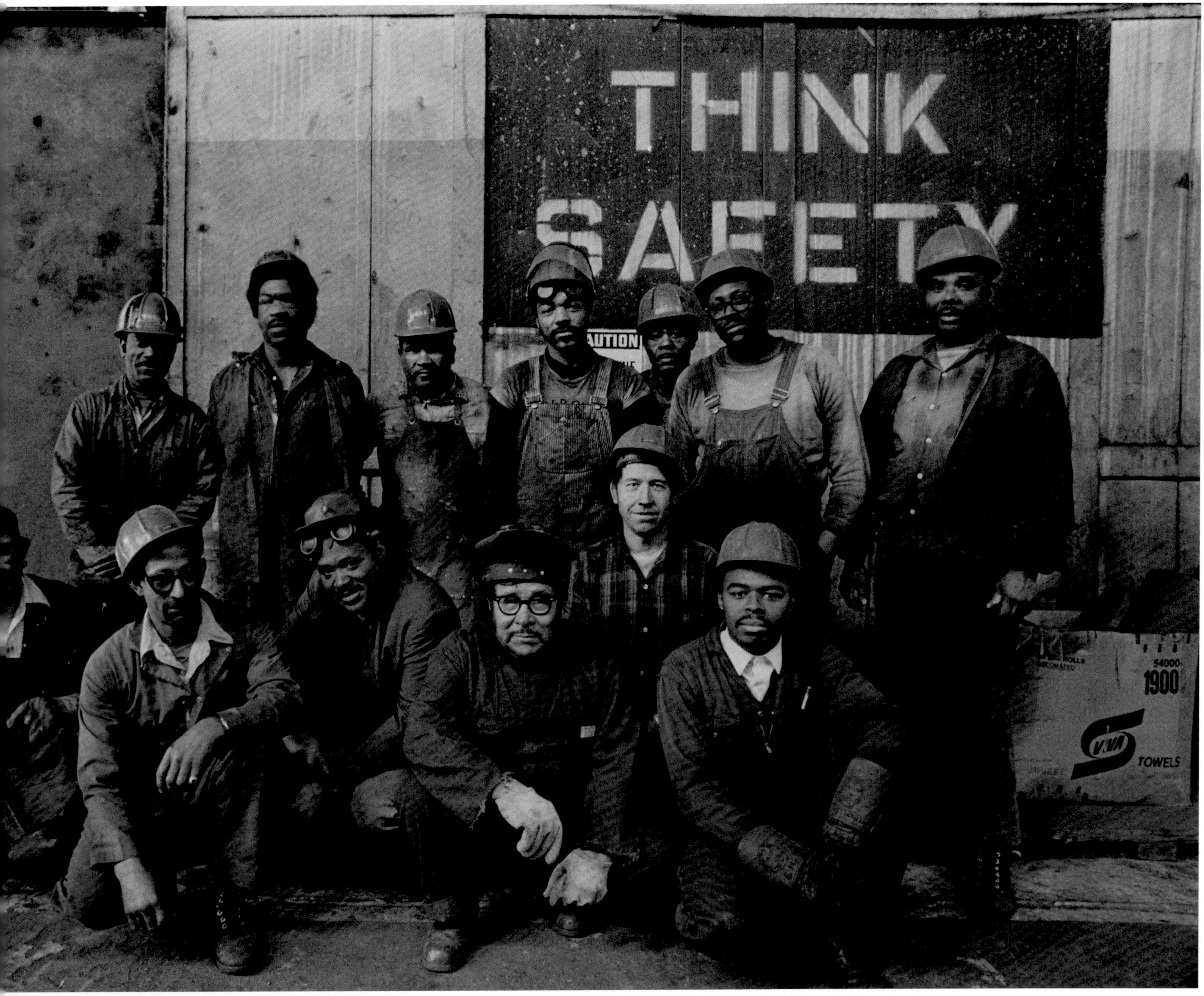
THINK
SAFETY
54000-
1900
VIVA
TOWELS

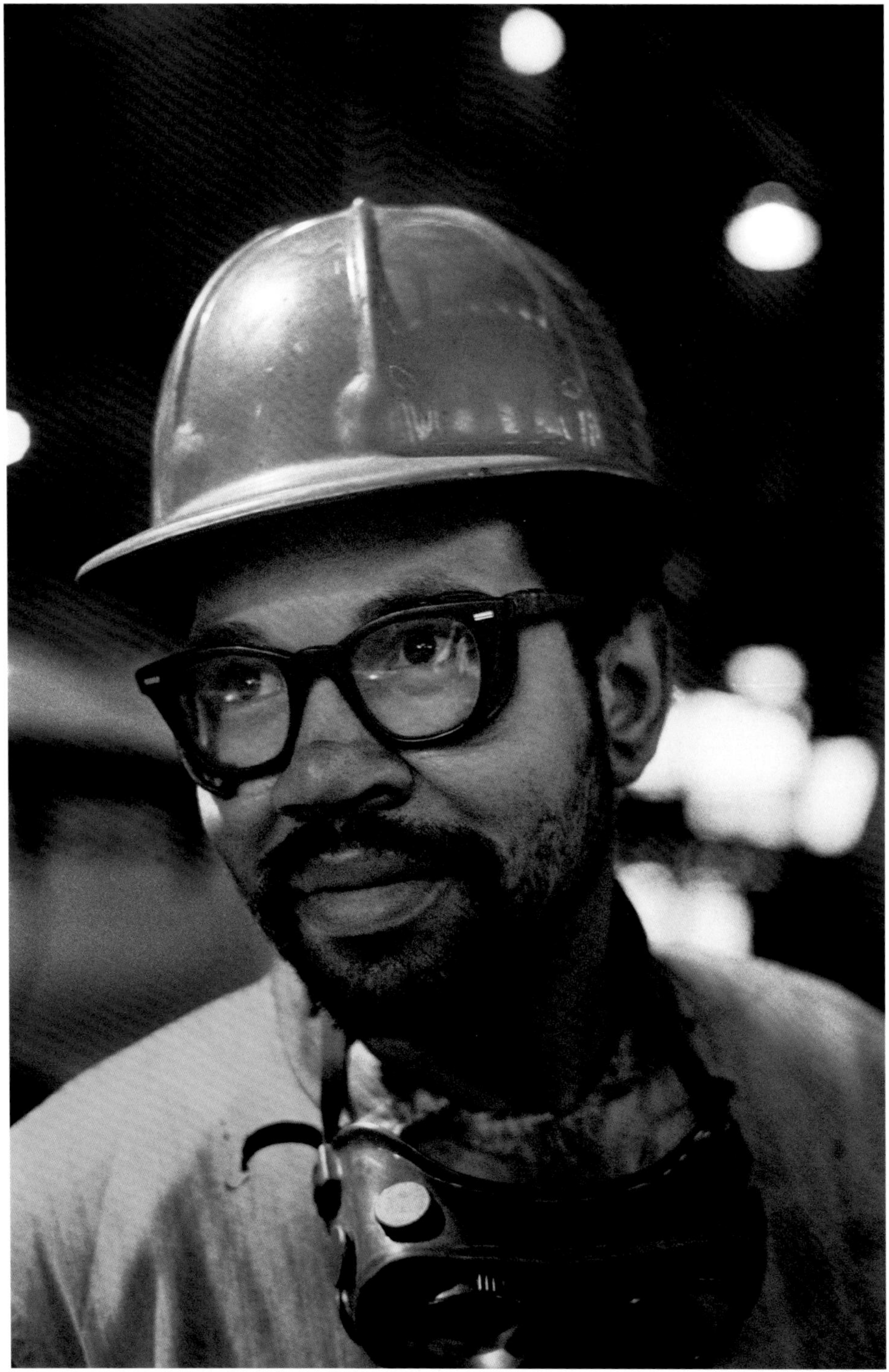

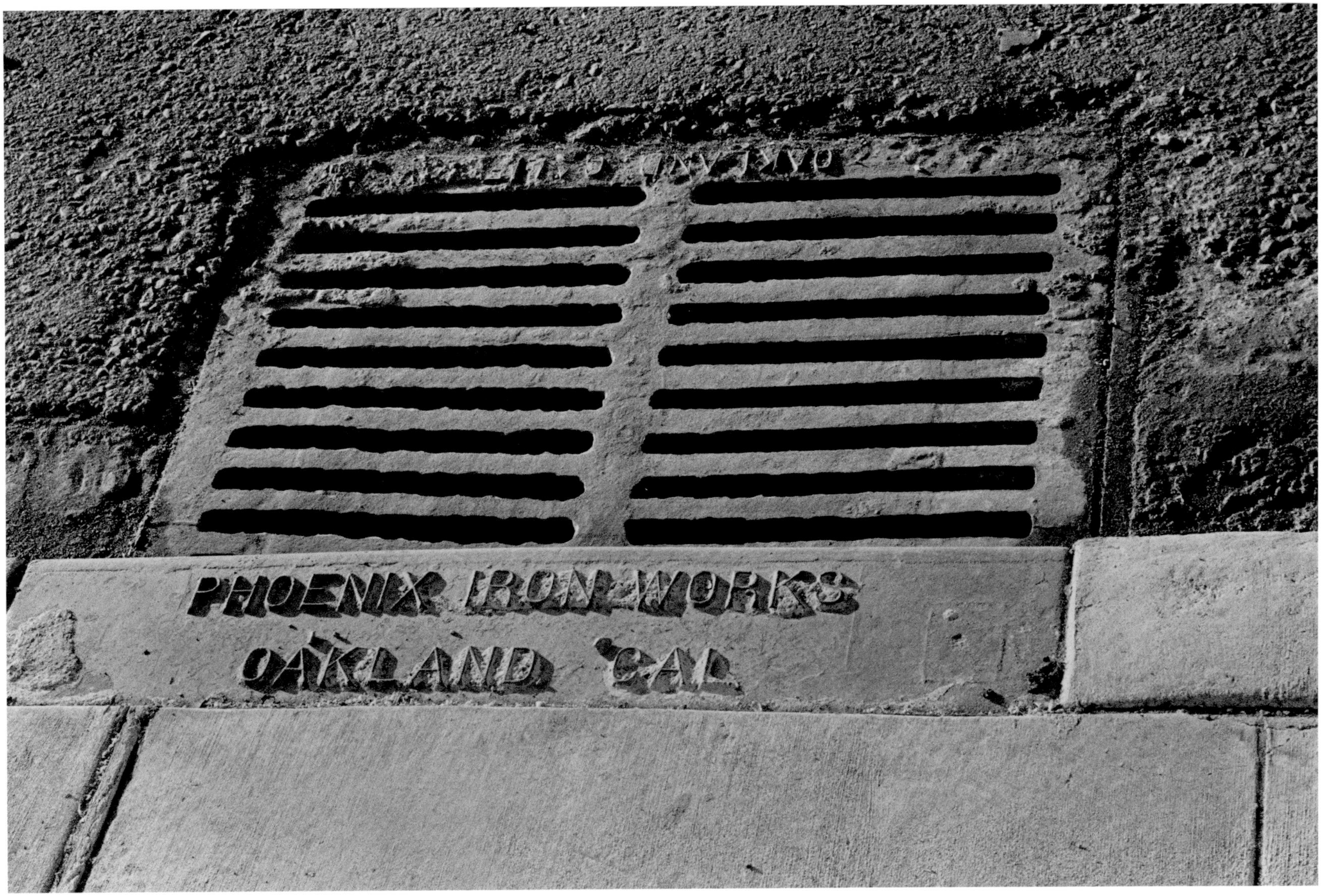
PHOENIX IRON WORKS
OAKLAND CAL

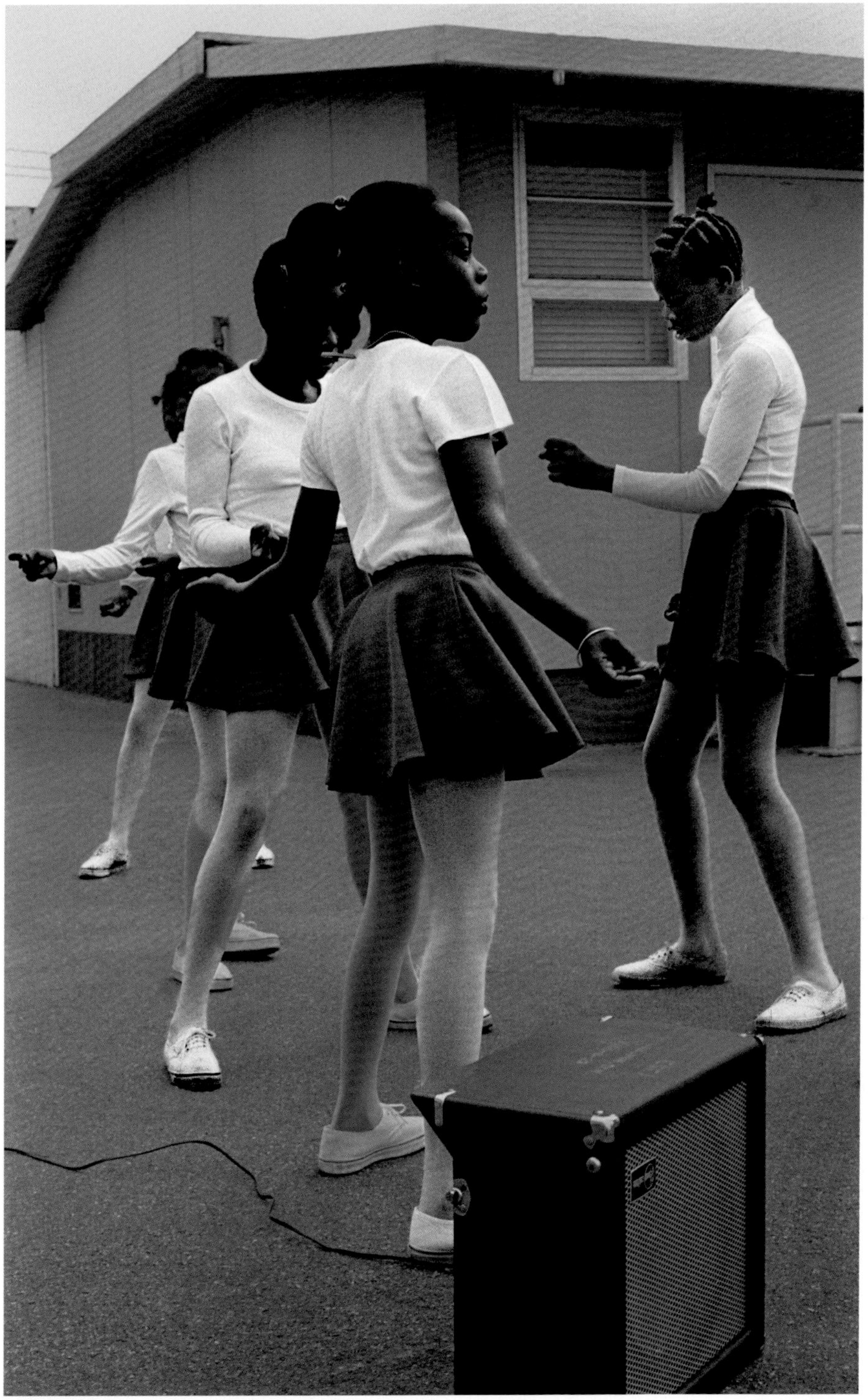

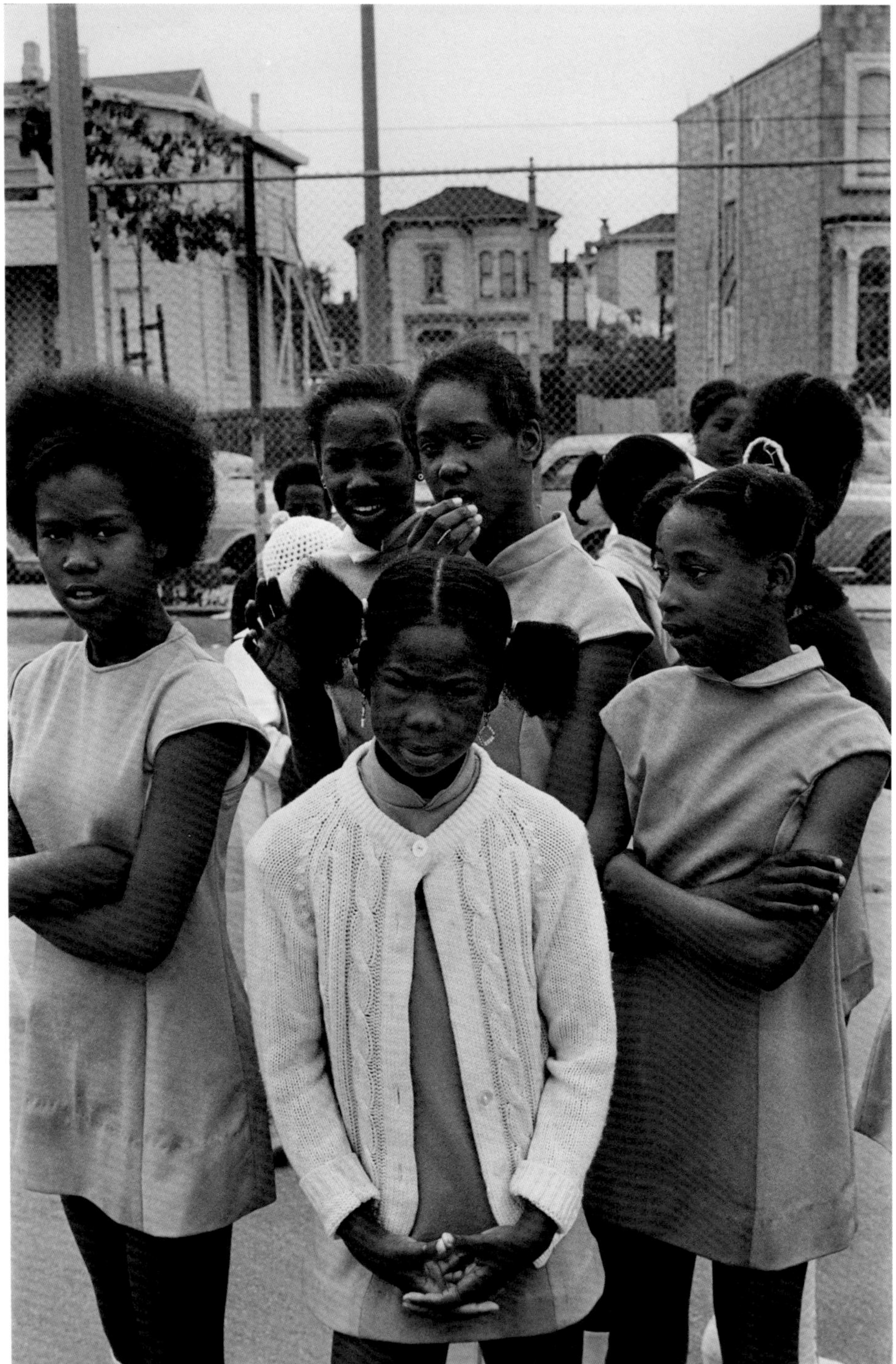

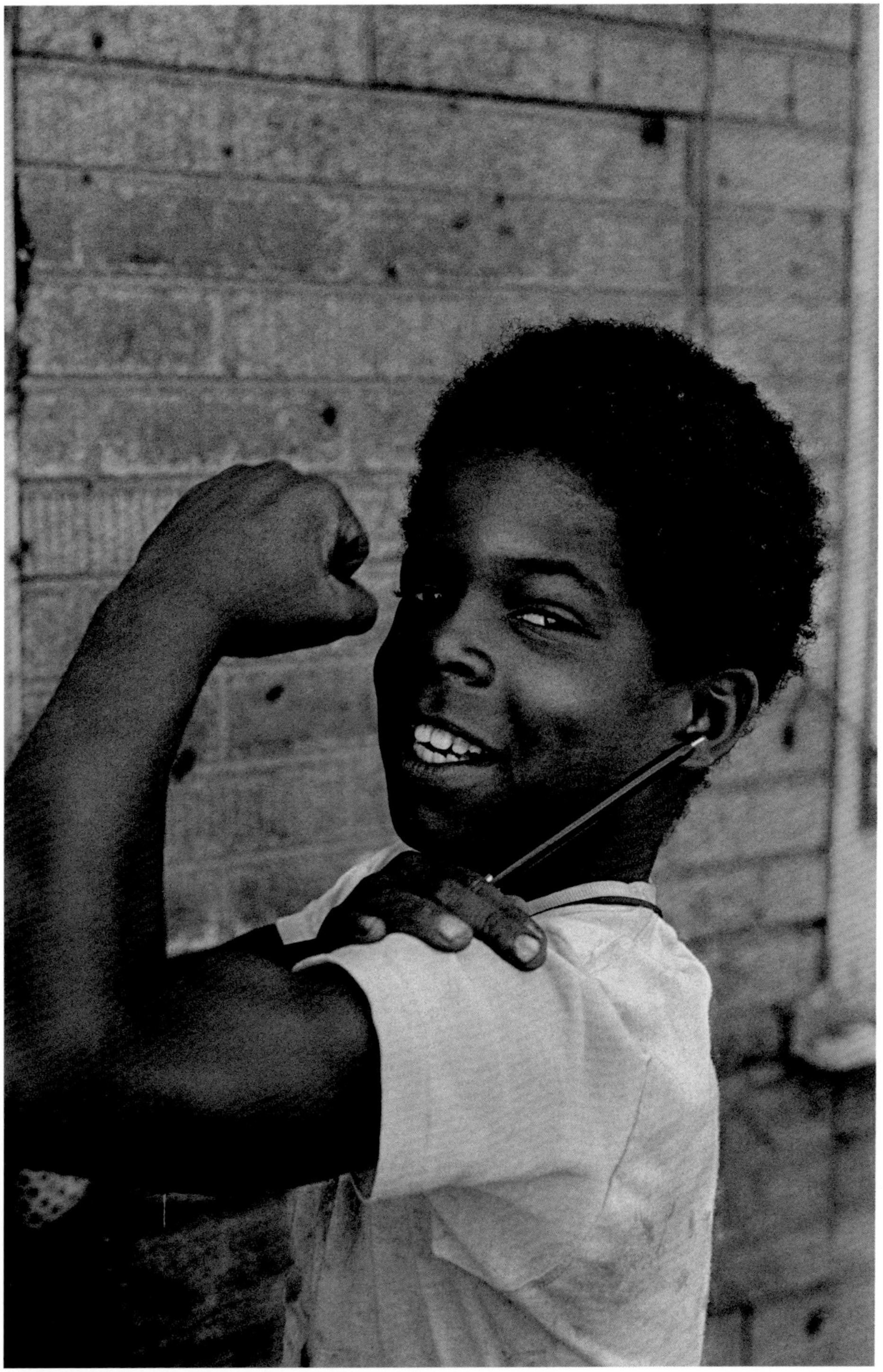

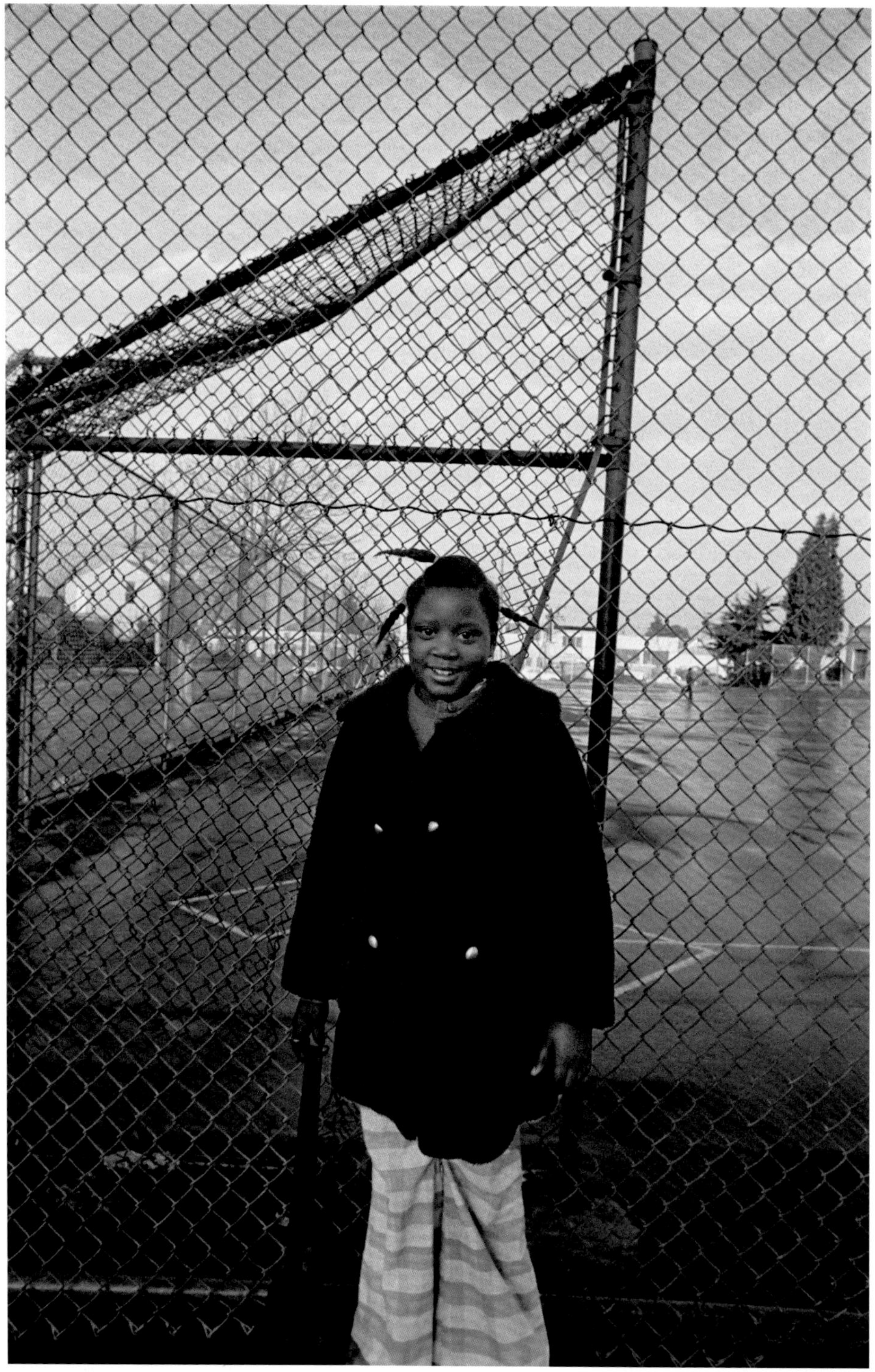

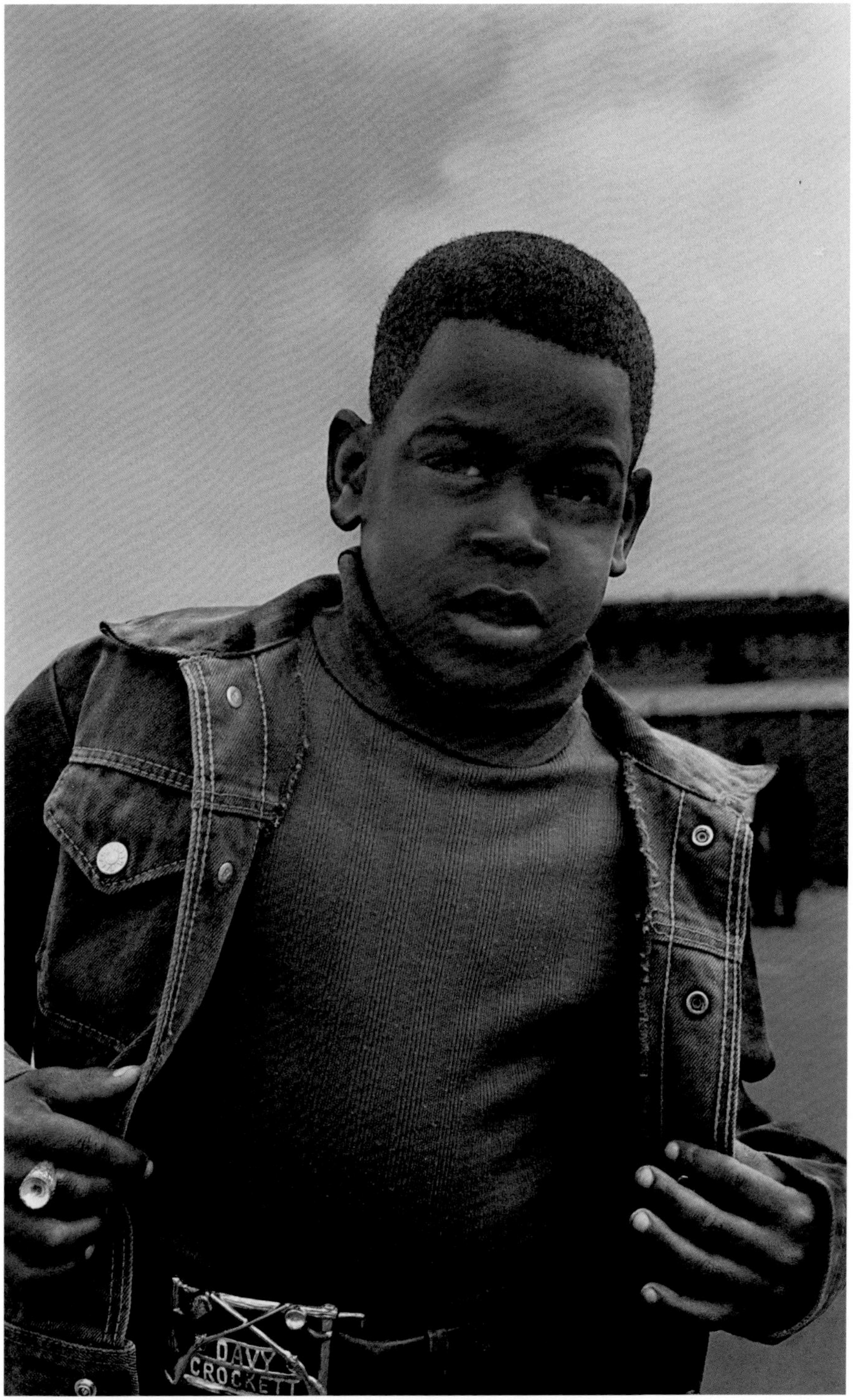
DAVY
CROCKETT

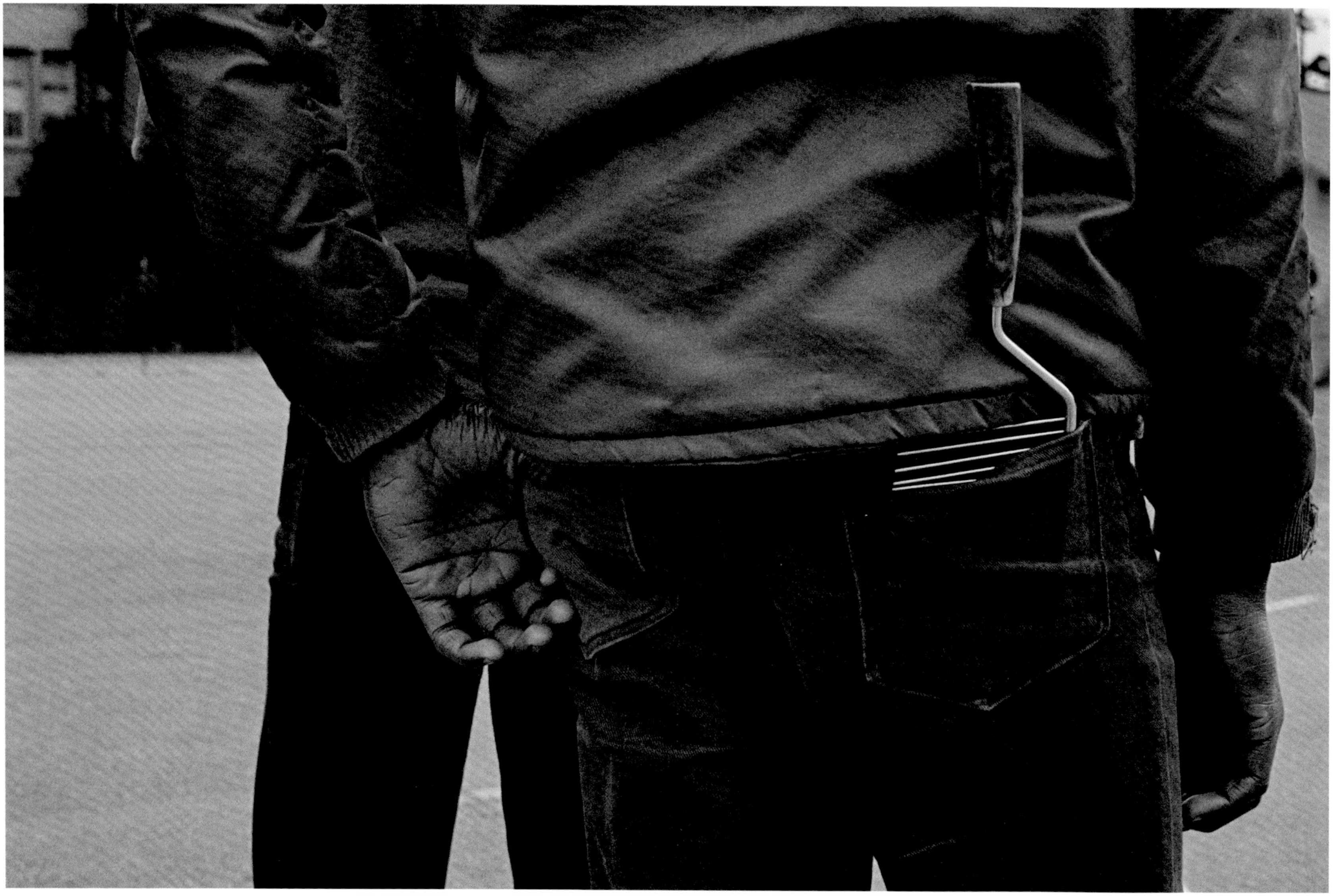

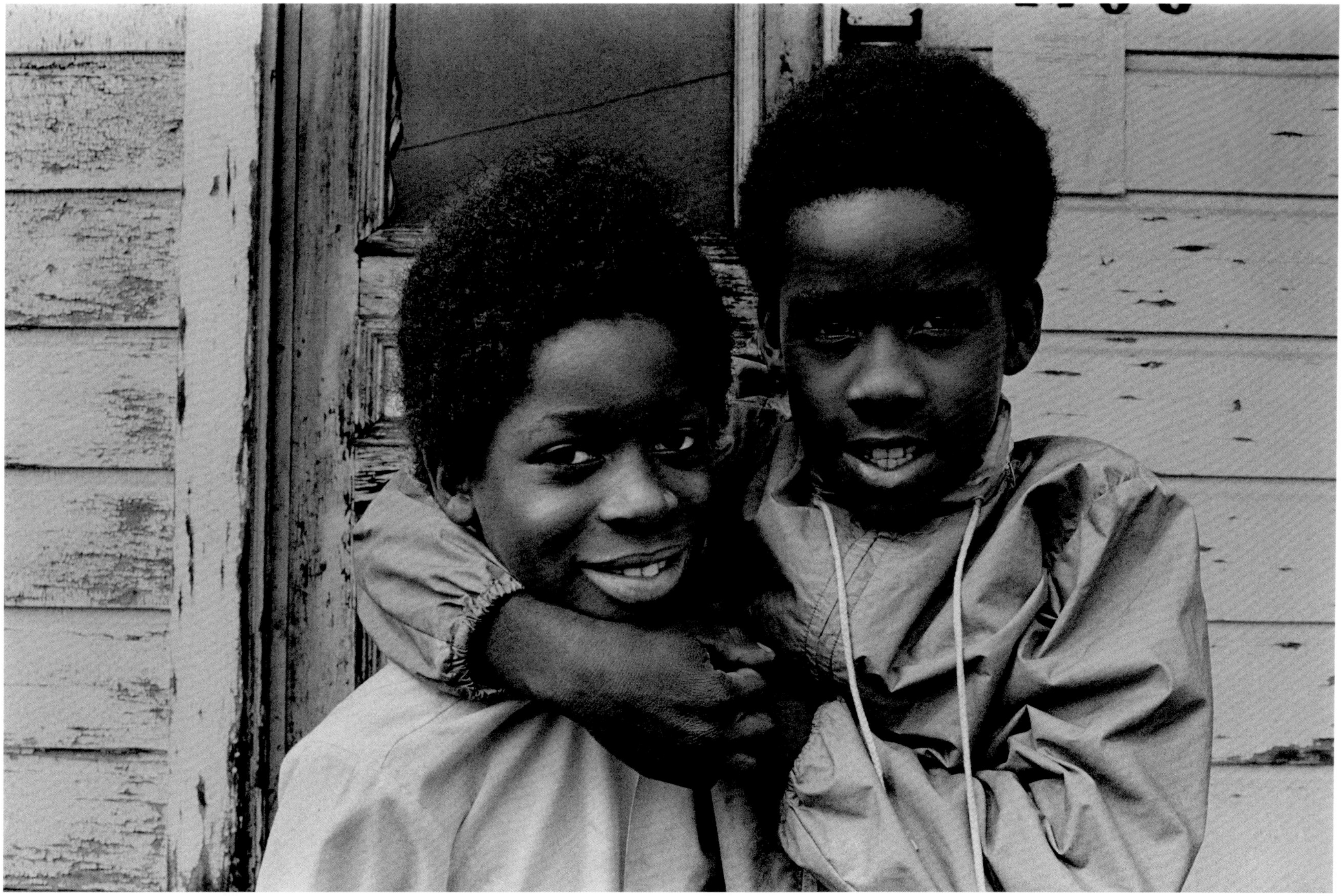

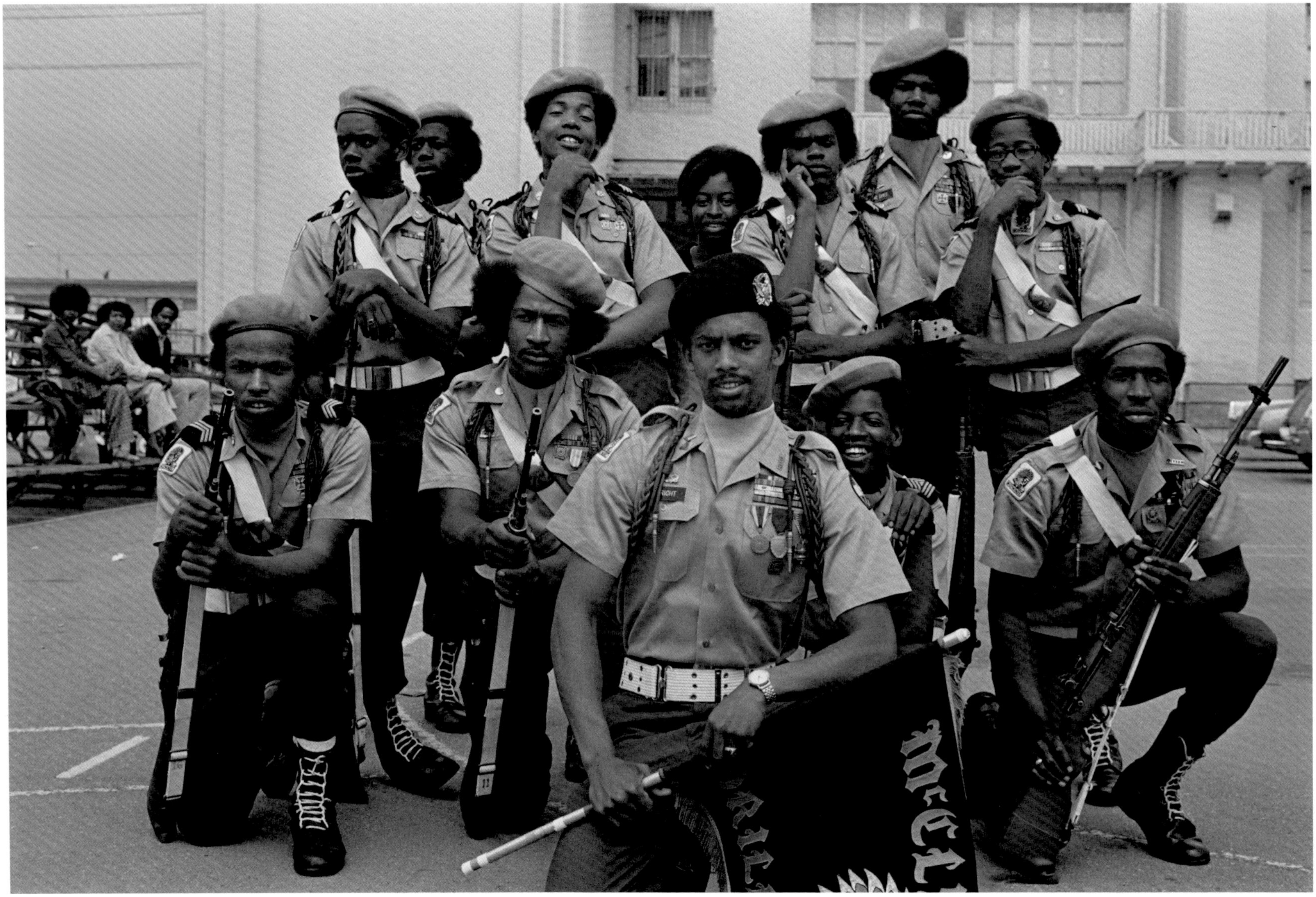

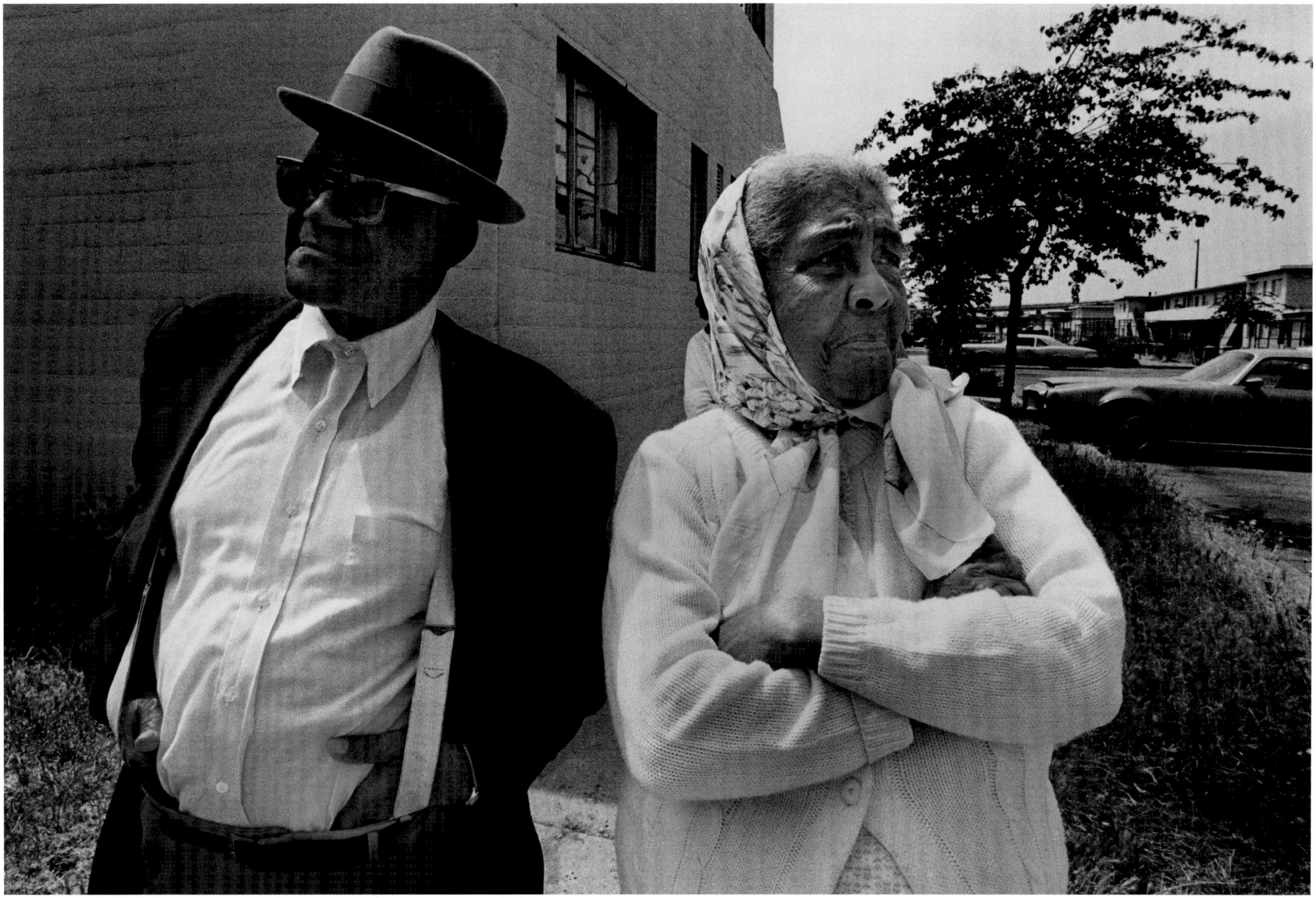

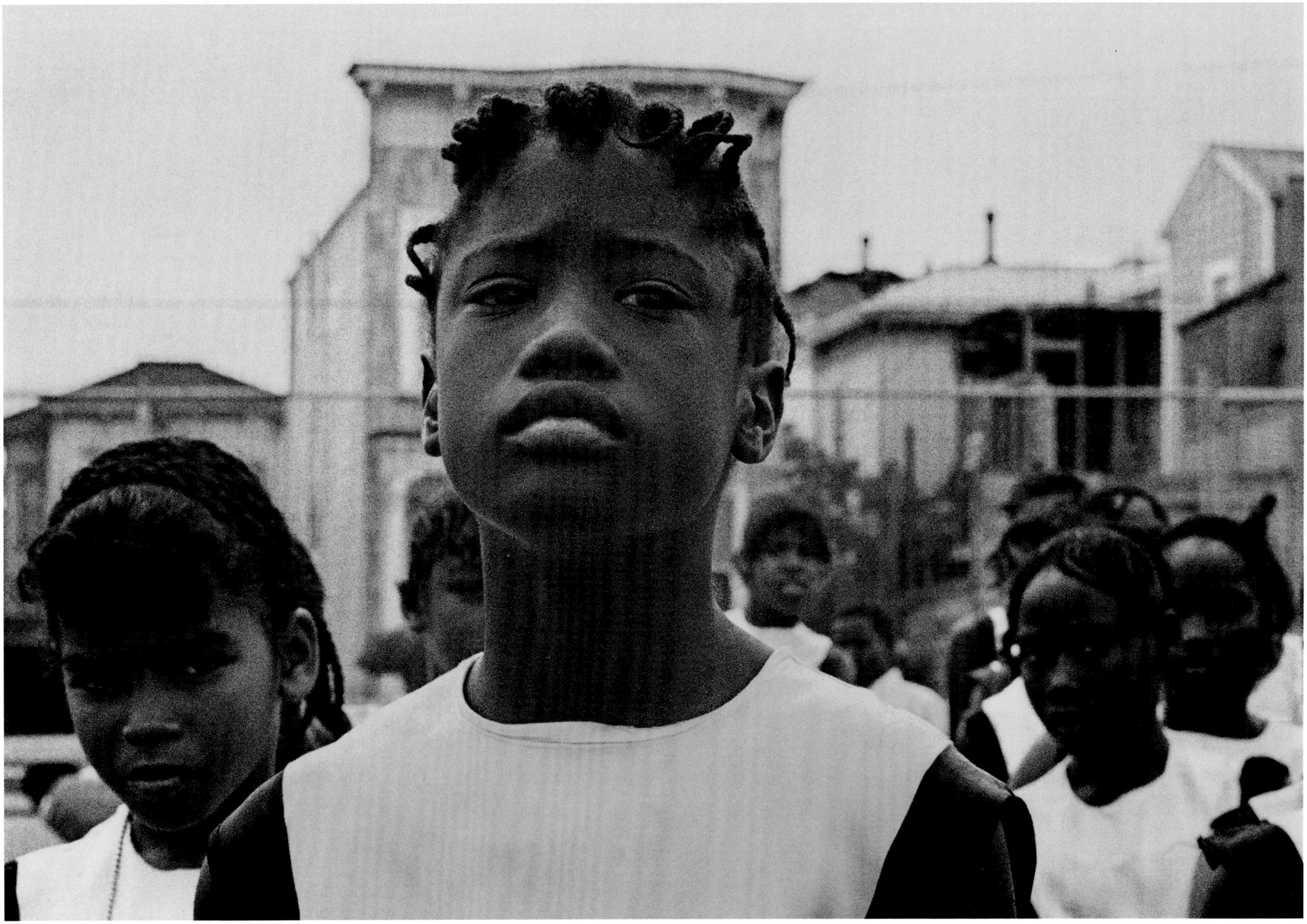

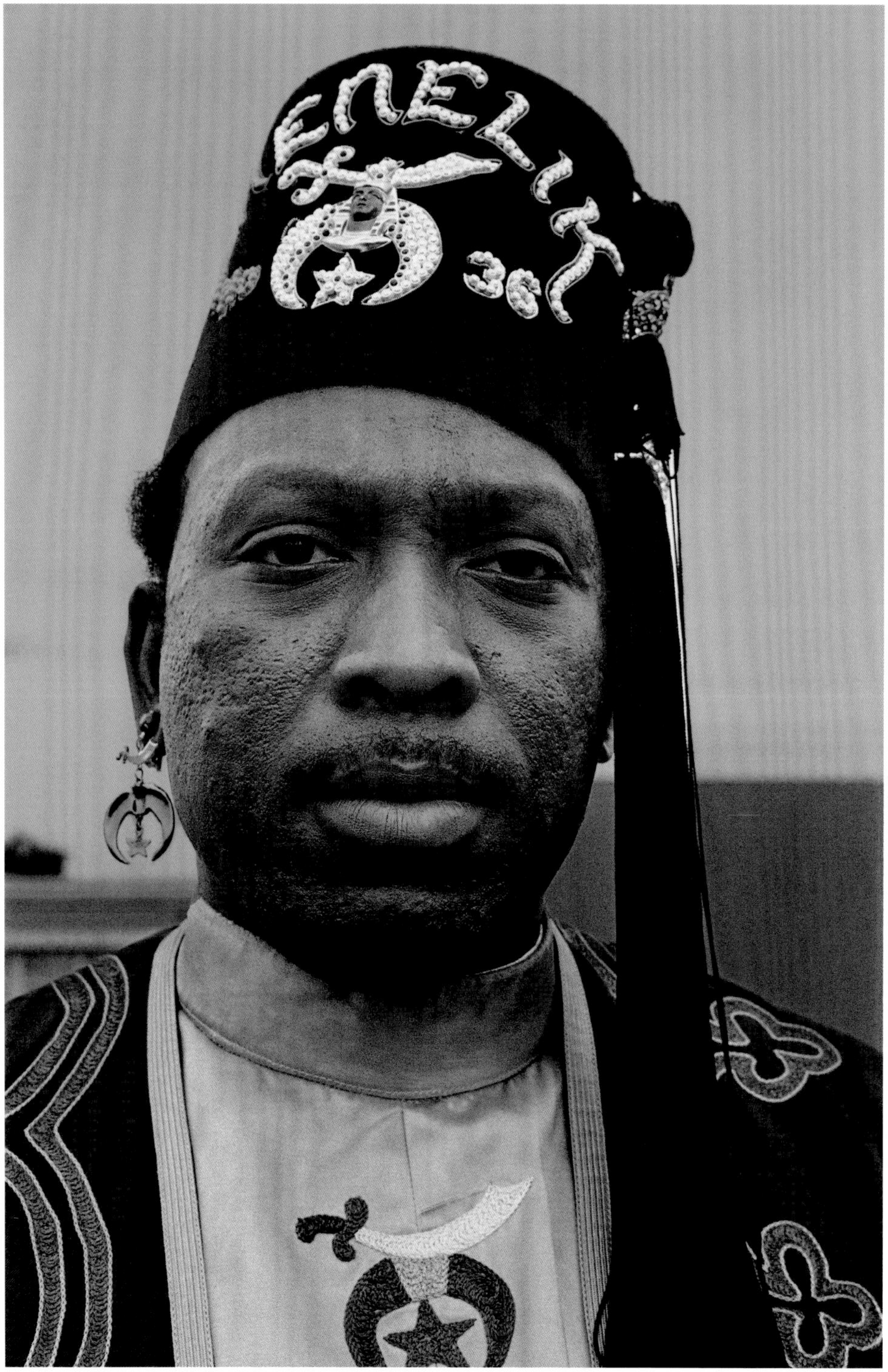
ENELIK
36

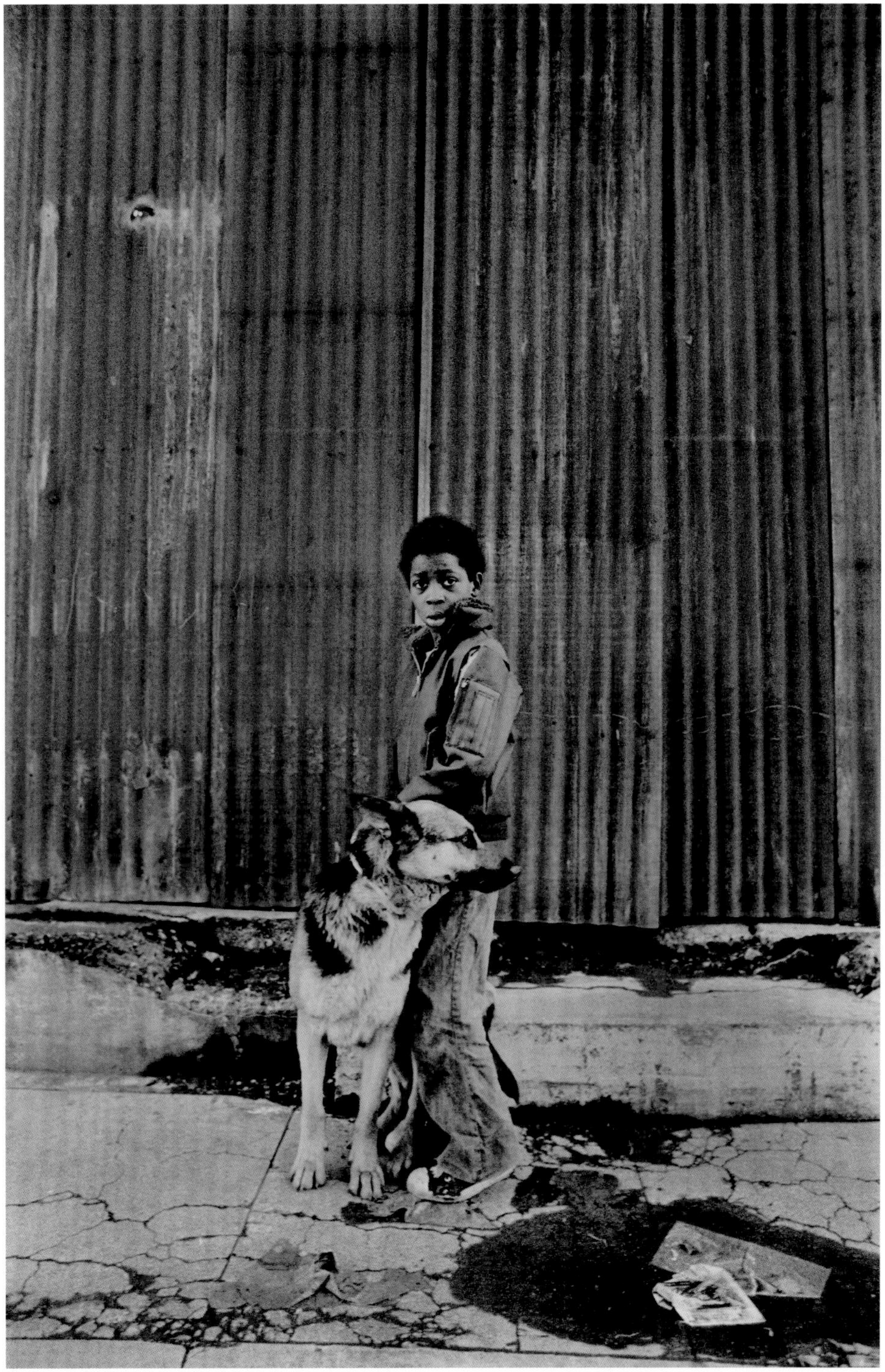

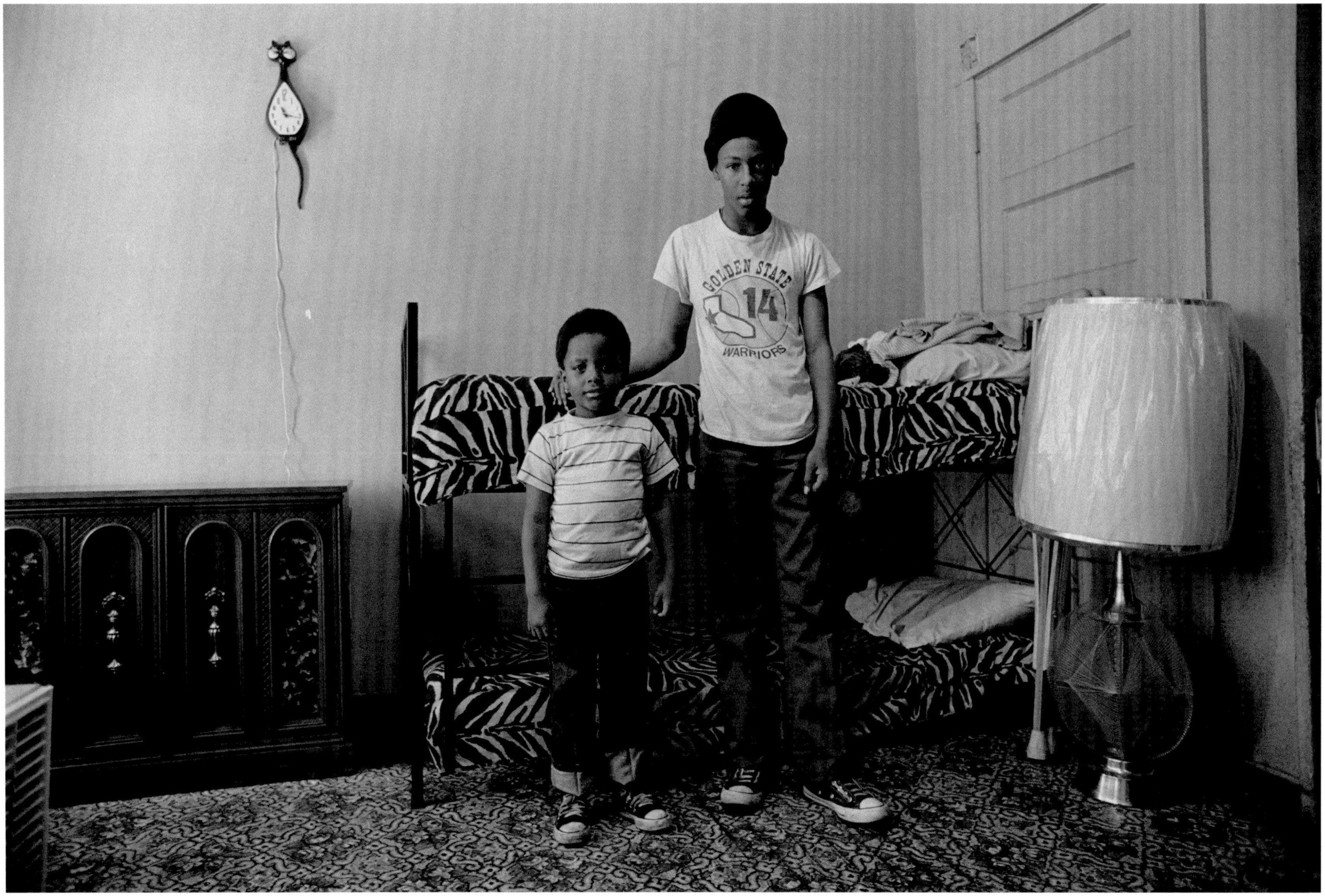
GOLDEN STATE
14
WARRIORS

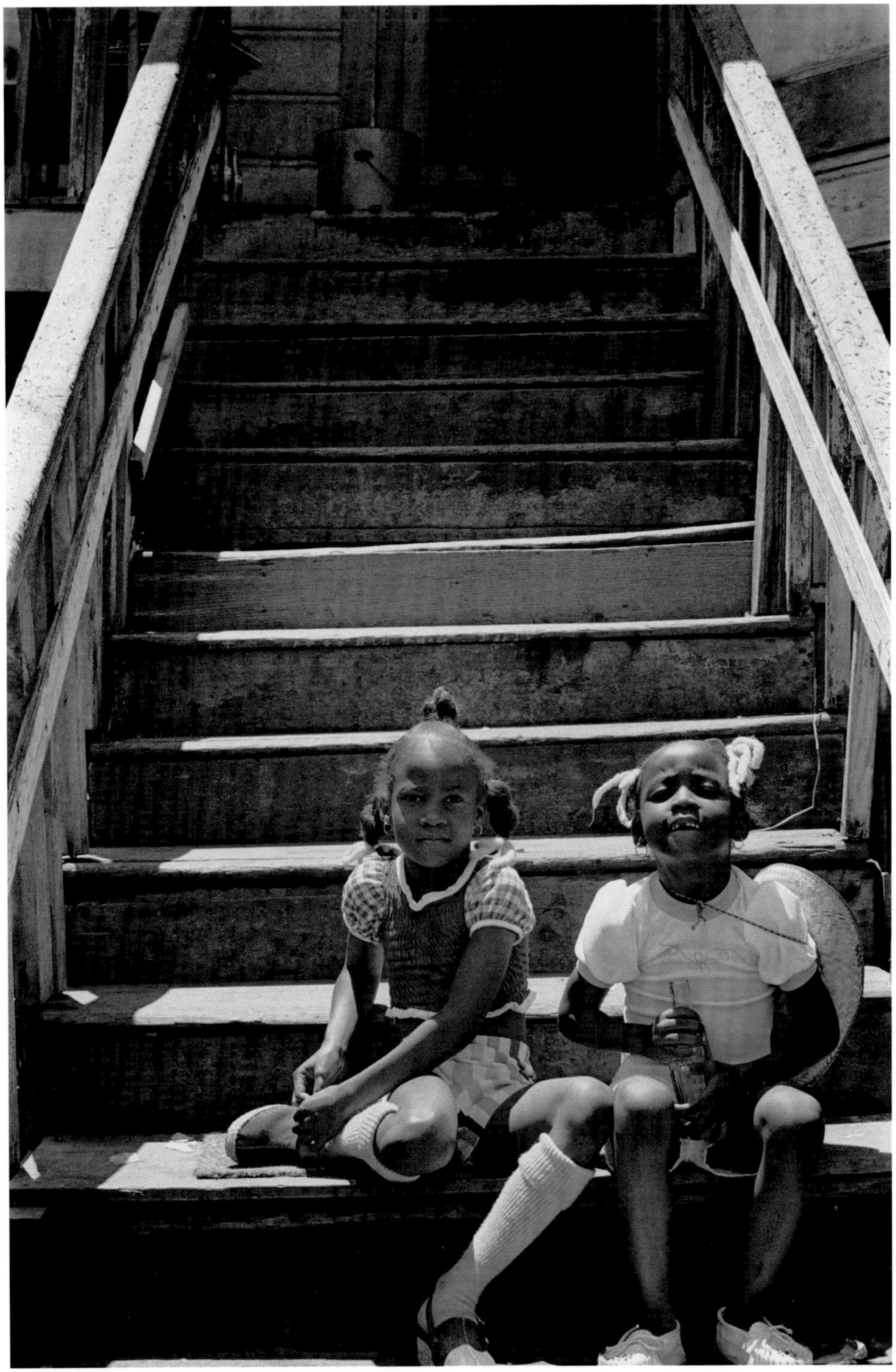

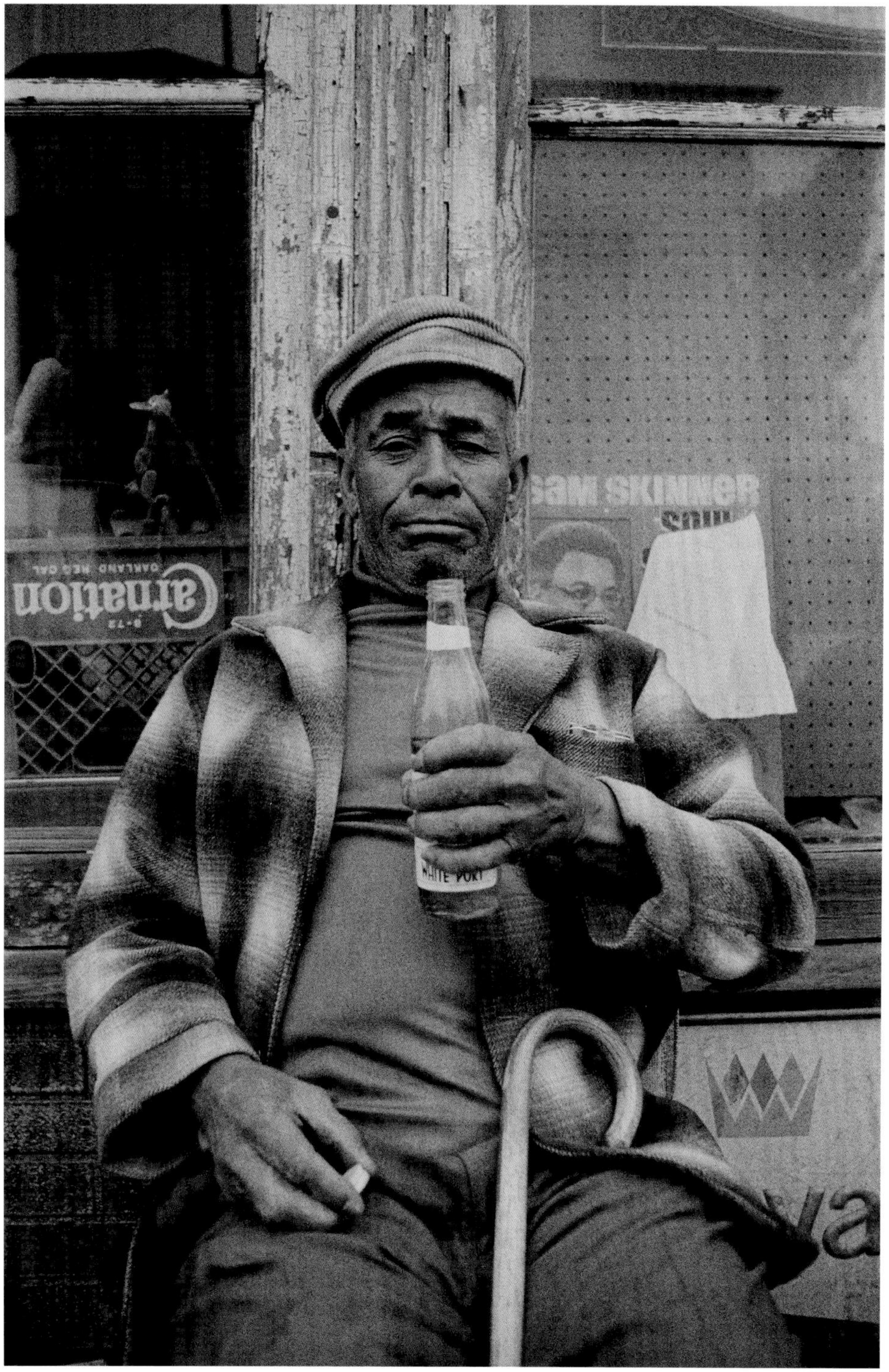
SAM SKINNER
WHITE PORT

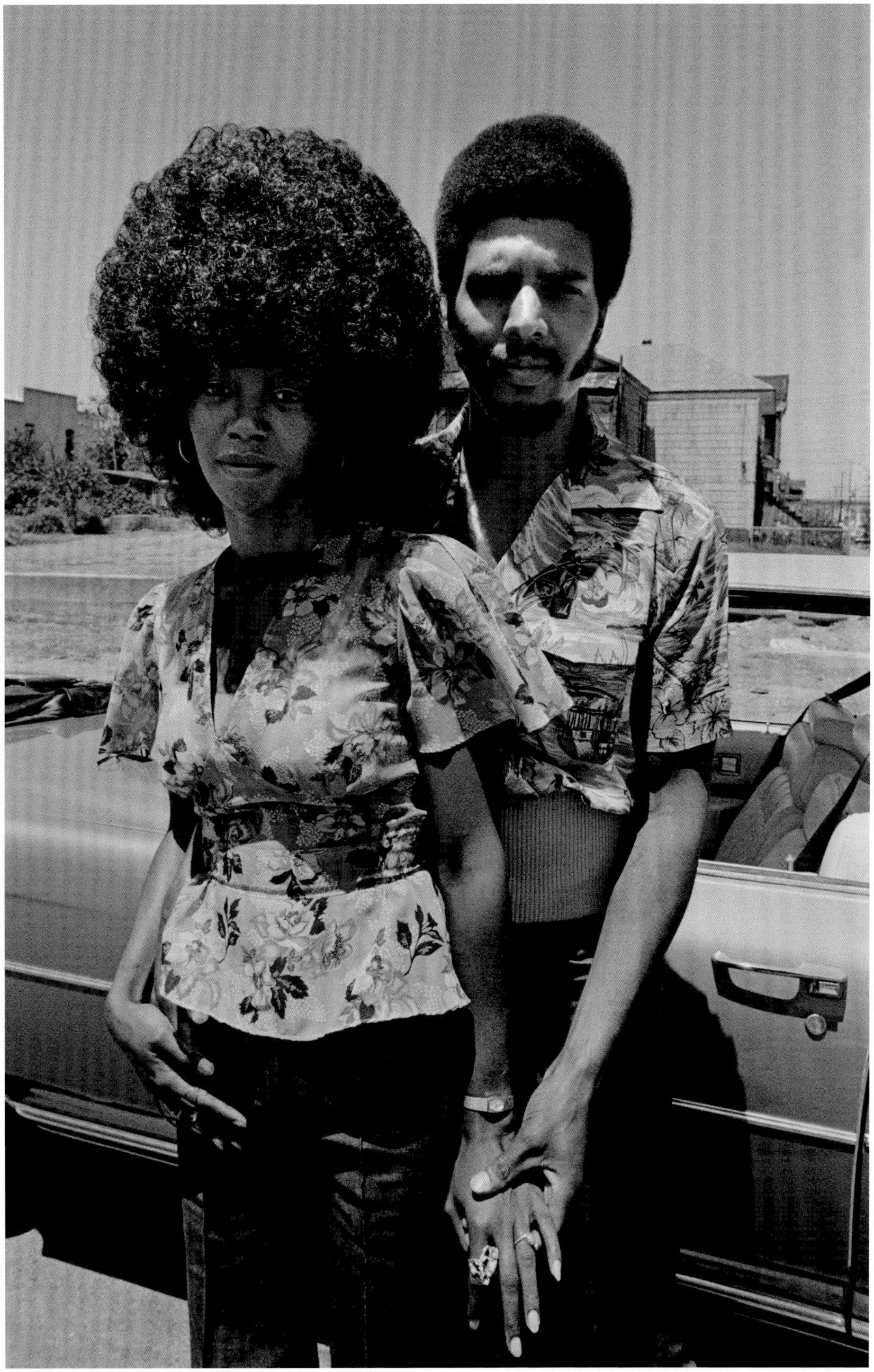

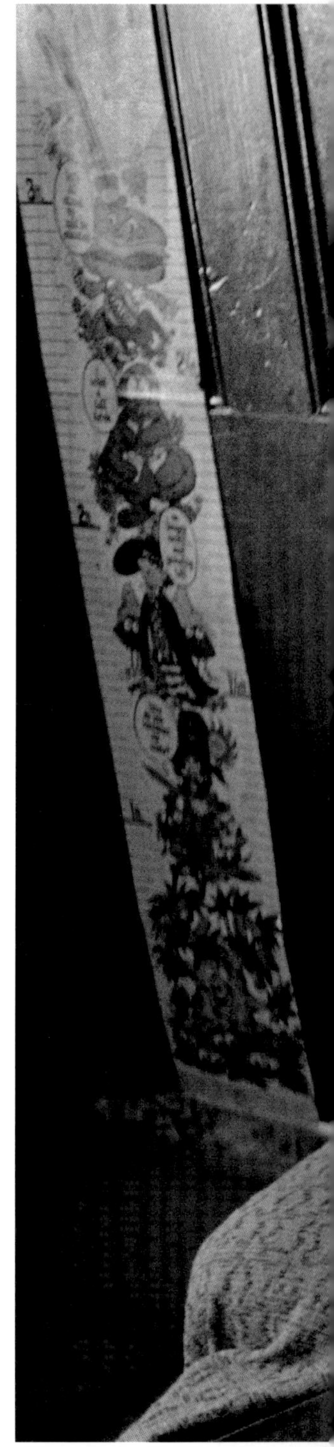

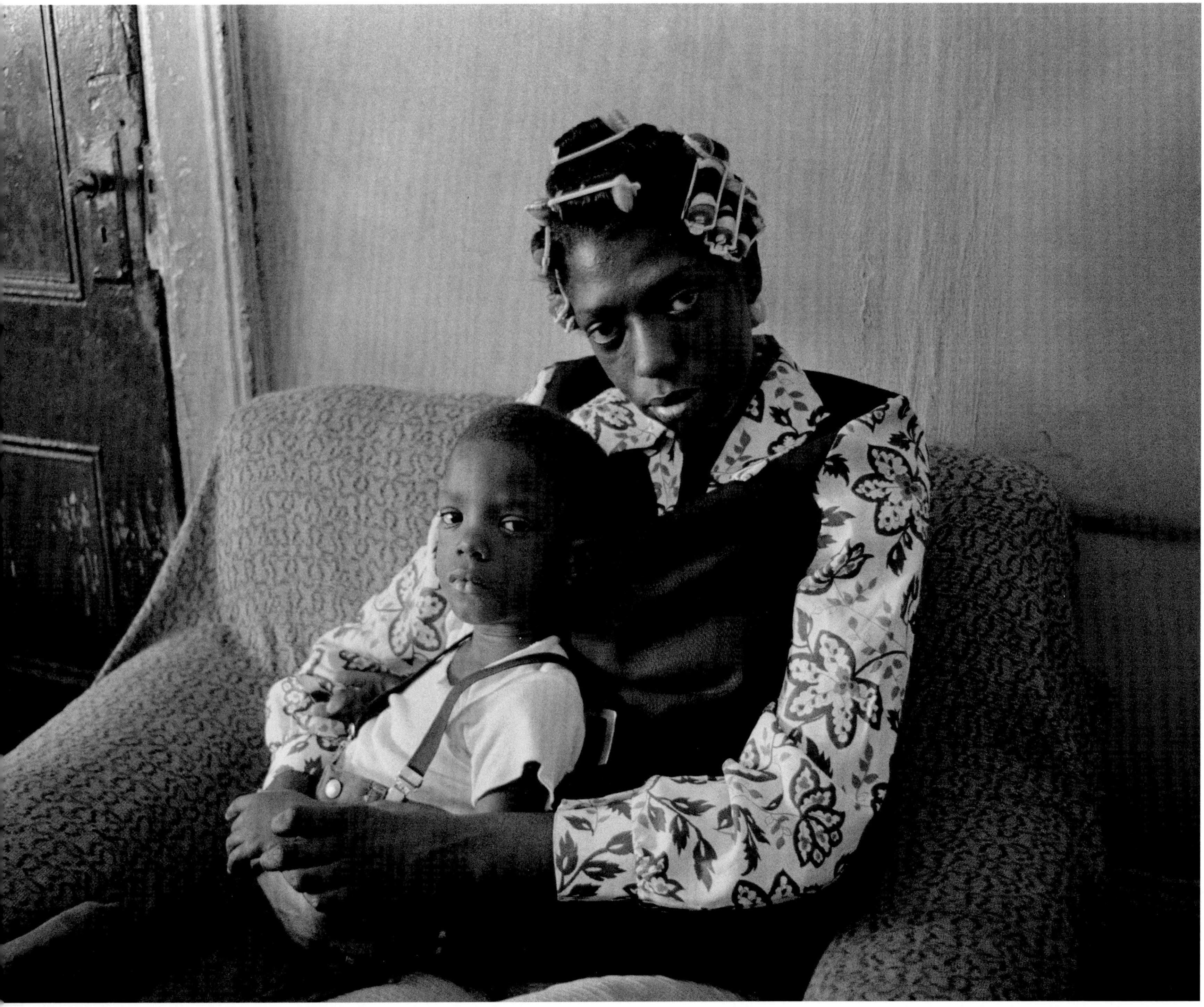

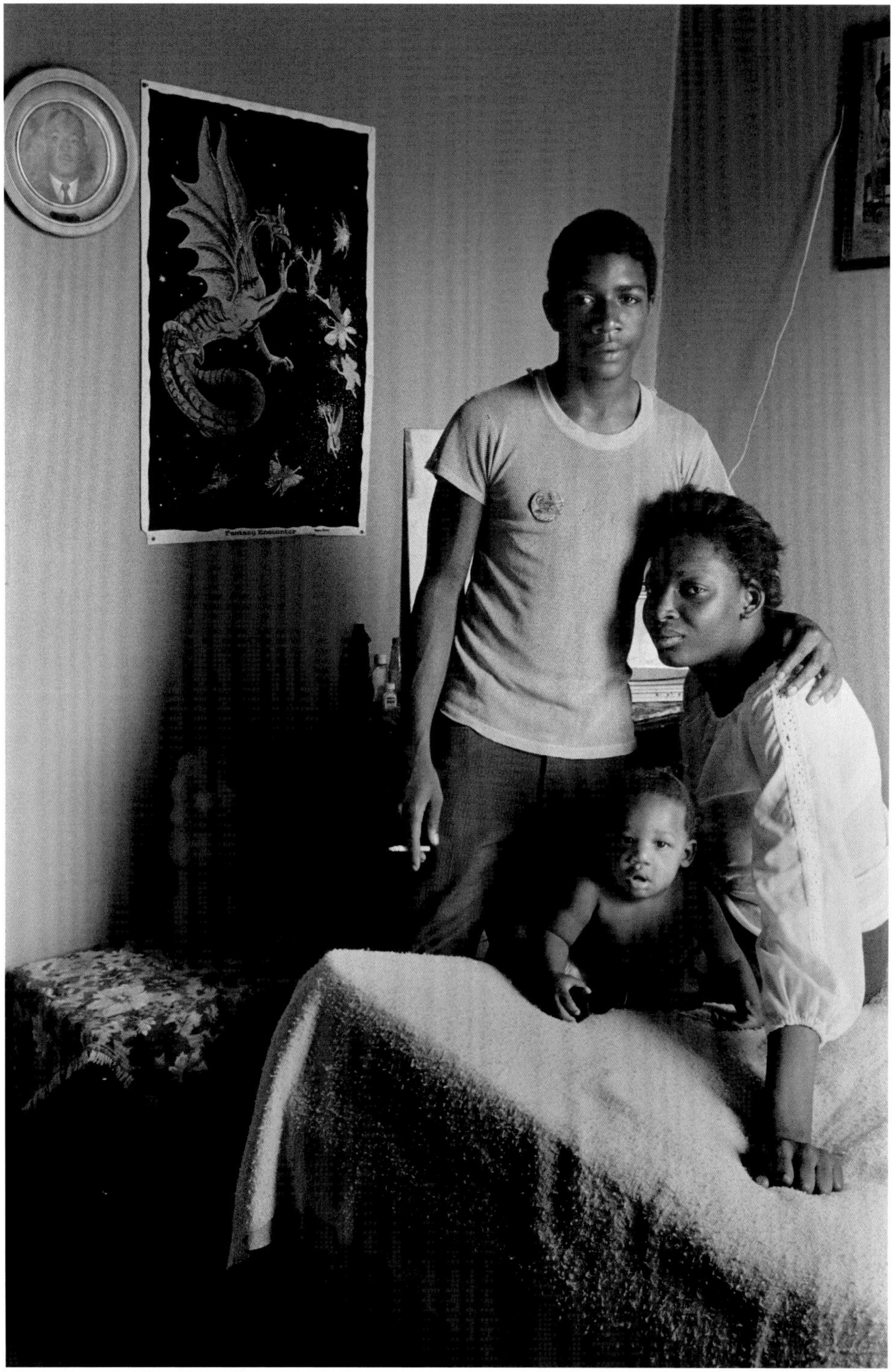

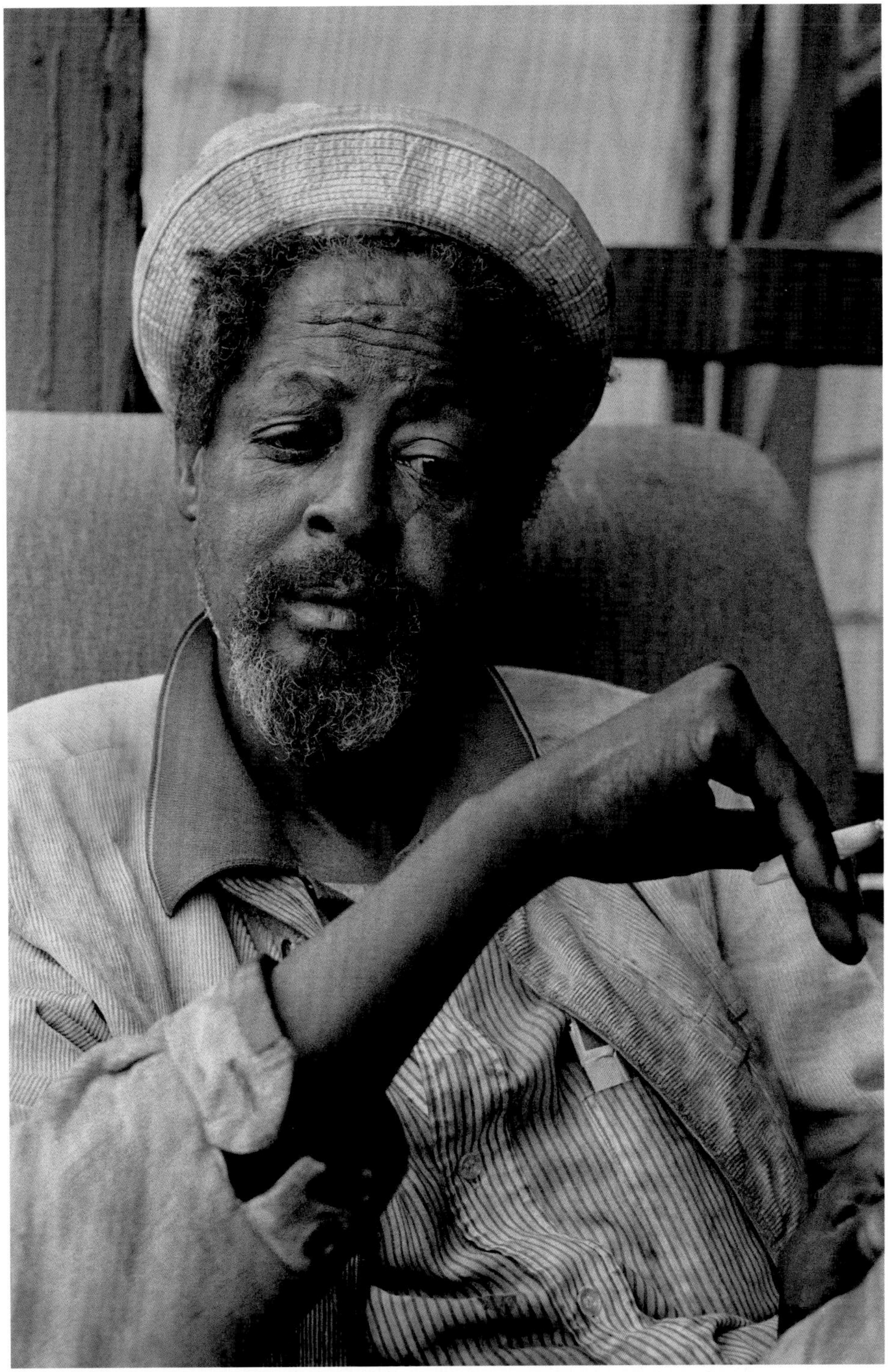

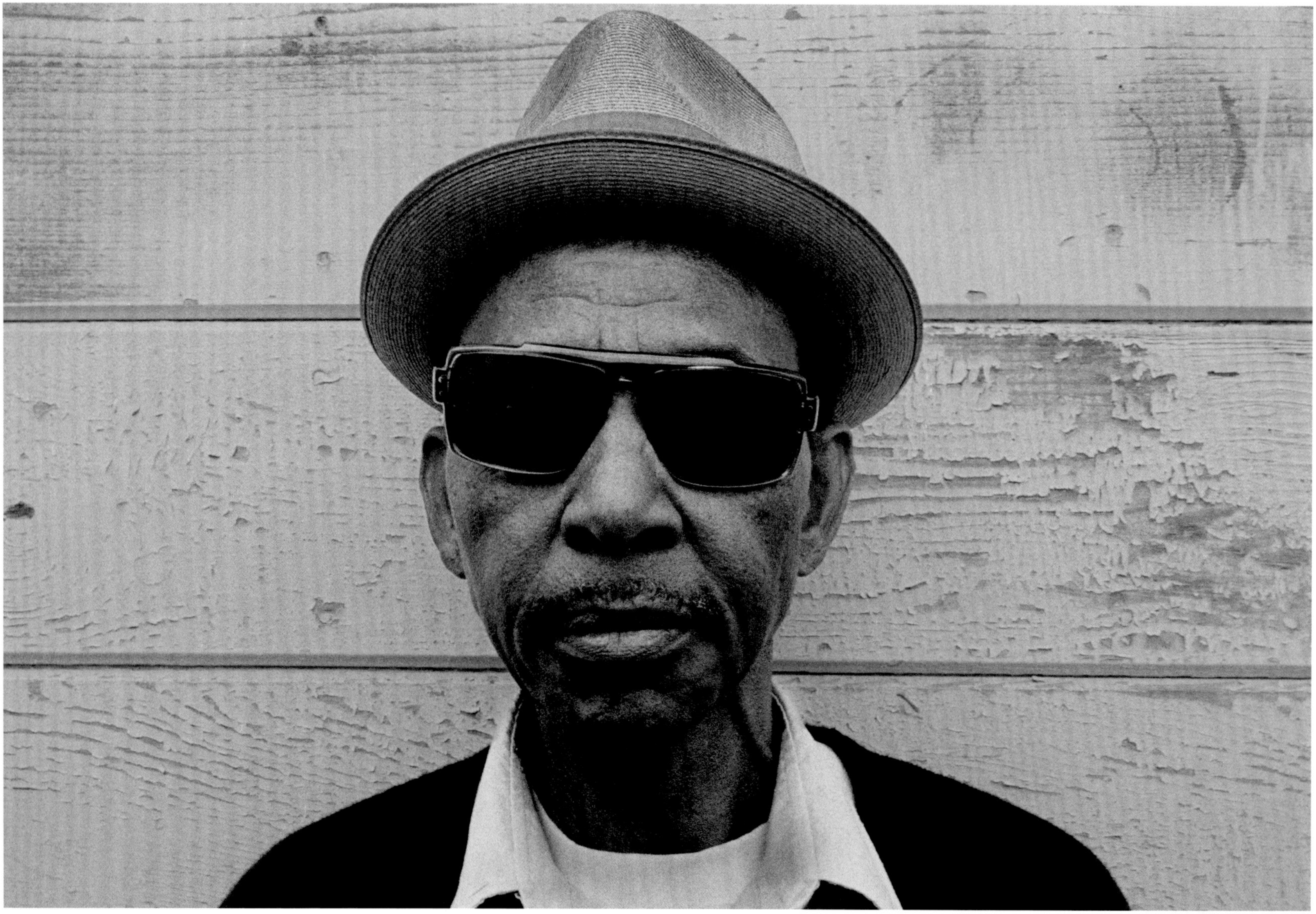

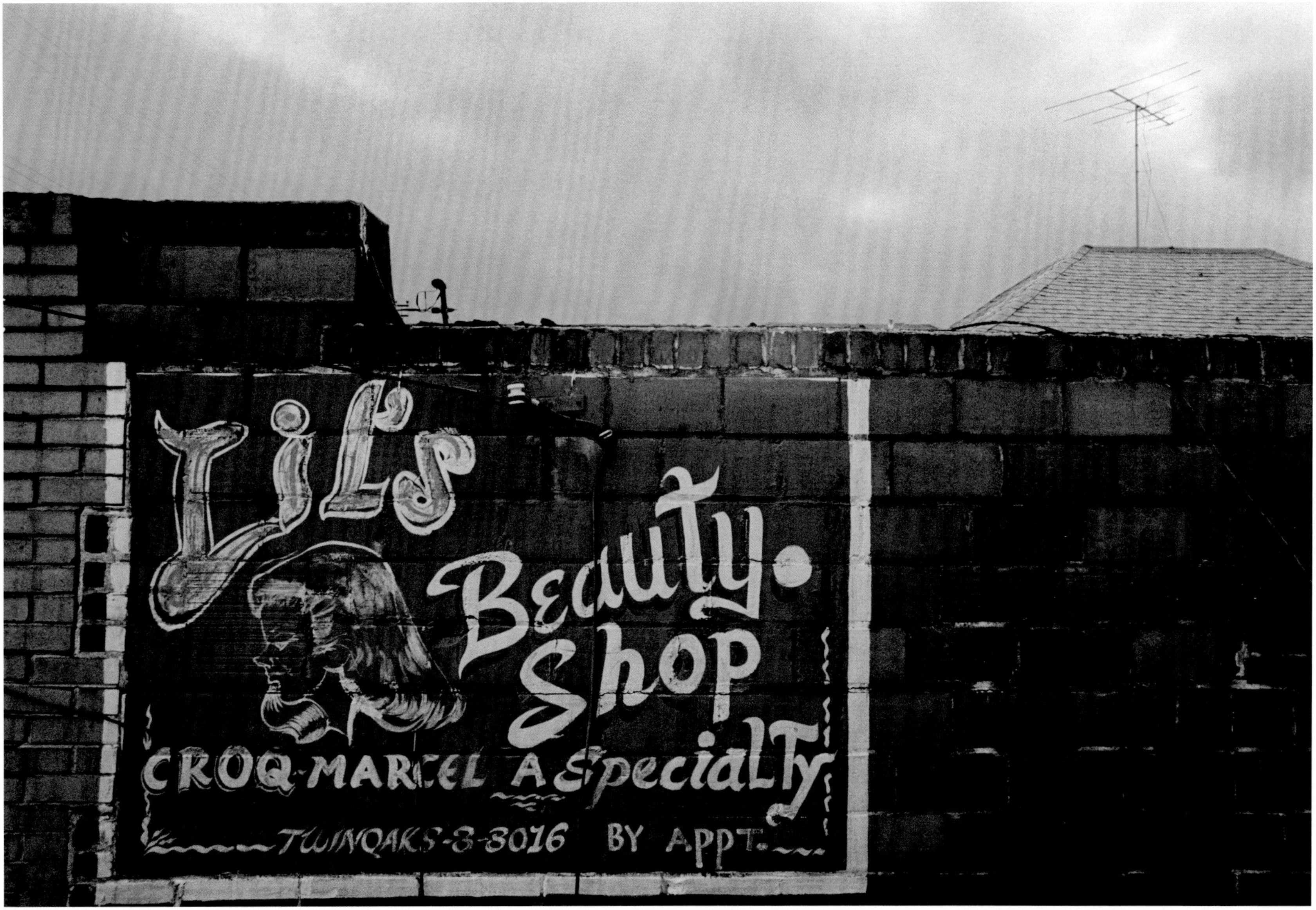
Lil's
Beauty
Shop
CROQ-MARCEL A SpecialTy
TWINOAKS-3-3016 BY APPT.

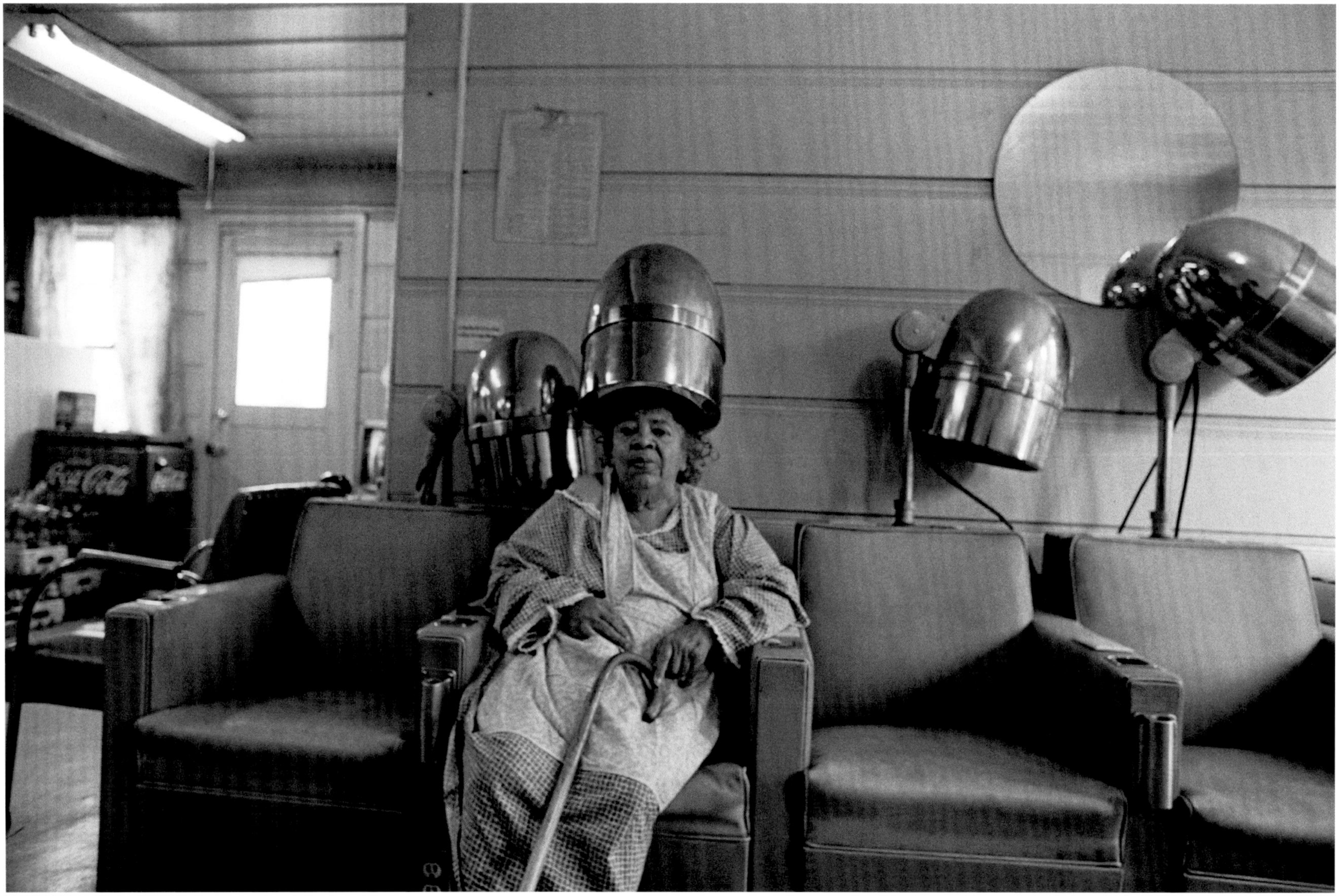
Coca-Cola

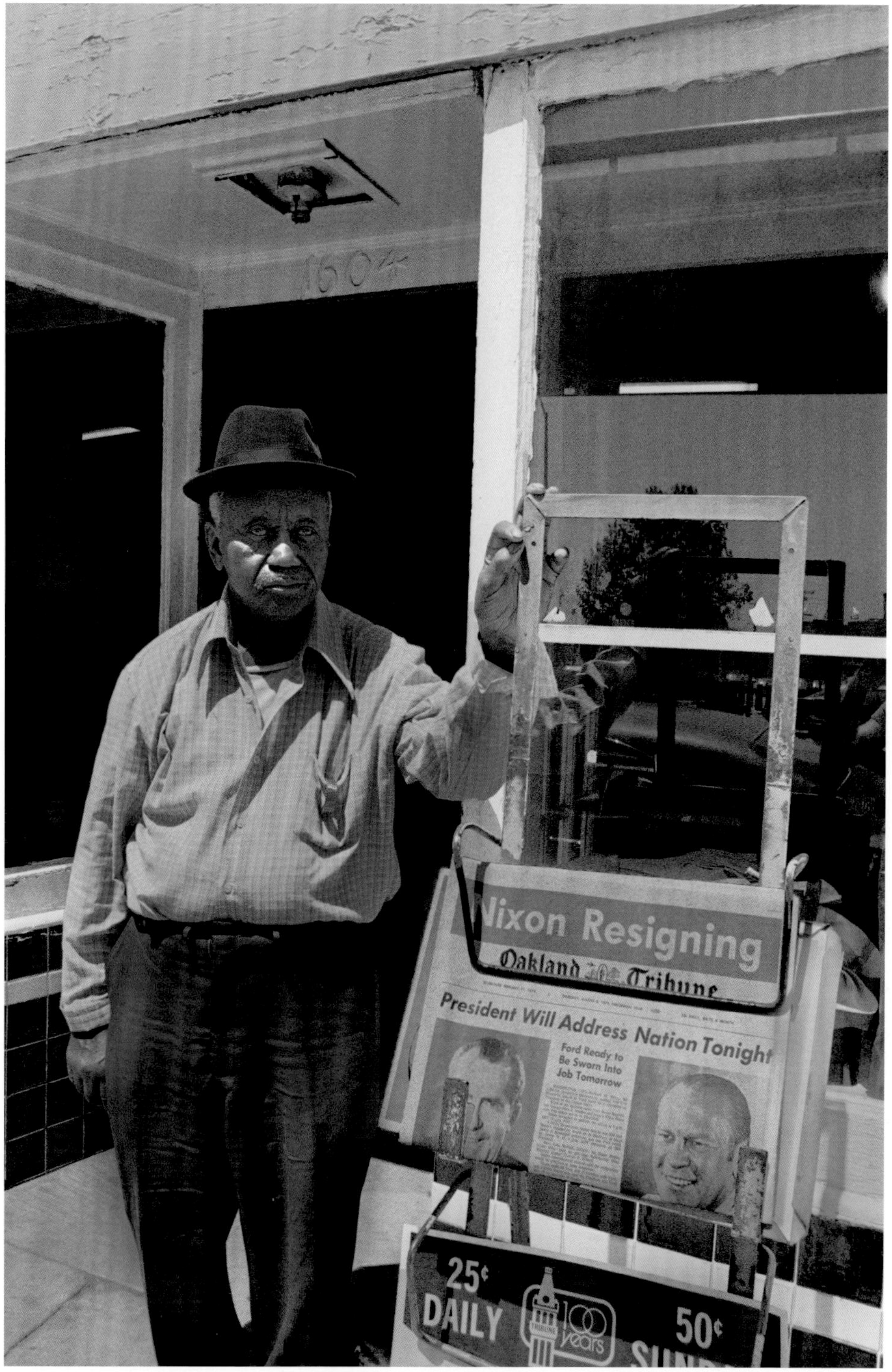
1604
Nixon Resigning
Oakland Tribune
President Will Address Nation Tonight
Ford Ready to Be Sworn Into Job Tomorrow
25¢ DAILY
100 years
50¢

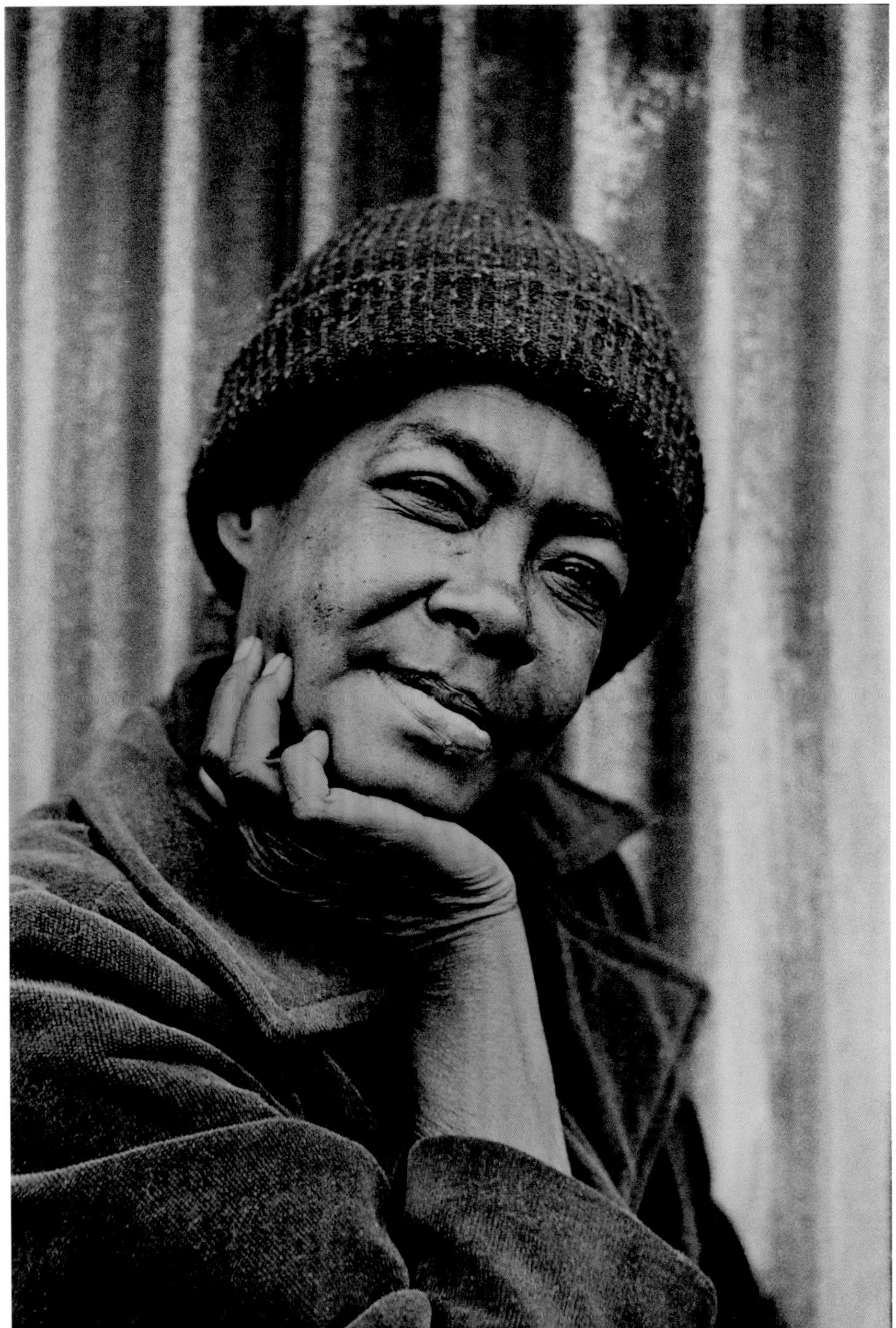

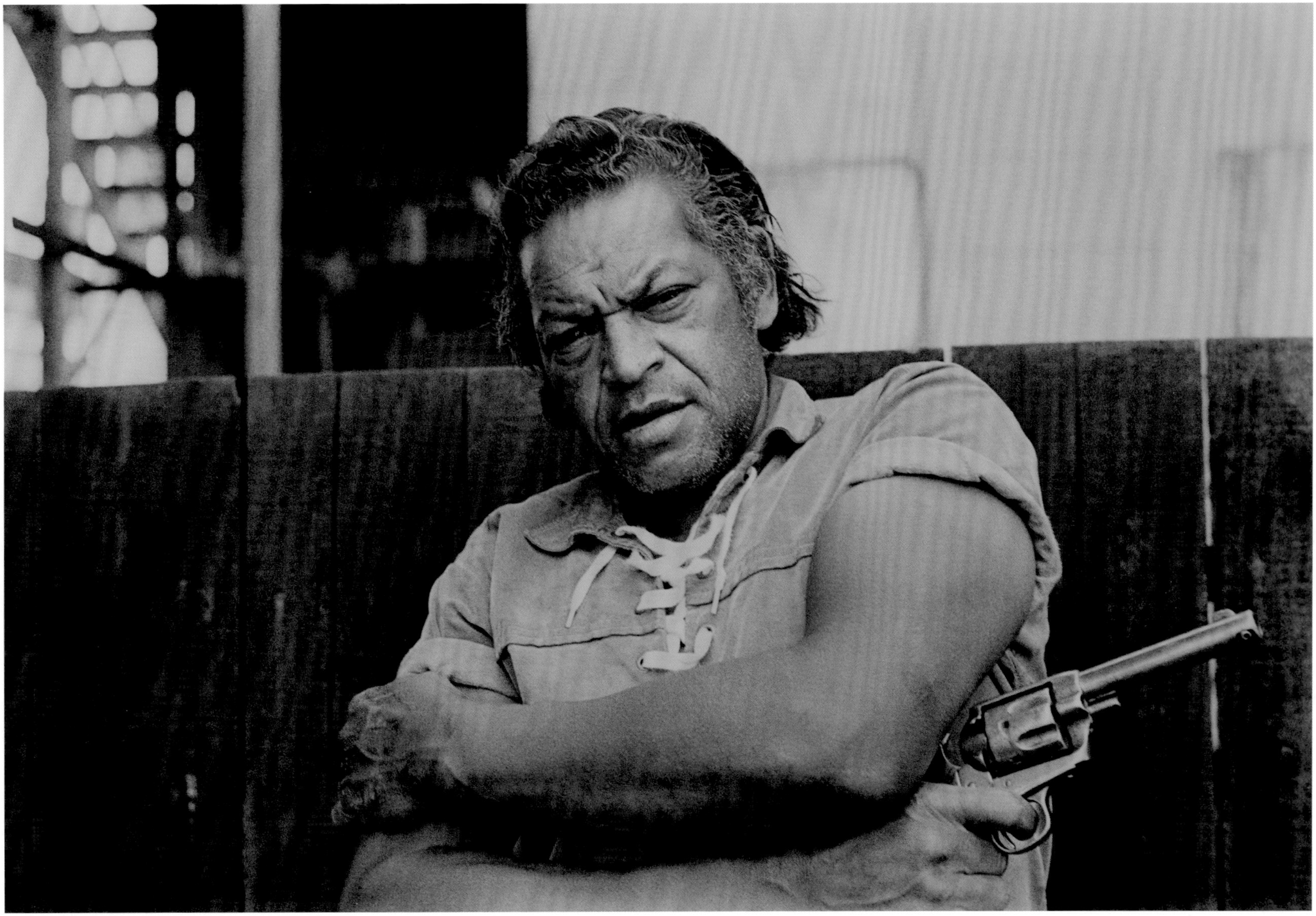

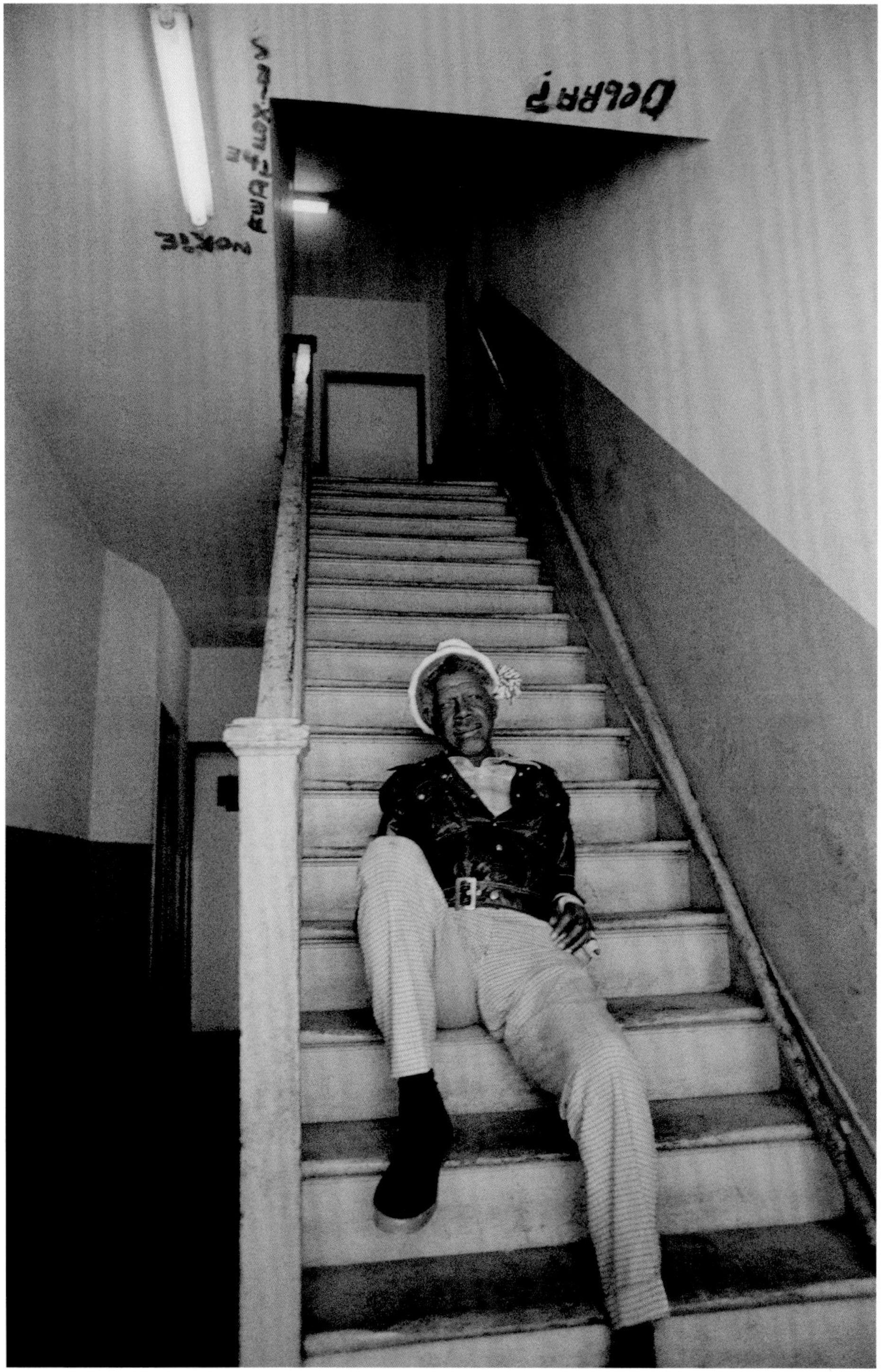

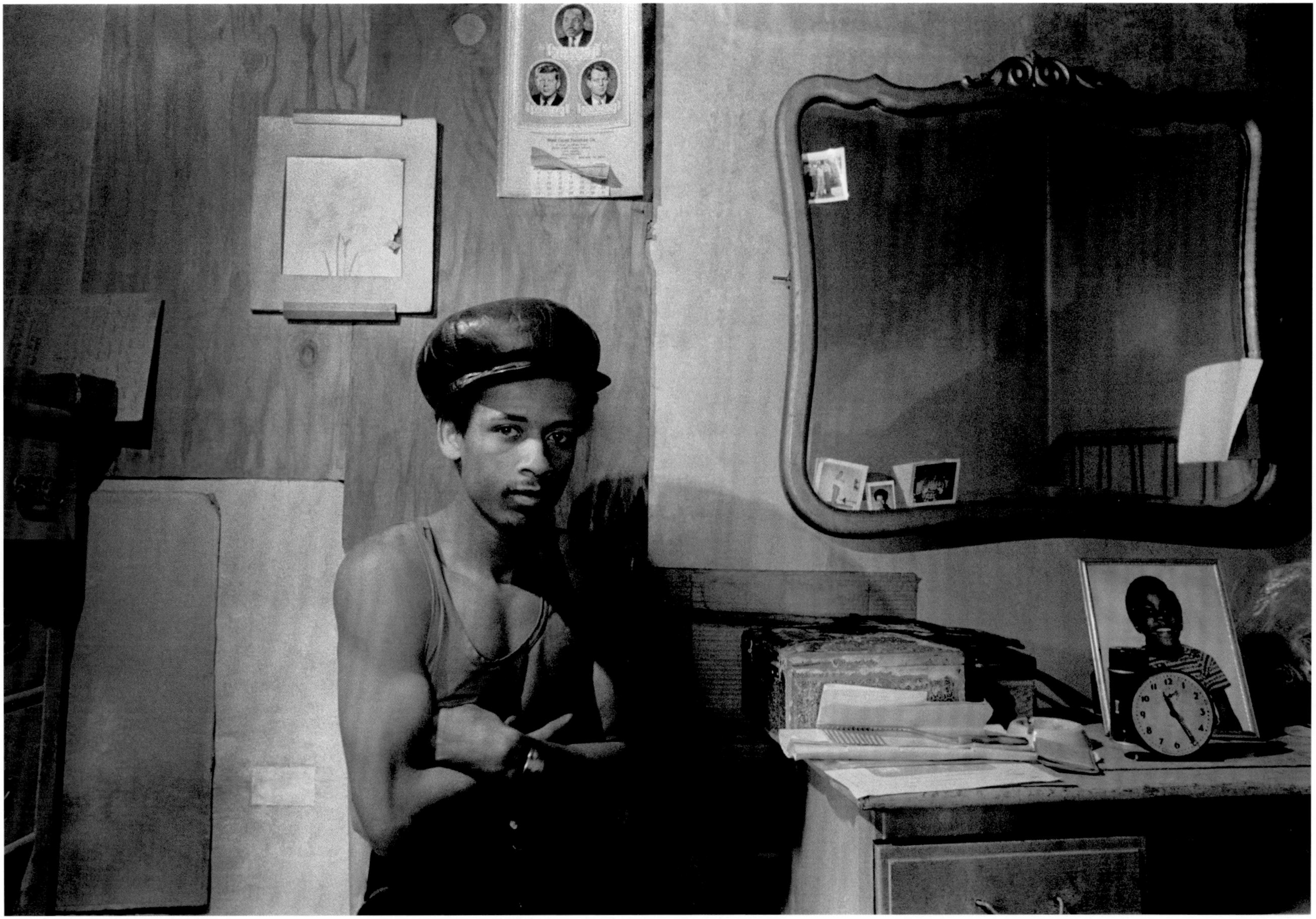

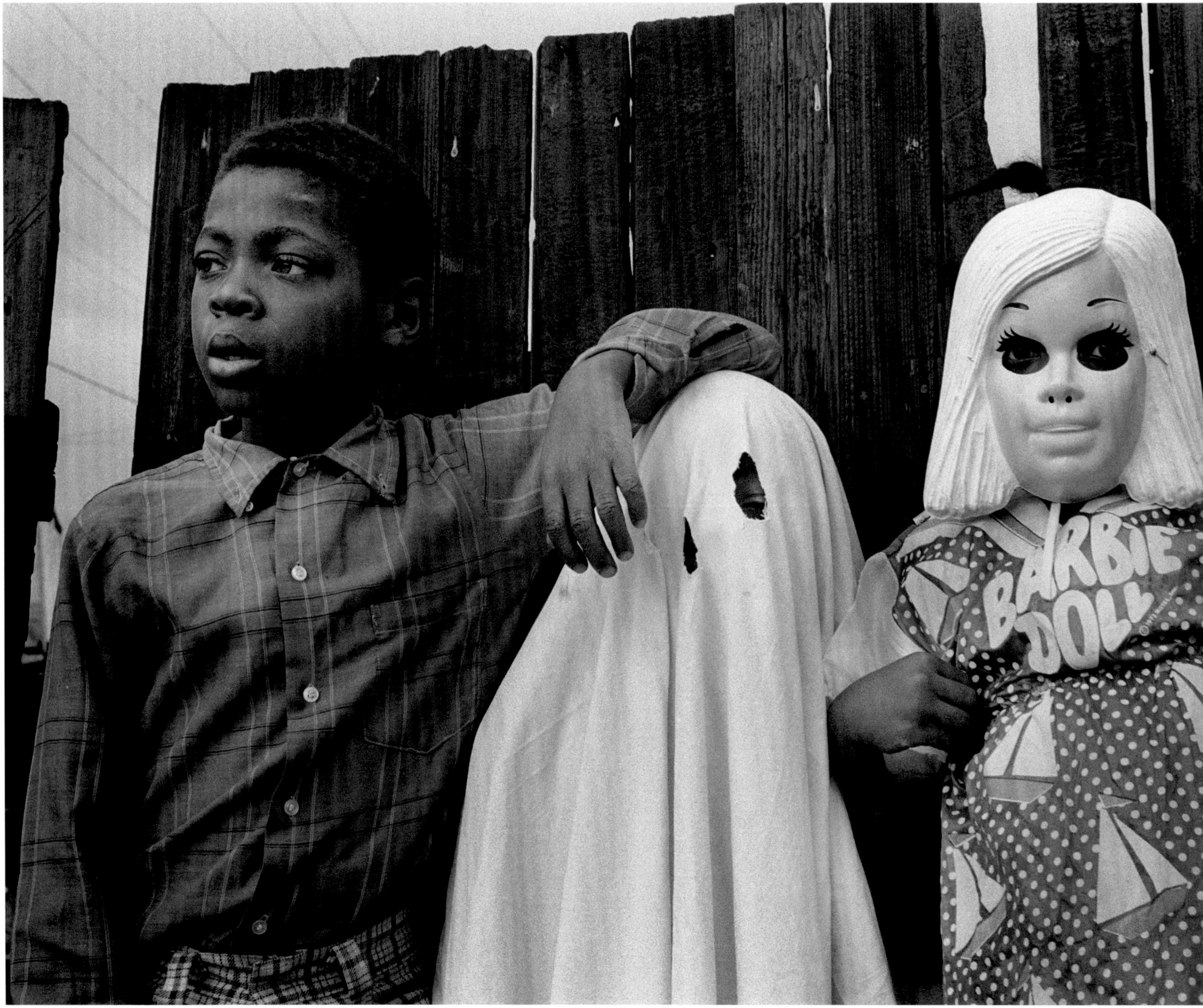
BARBIE DOLL

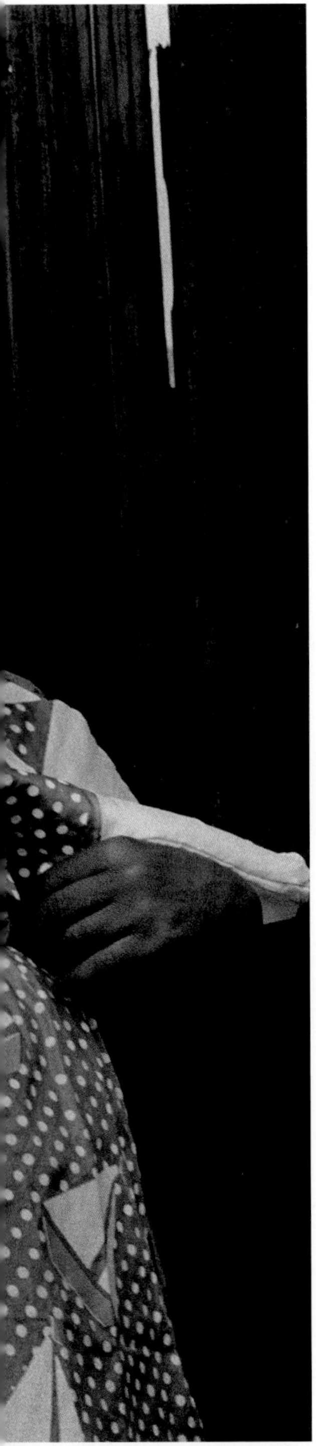

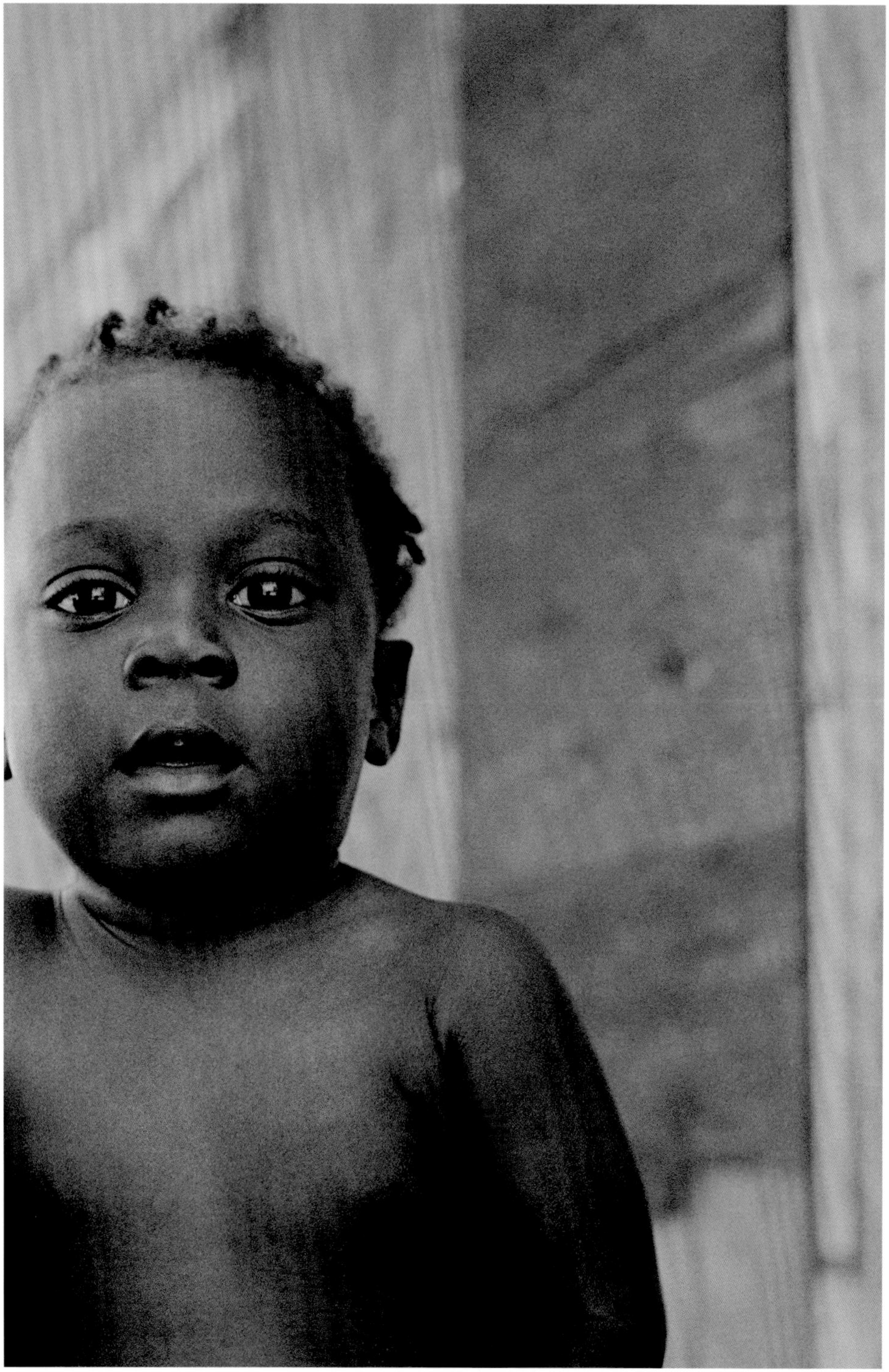

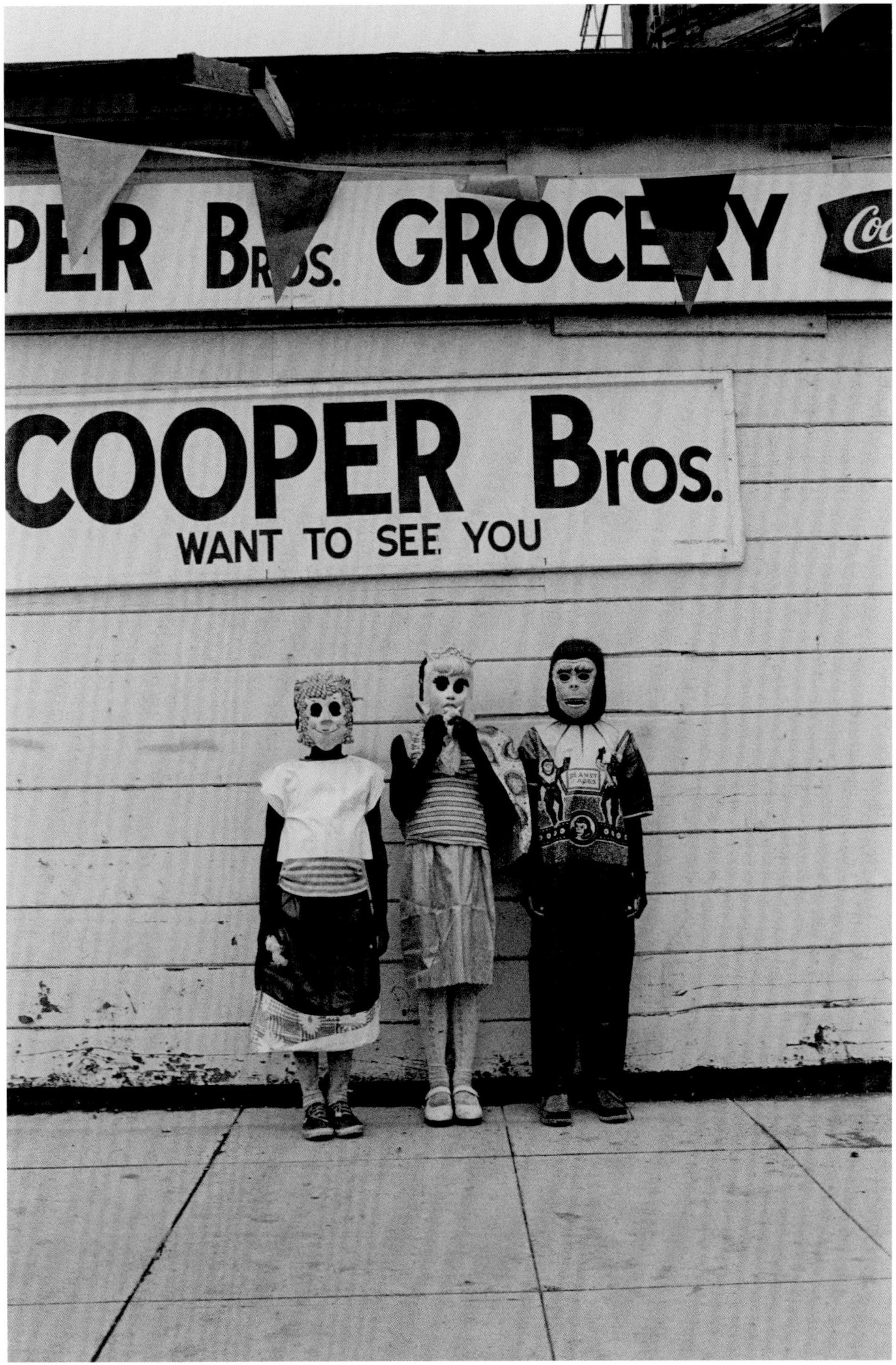
PER Bros. GROCERY
COOPER Bros.
WANT TO SEE YOU

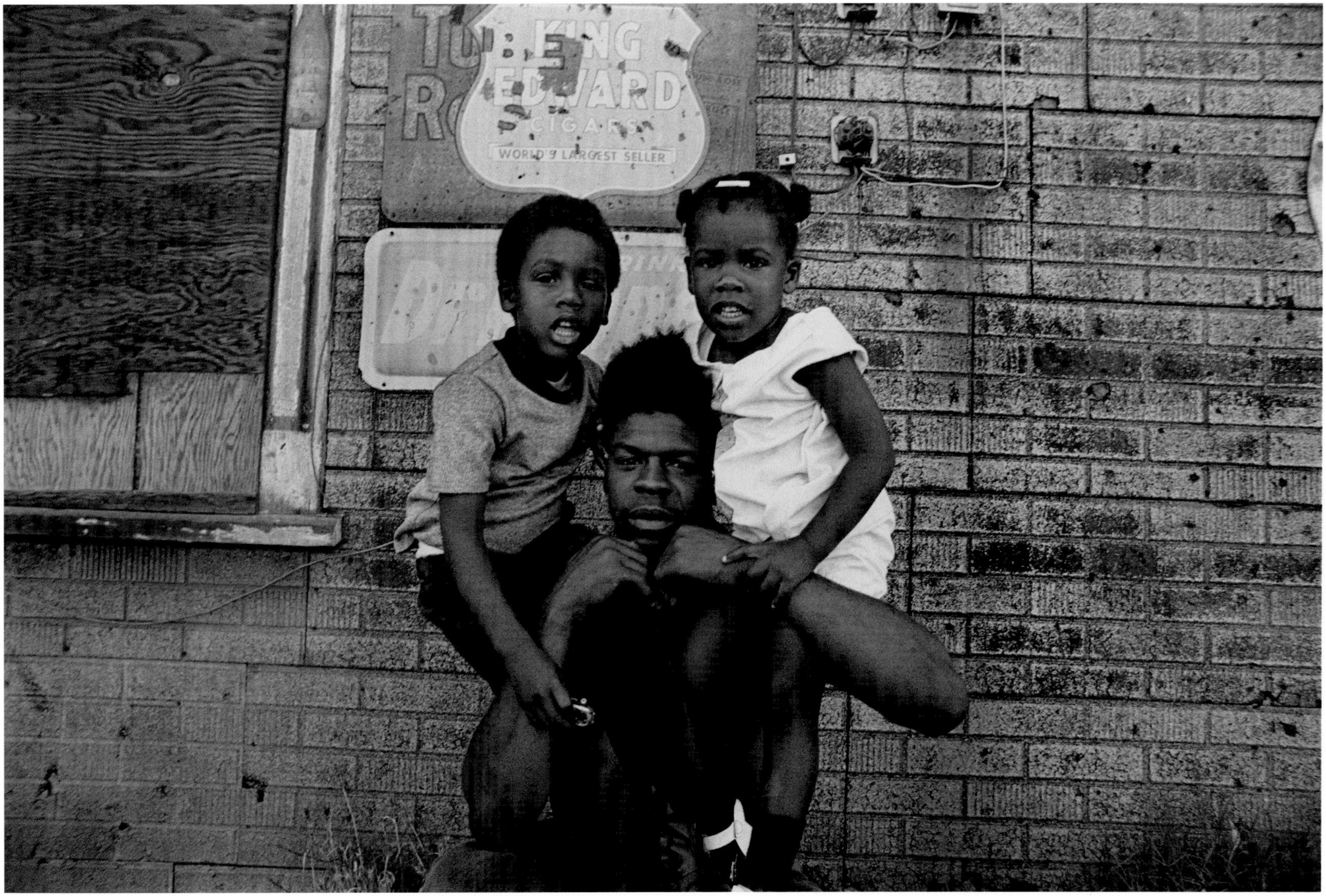
KING
EDWARD
CIGARS
WORLD'S LARGEST SELLER

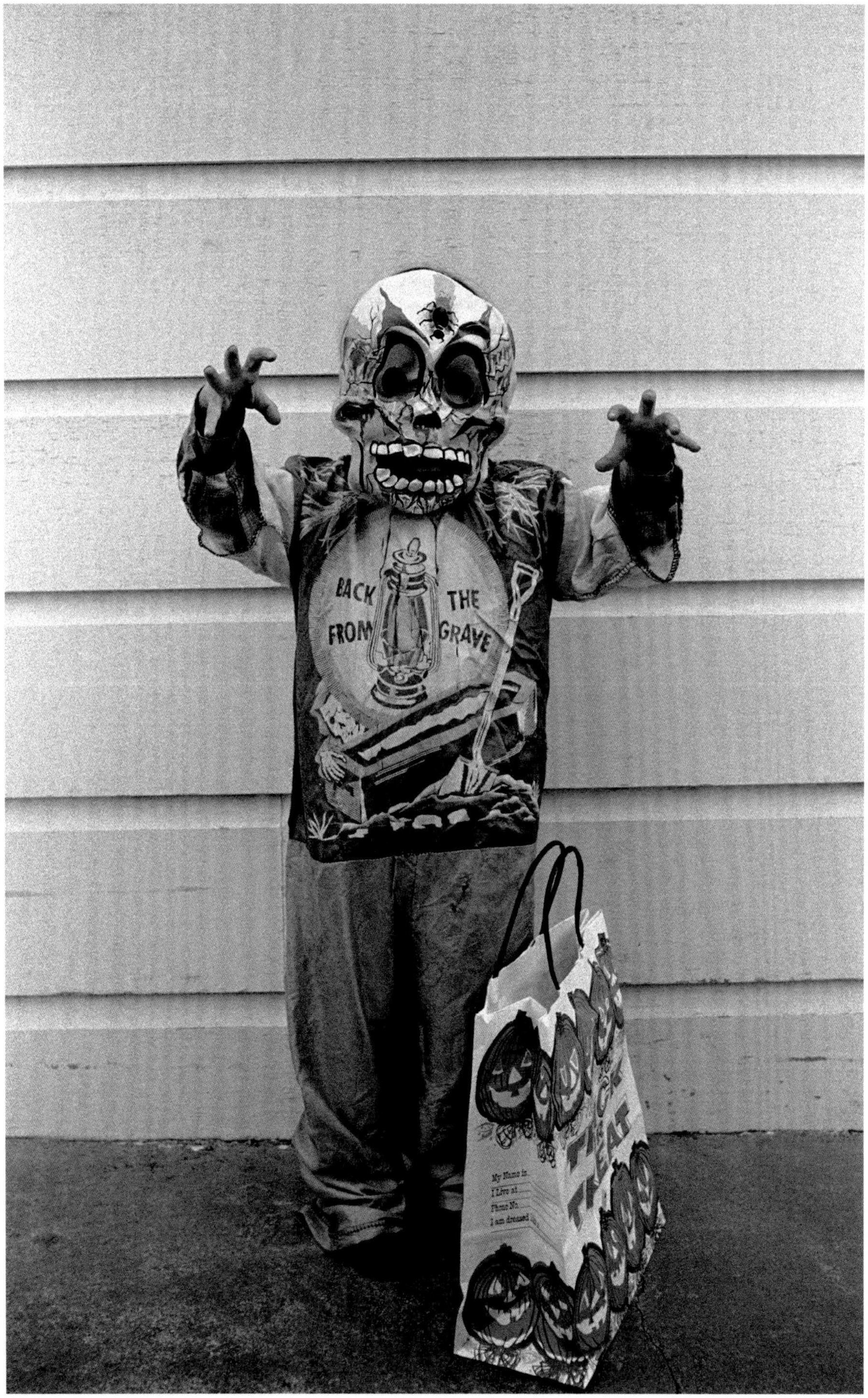
BACK FROM
THE GRAVE

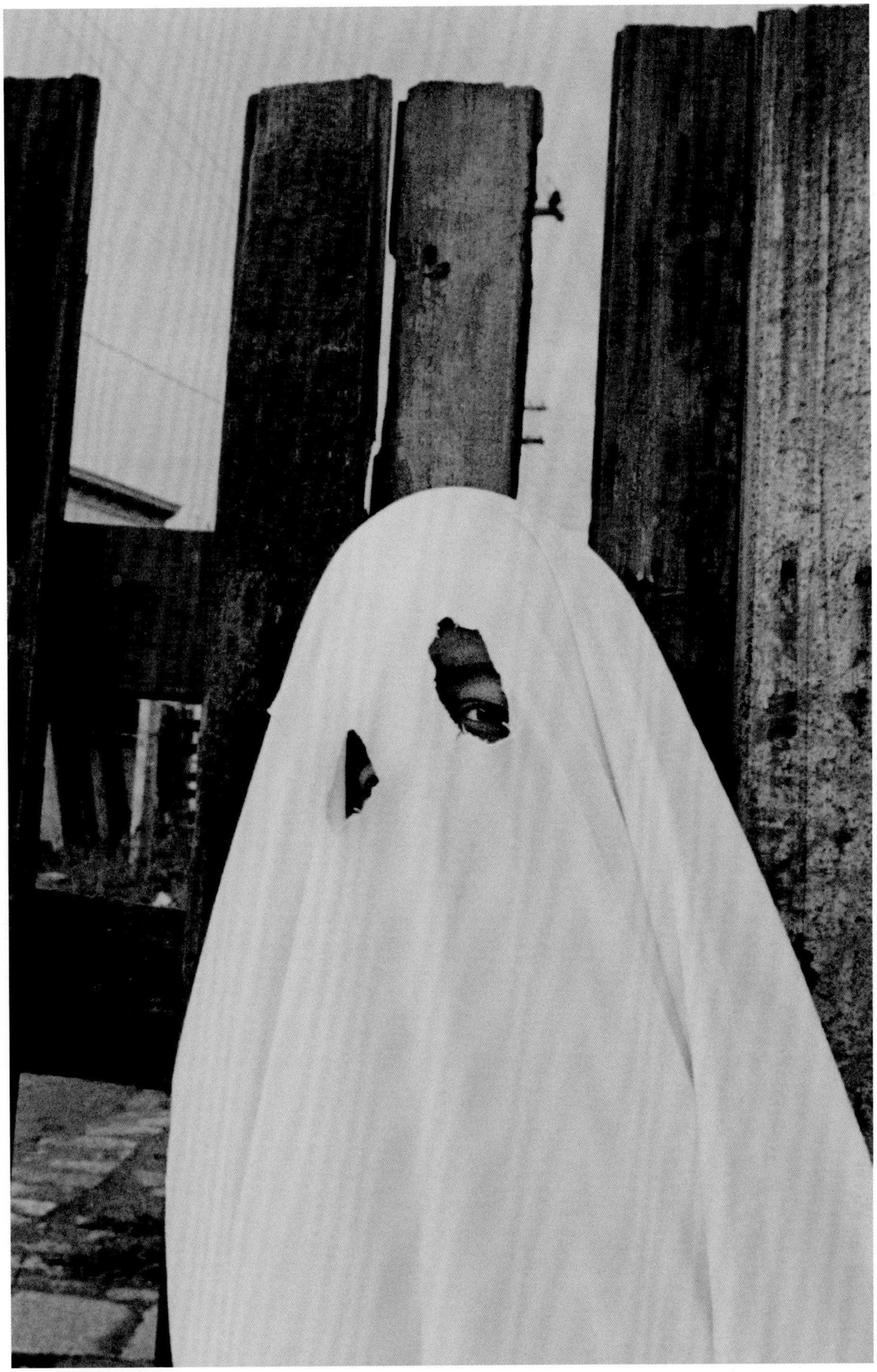

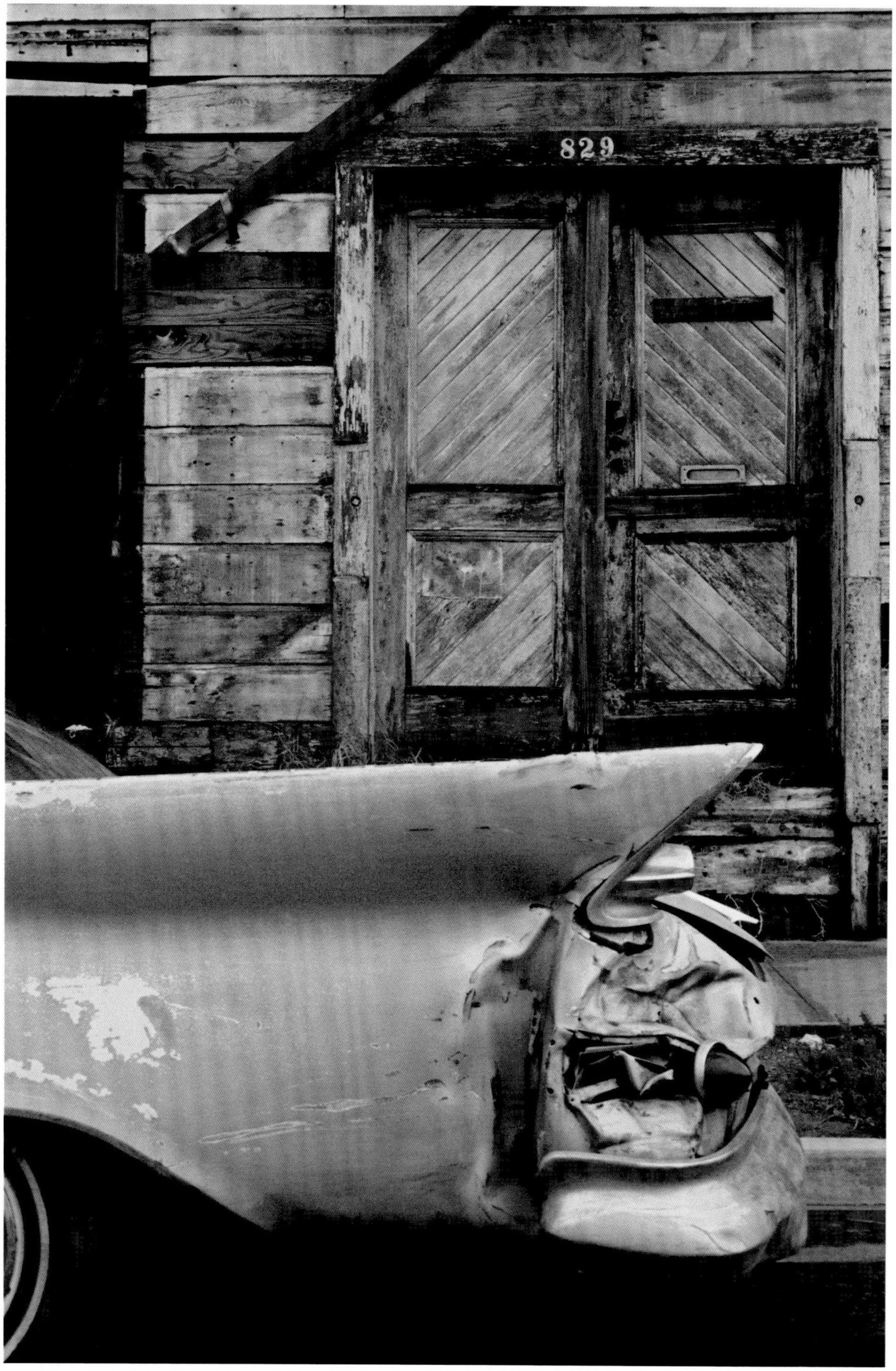
829

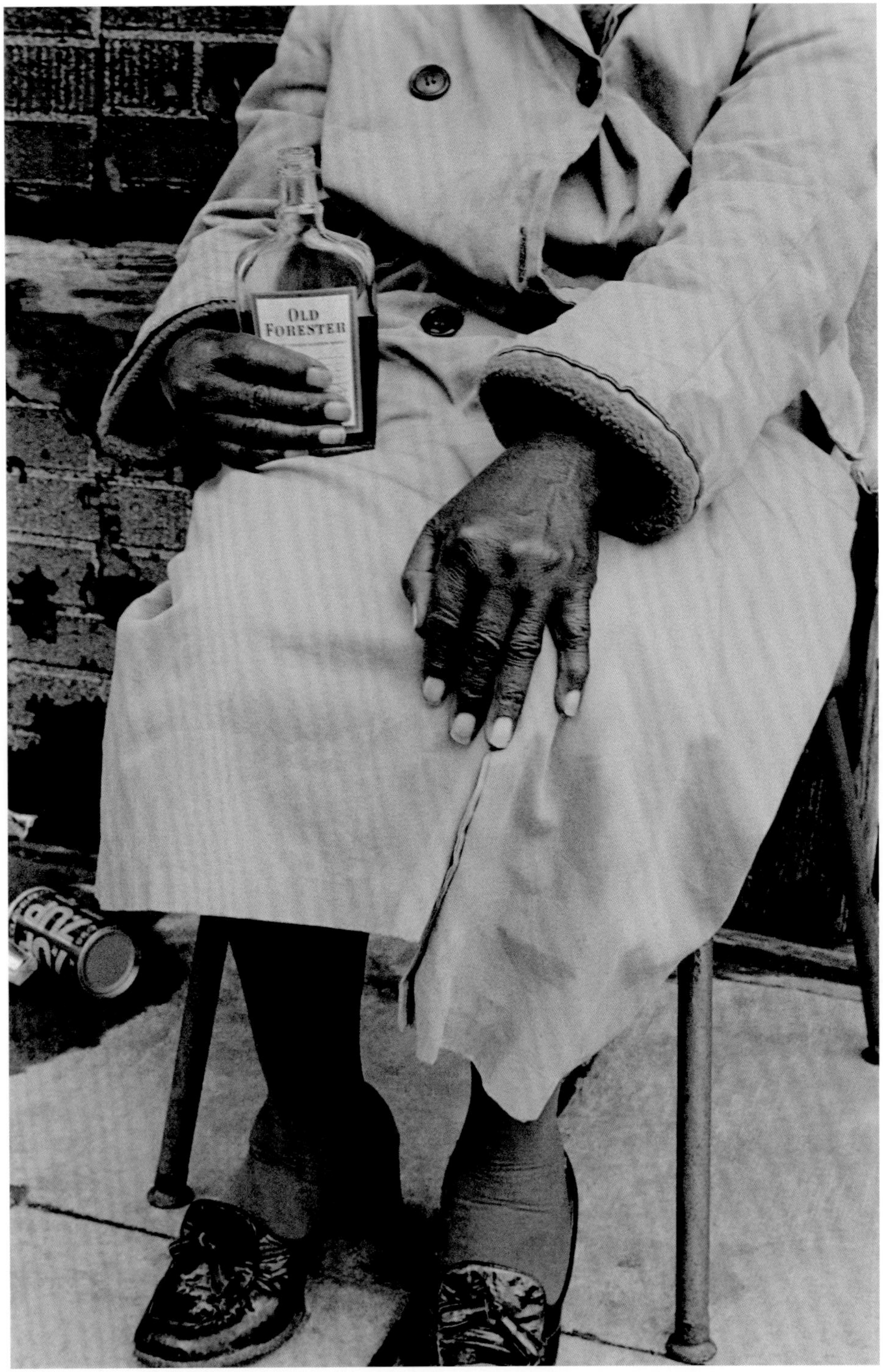
OLD
FORESTER

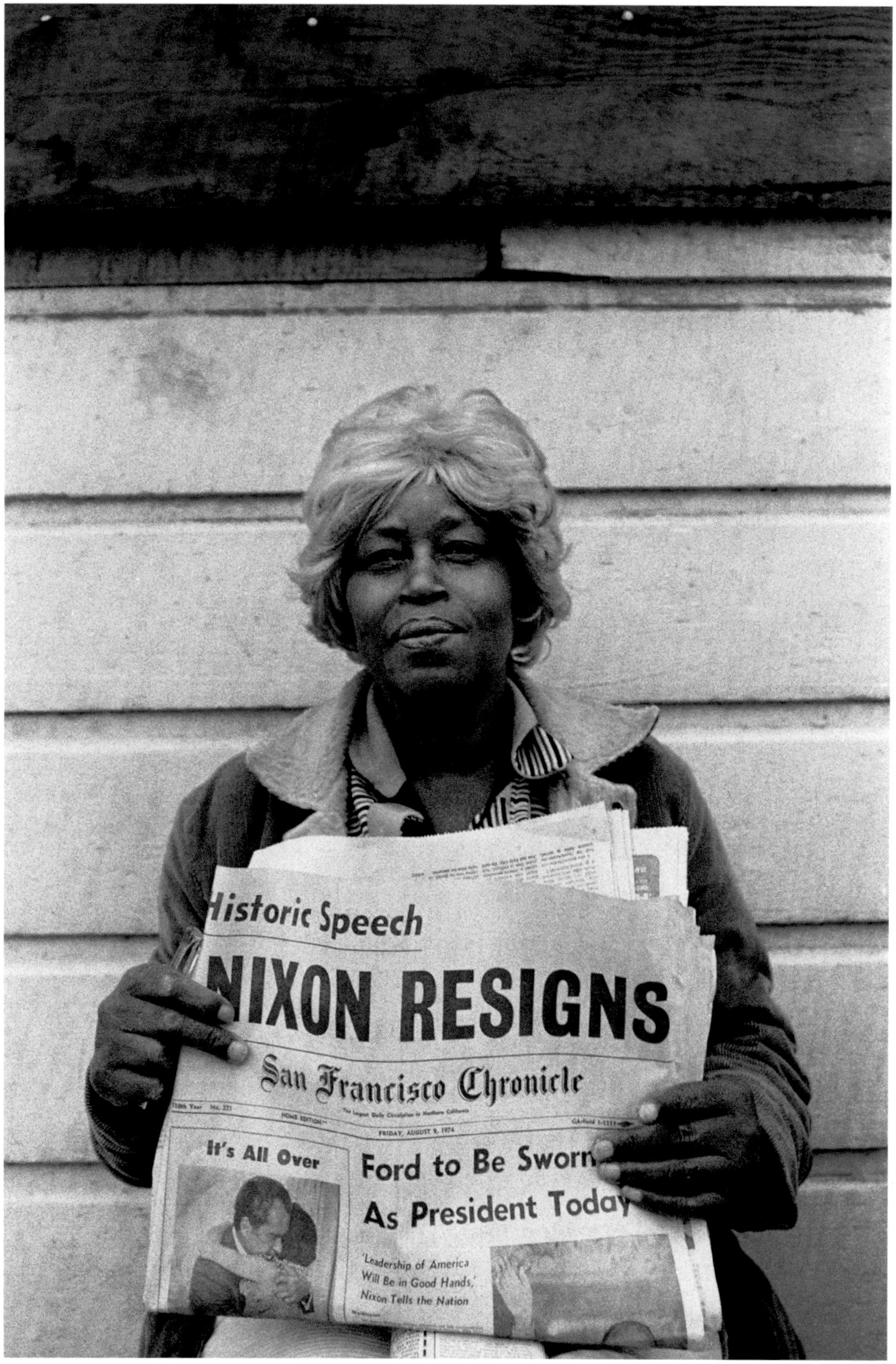
Historic Speech
NIXON RESIGNS
San Francisco Chronicle
It's All Over
Ford to Be Sworn
As President Today
'Leadership of America
Will Be in Good Hands,'
Nixon Tells the Nation

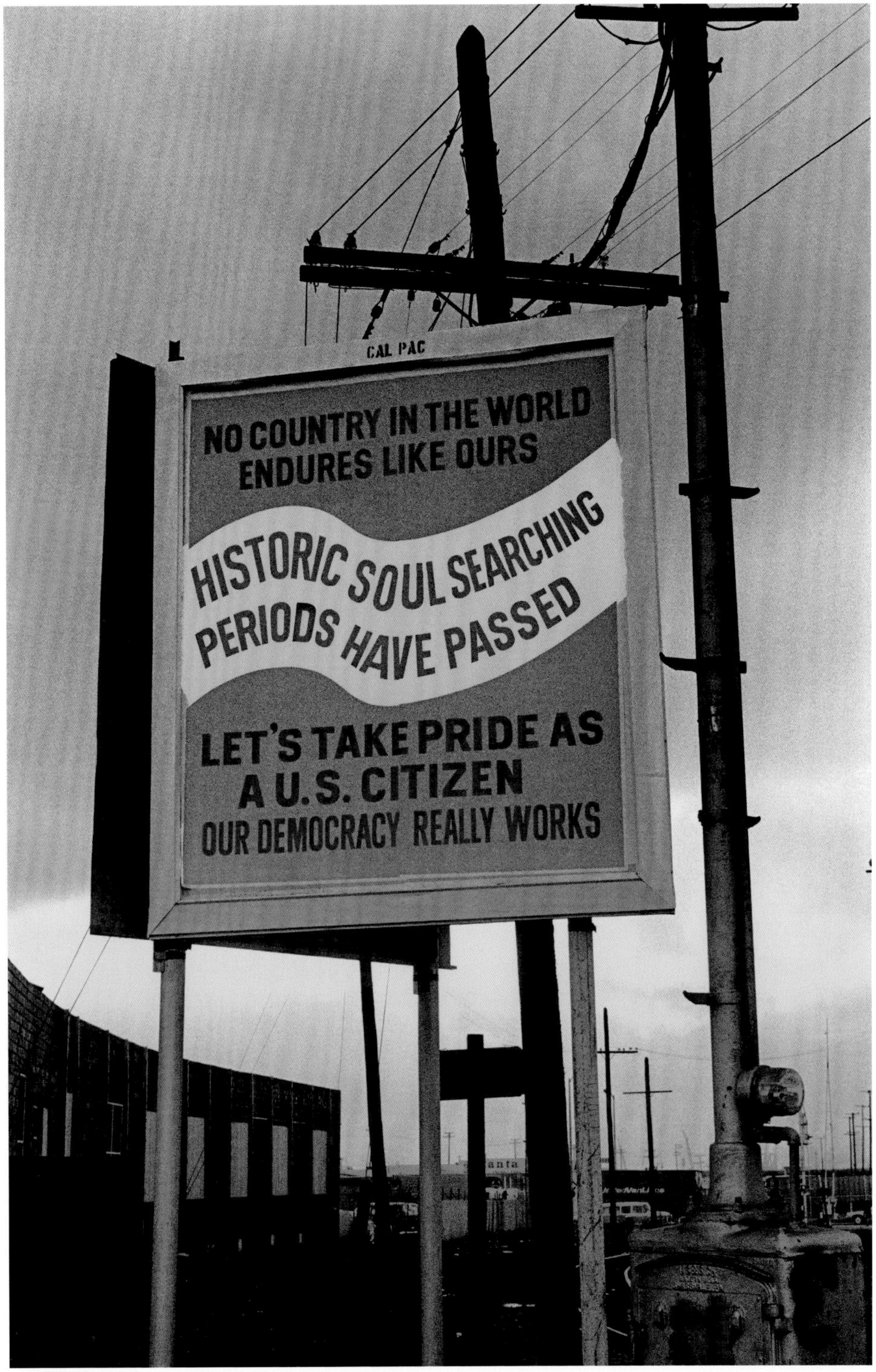
CAL PAC
NO COUNTRY IN THE WORLD
ENDURES LIKE OURS
HISTORIC SOUL SEARCHING
PERIODS HAVE PASSED
LET'S TAKE PRIDE AS
A U.S. CITIZEN
OUR DEMOCRACY REALLY WORKS

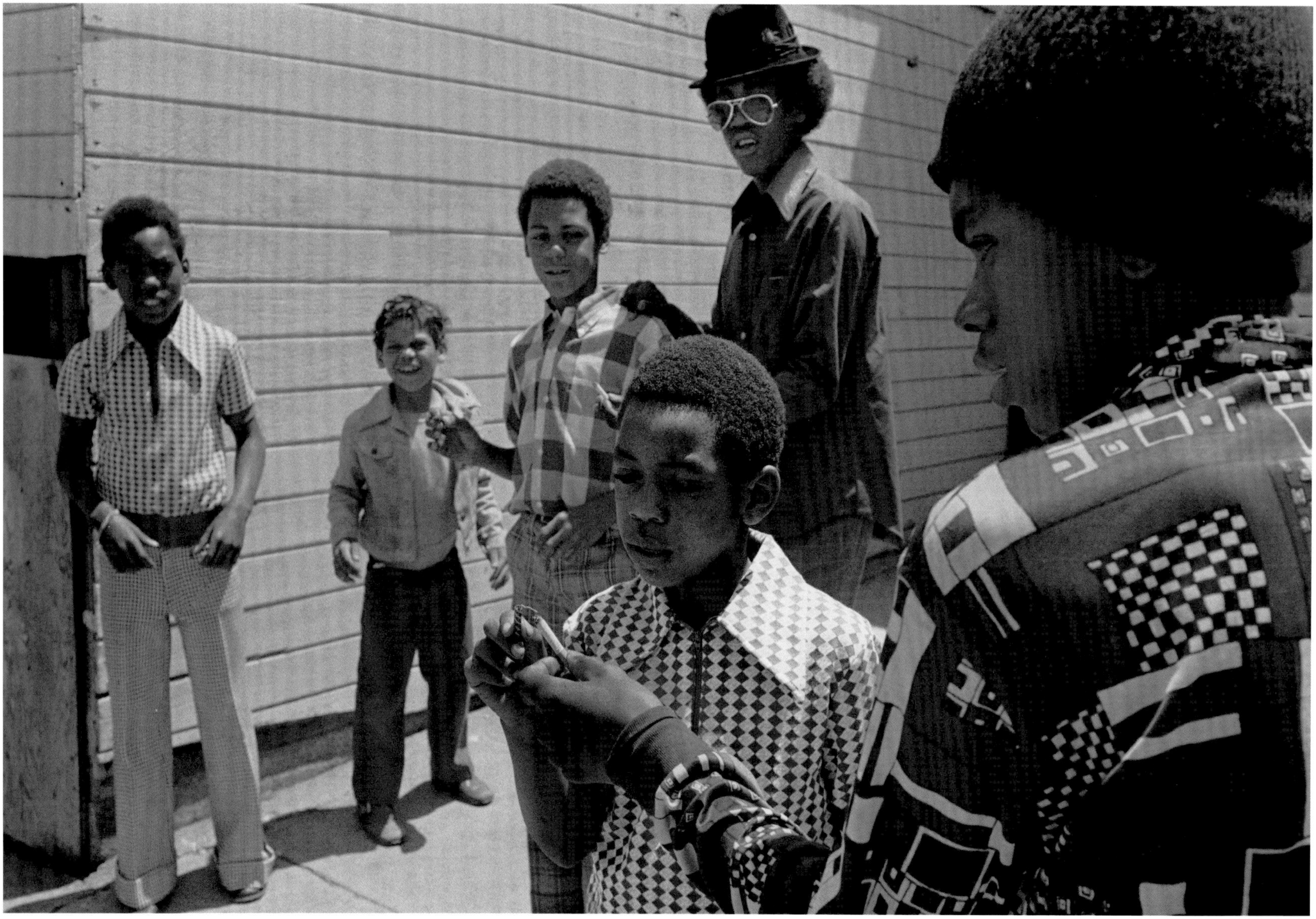

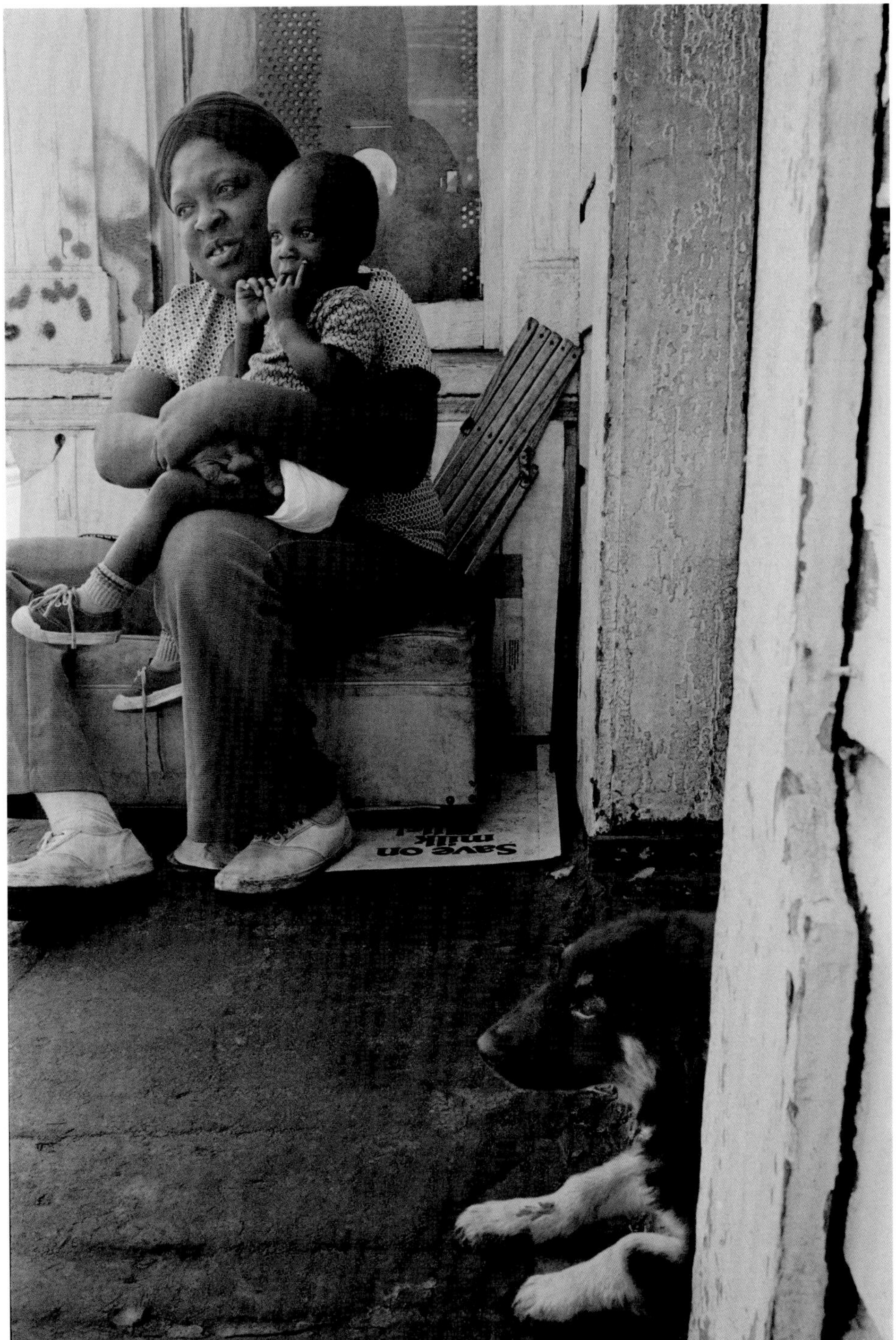
Save on
milk

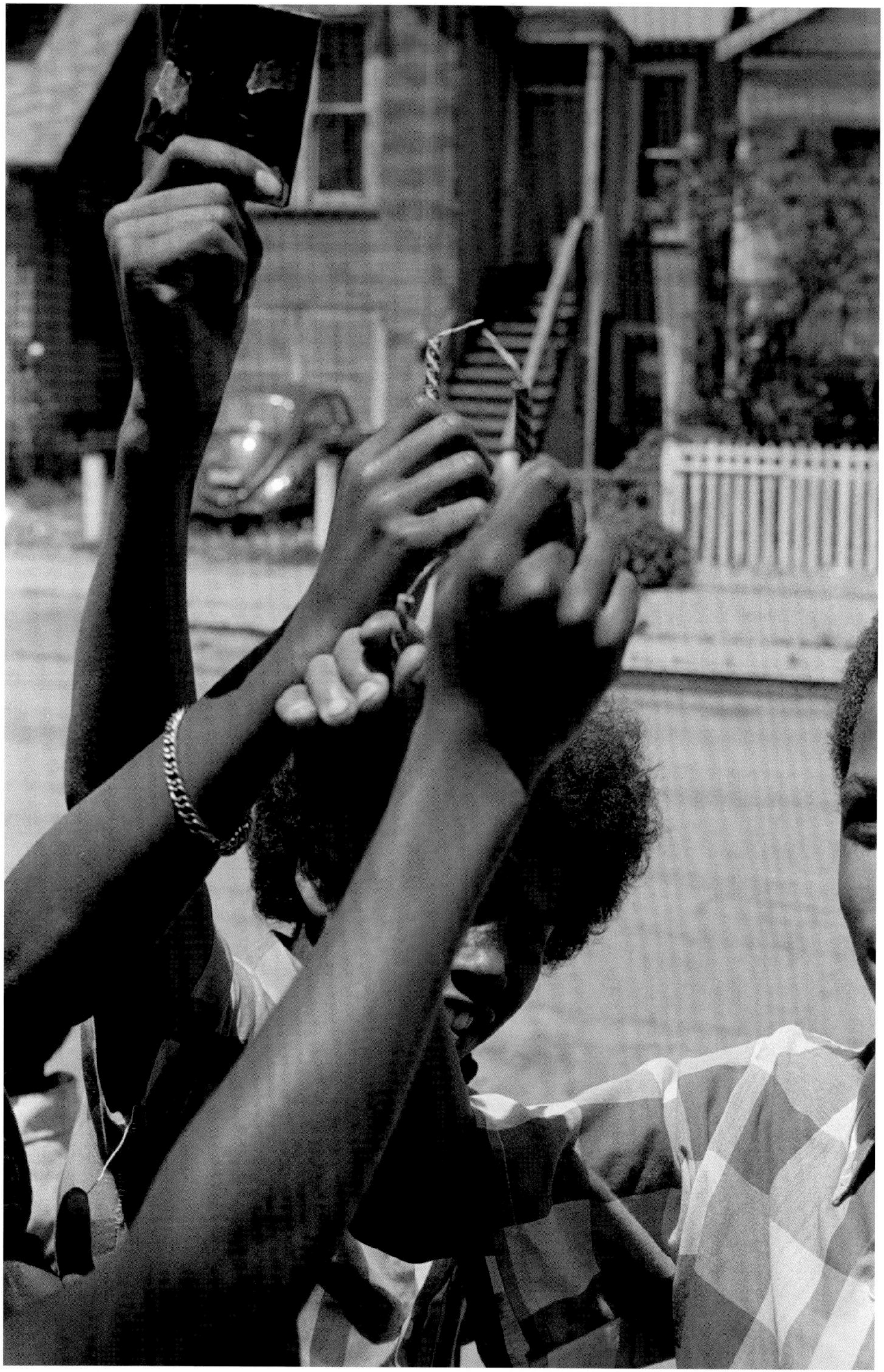

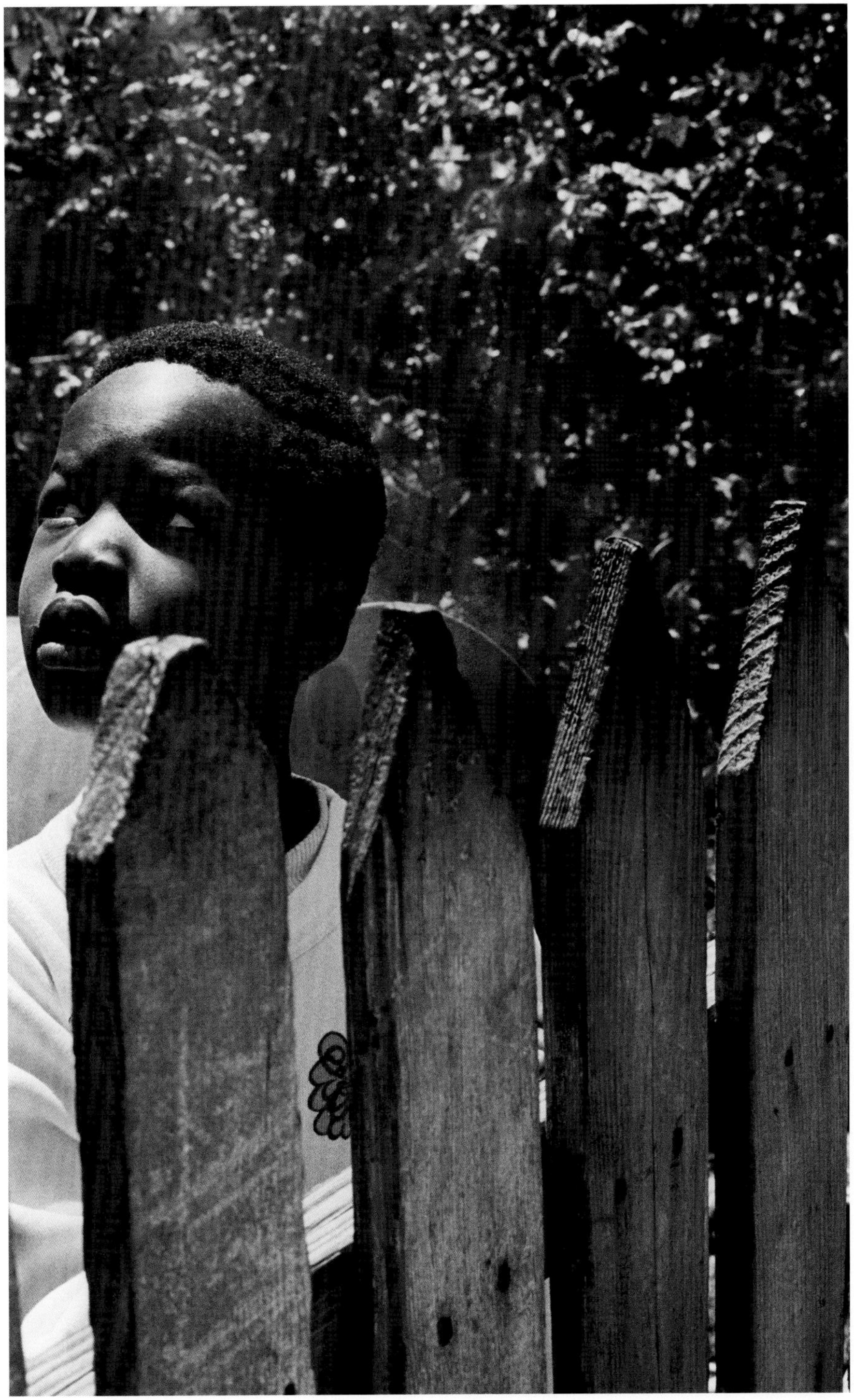

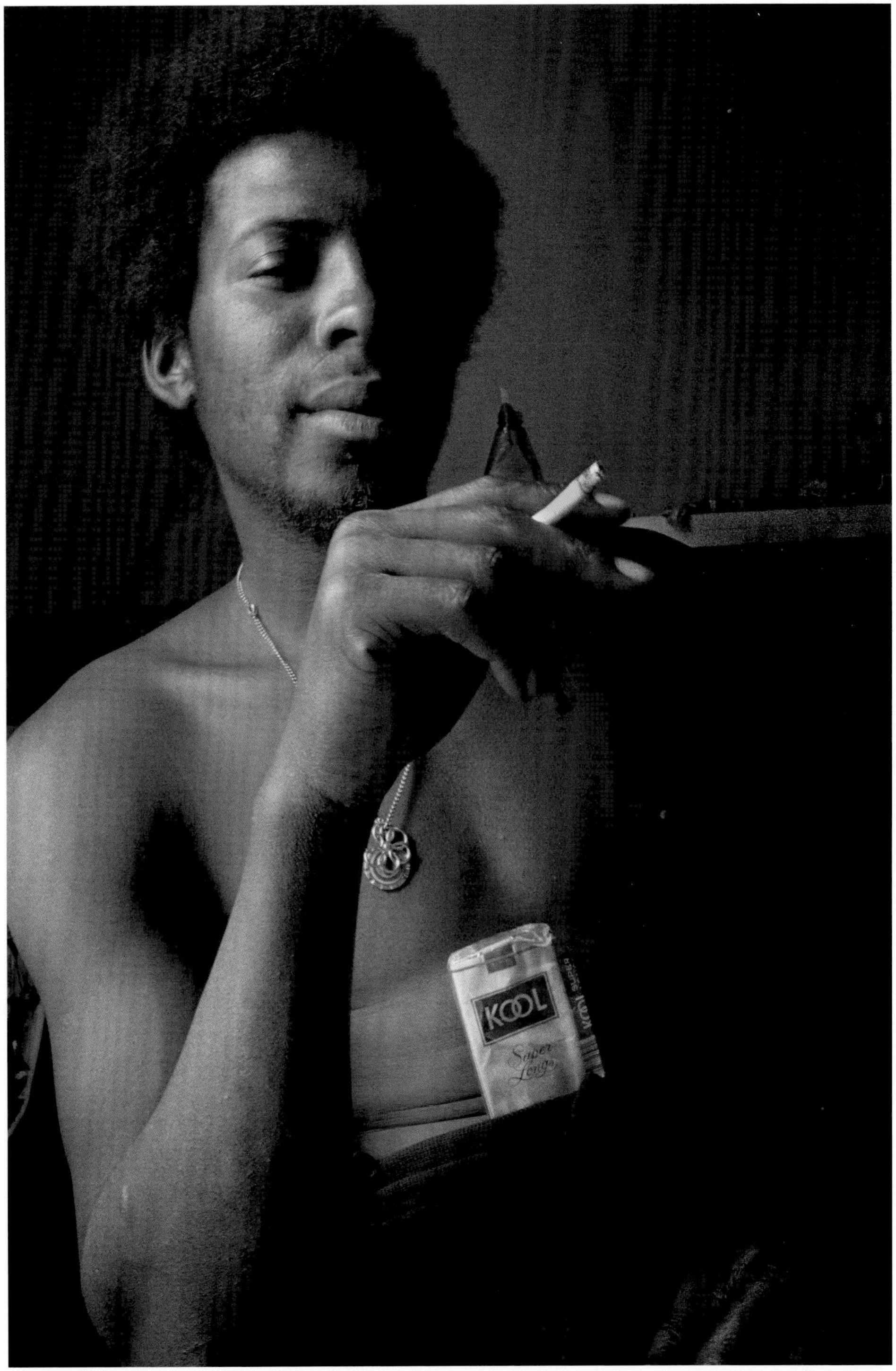
KOOL
Super Longs

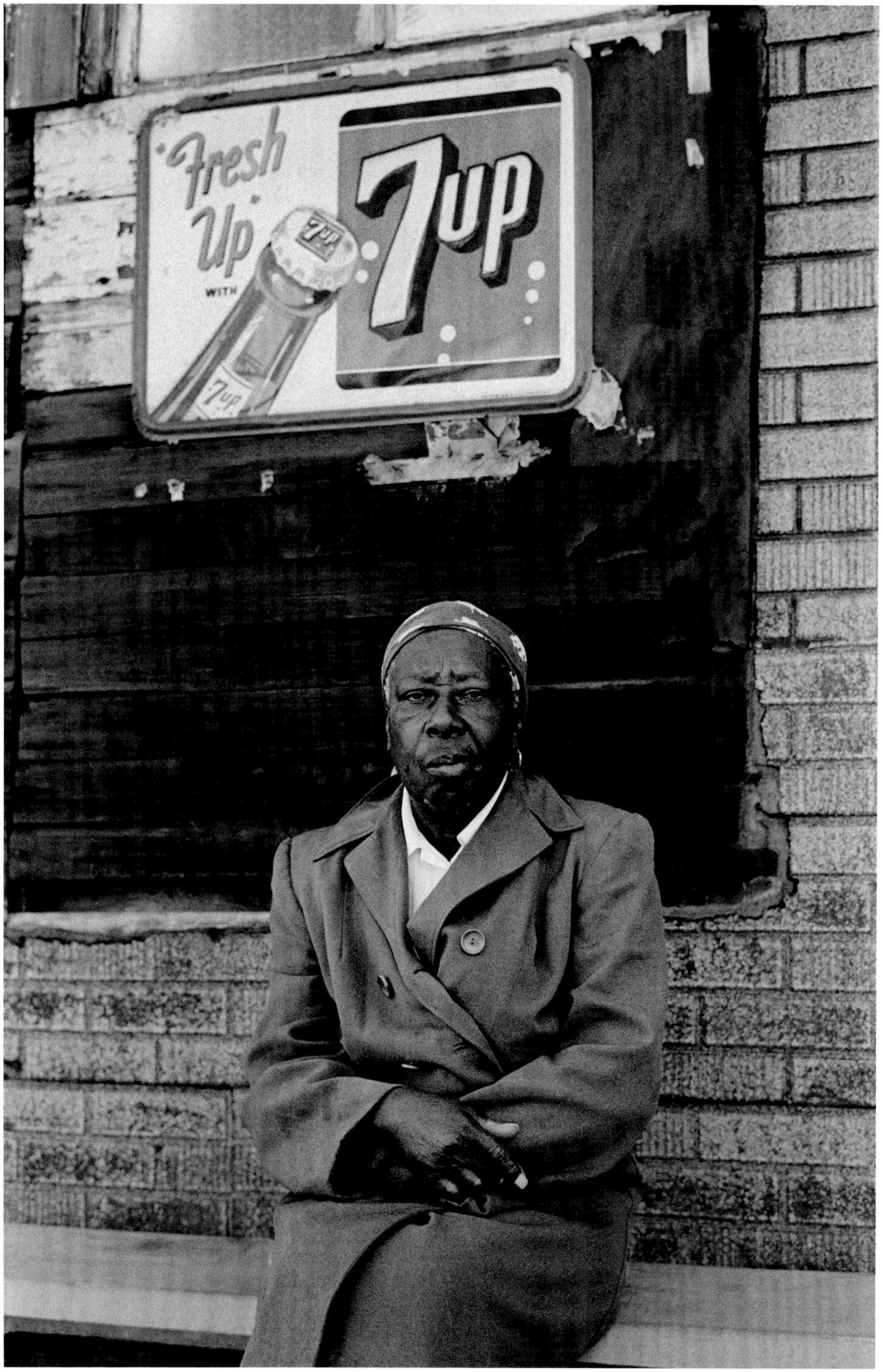
"Fresh Up" WITH
7up

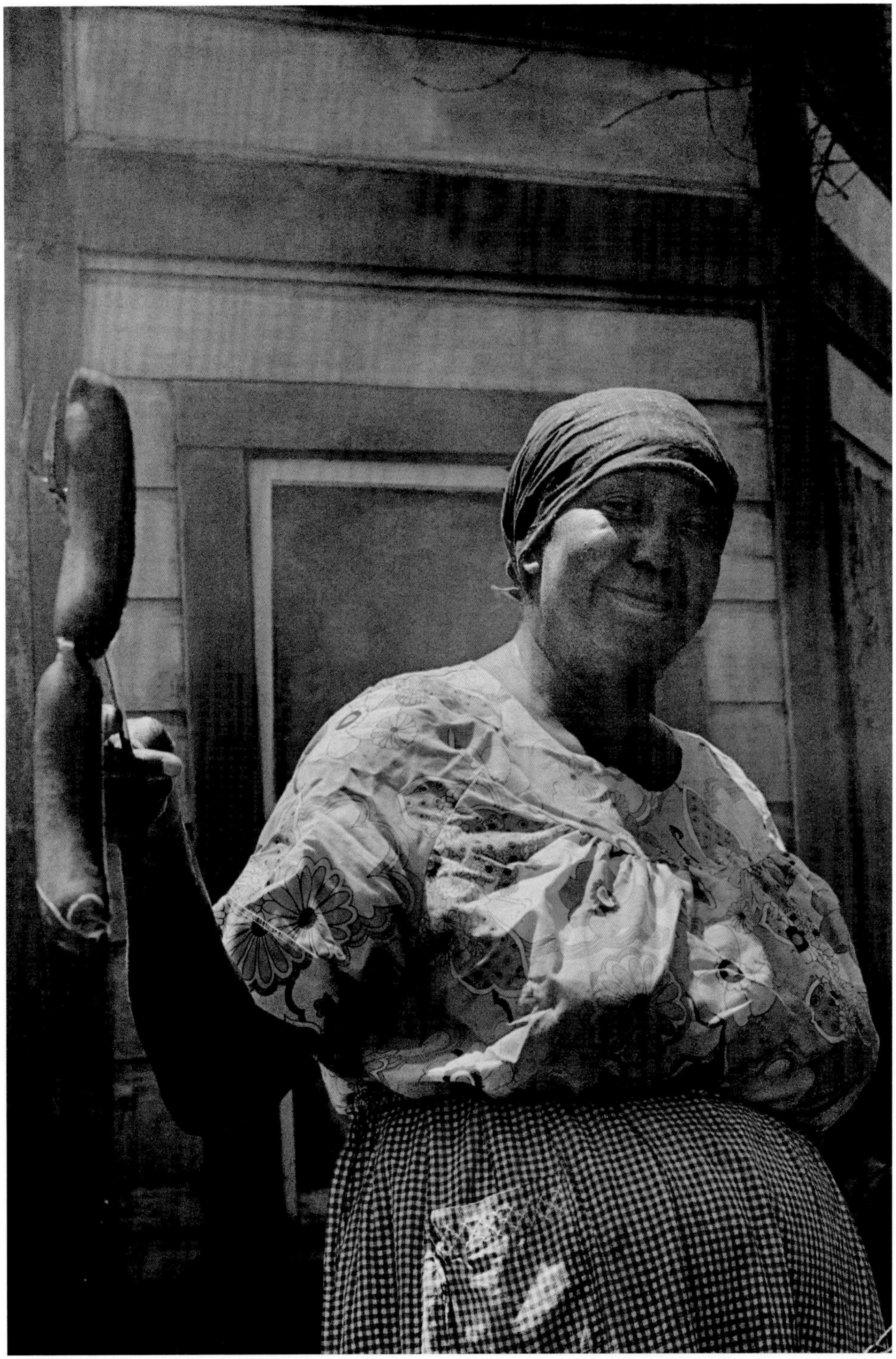

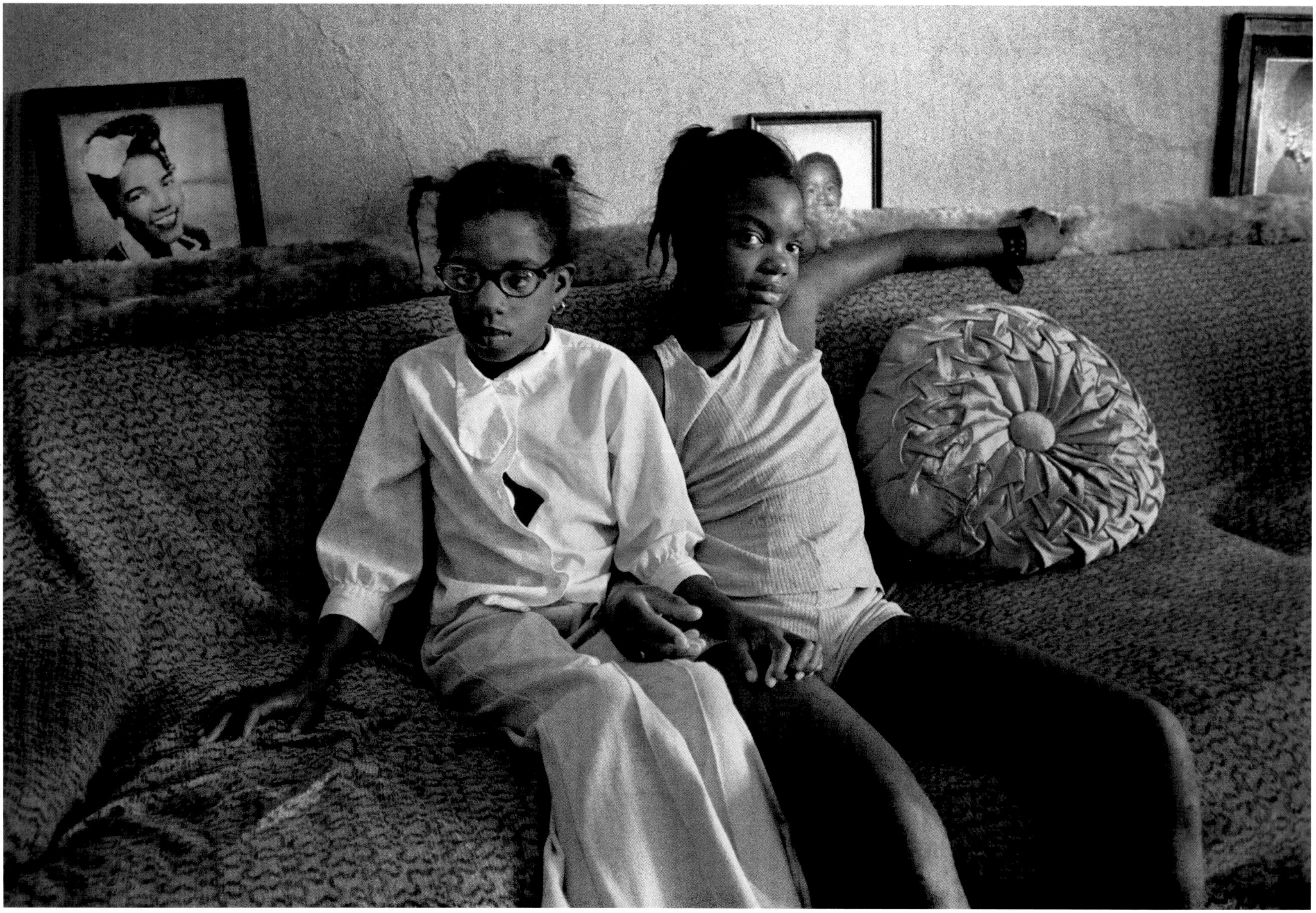

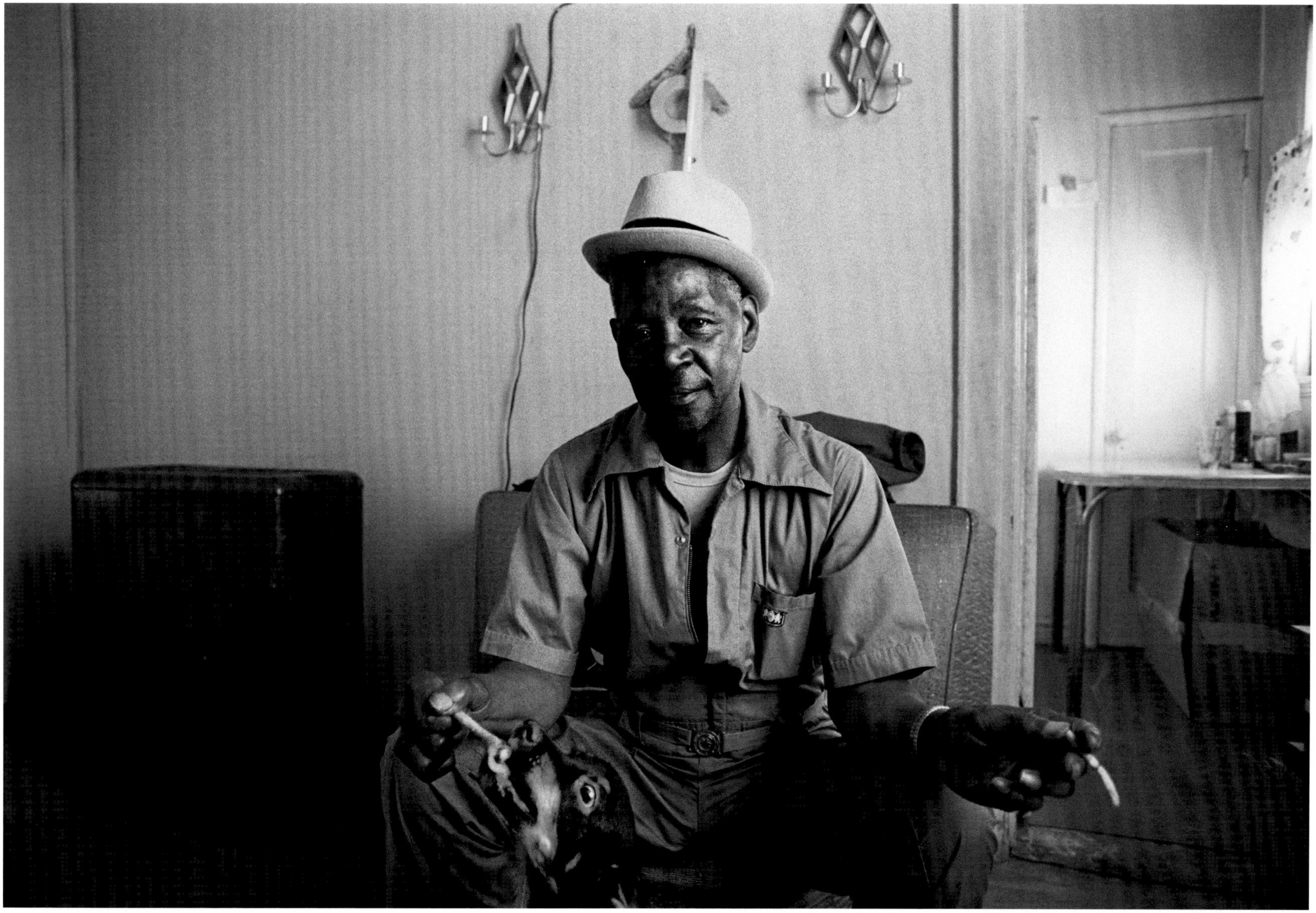

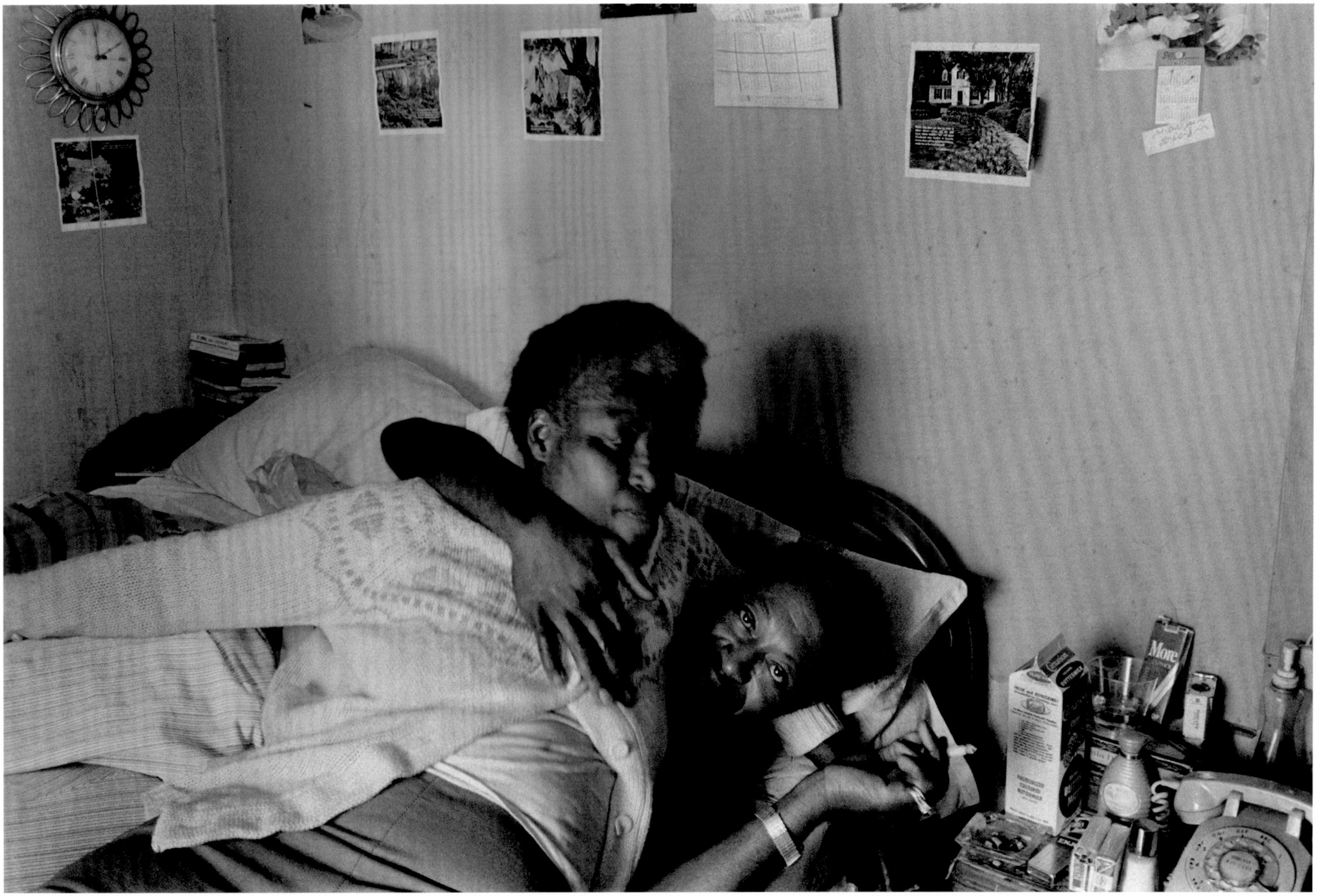
More

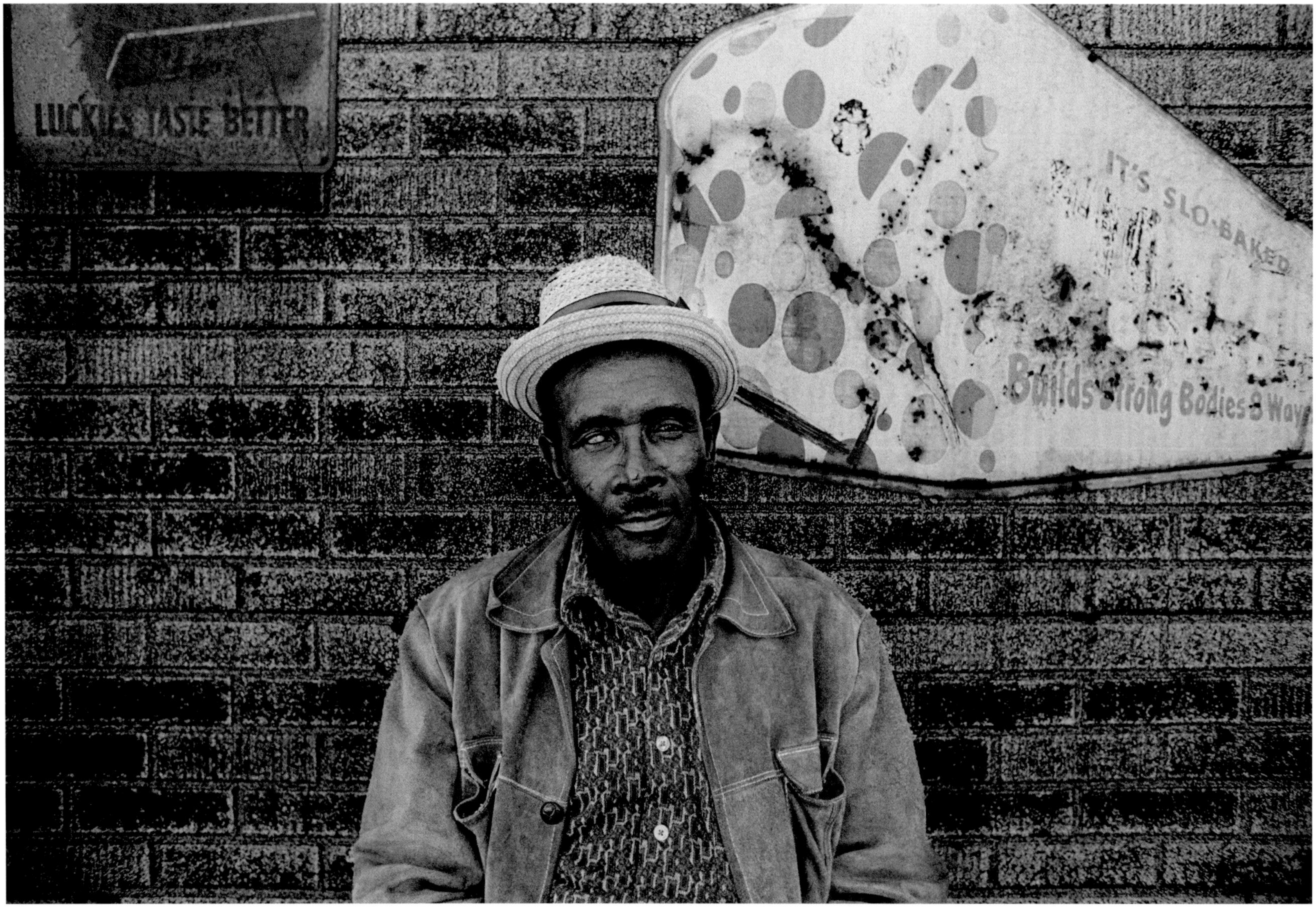
LUCKIES TASTE BETTER
IT'S SLO-BAKED
Builds Strong Bodies 8 Way

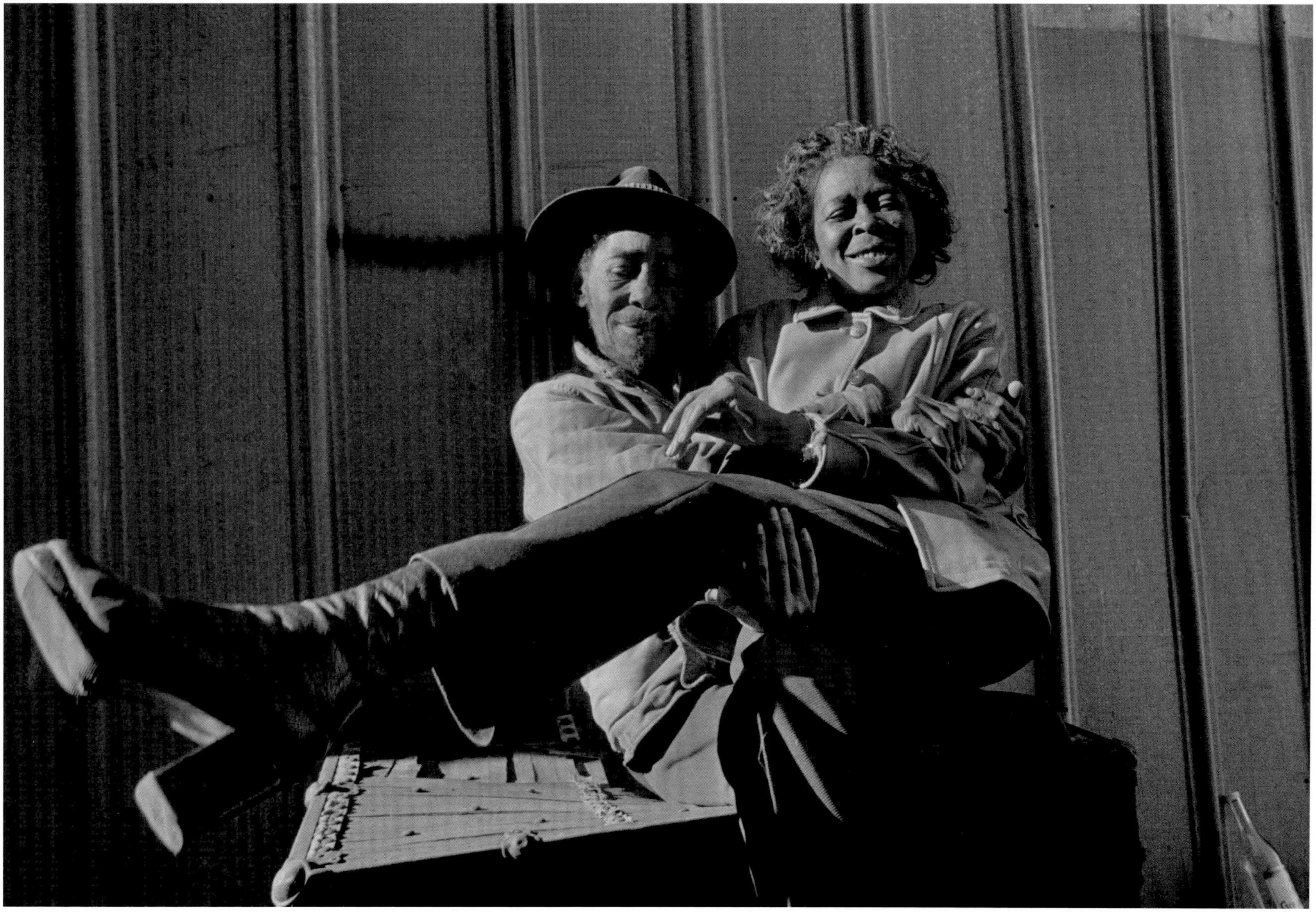

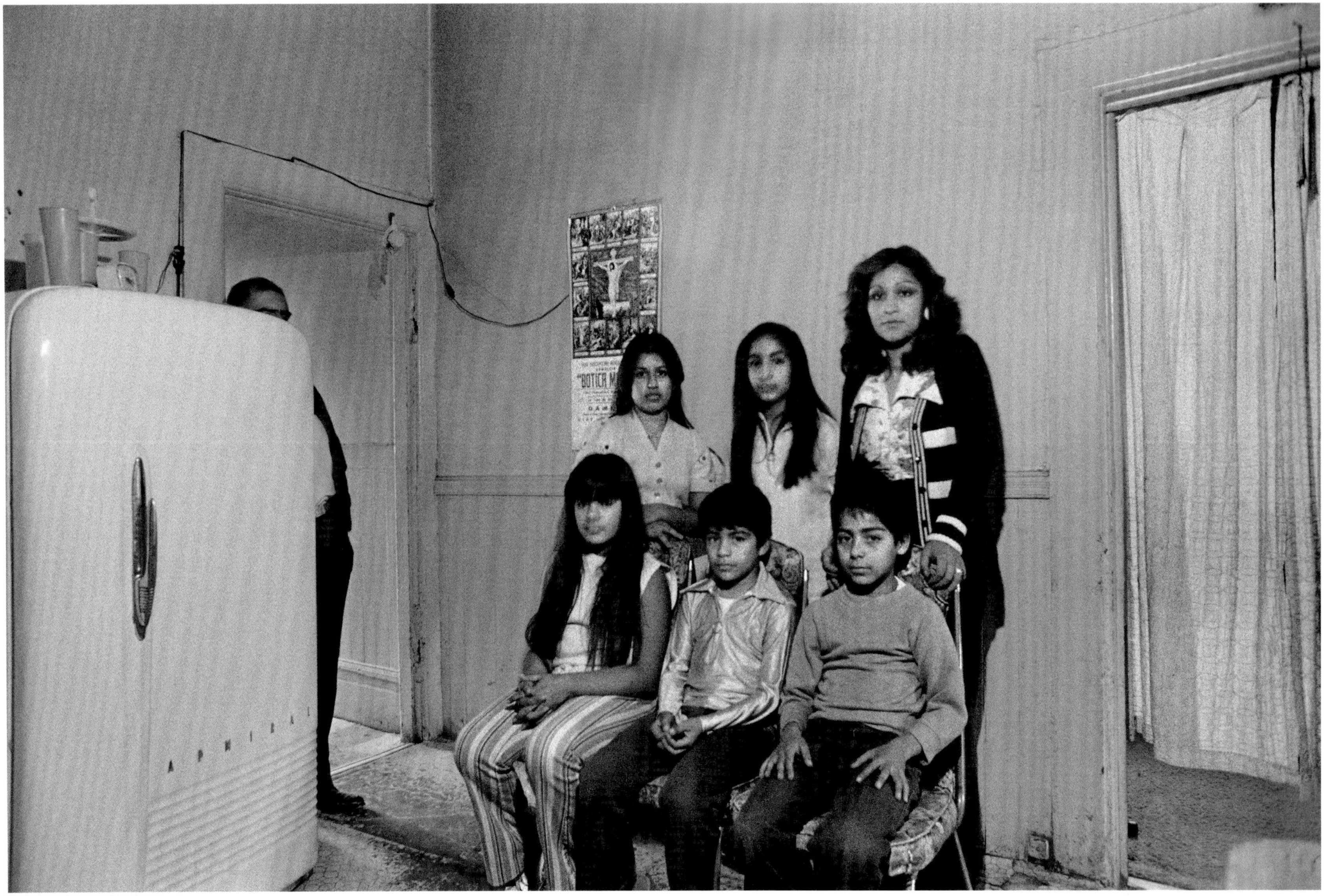

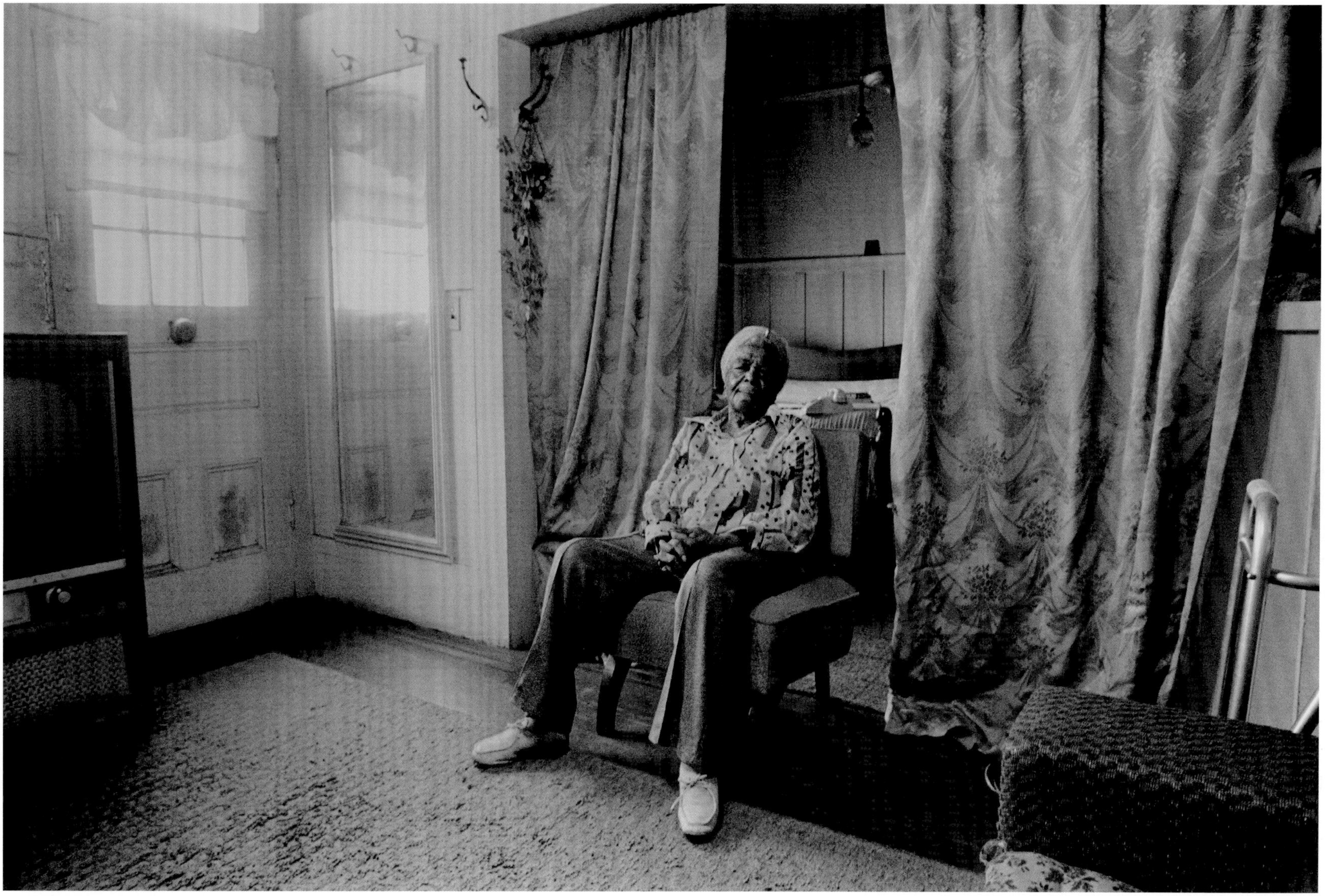

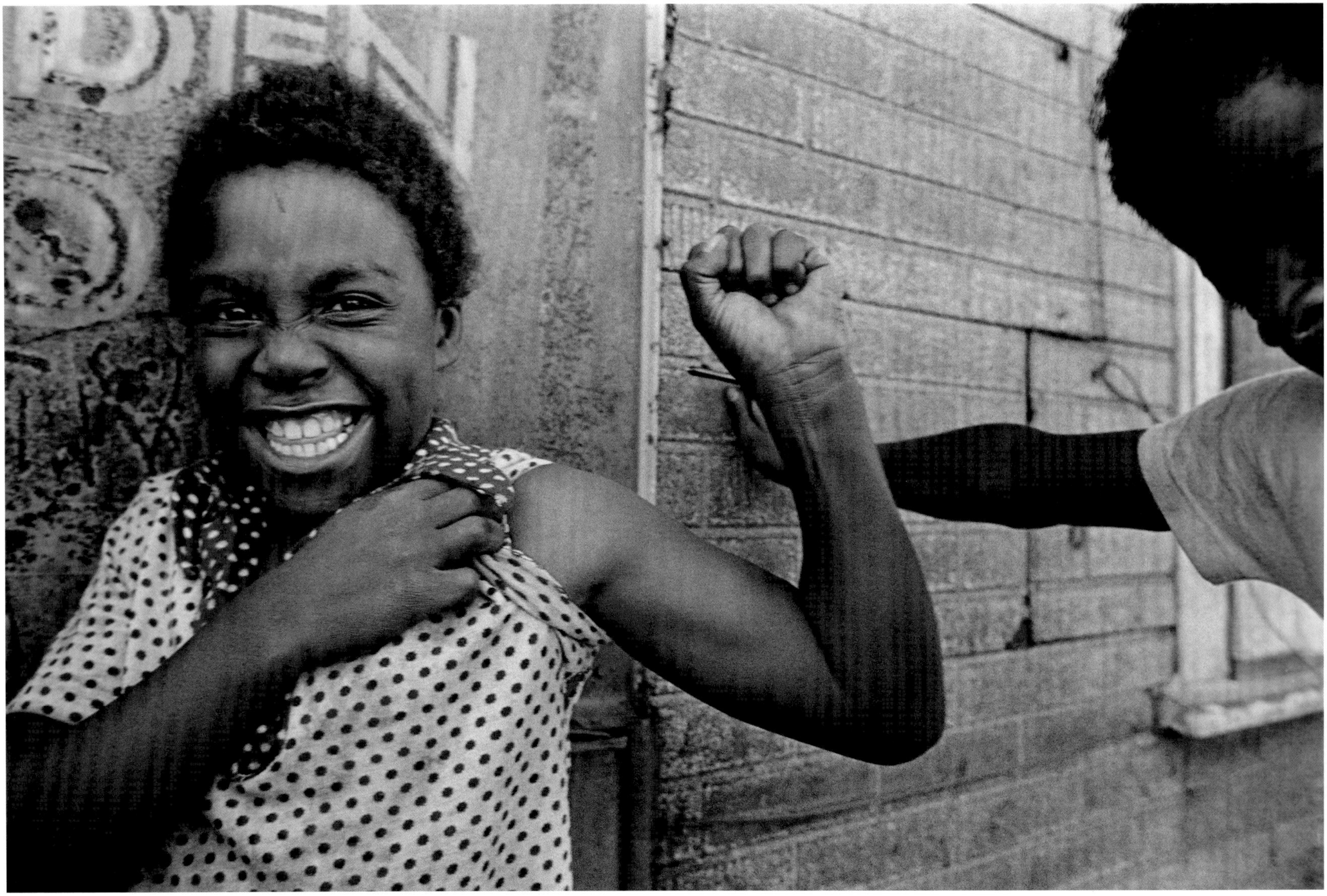

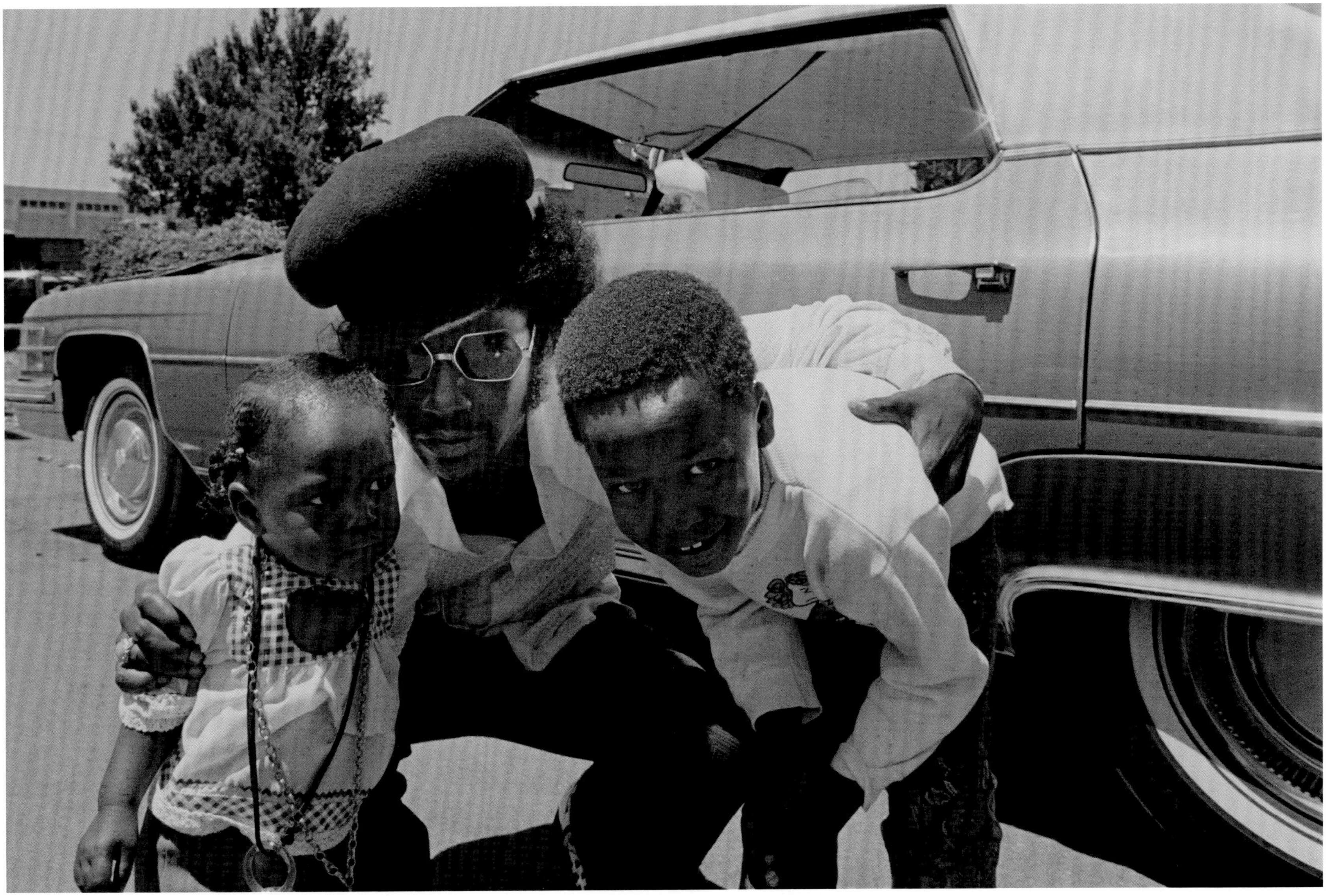

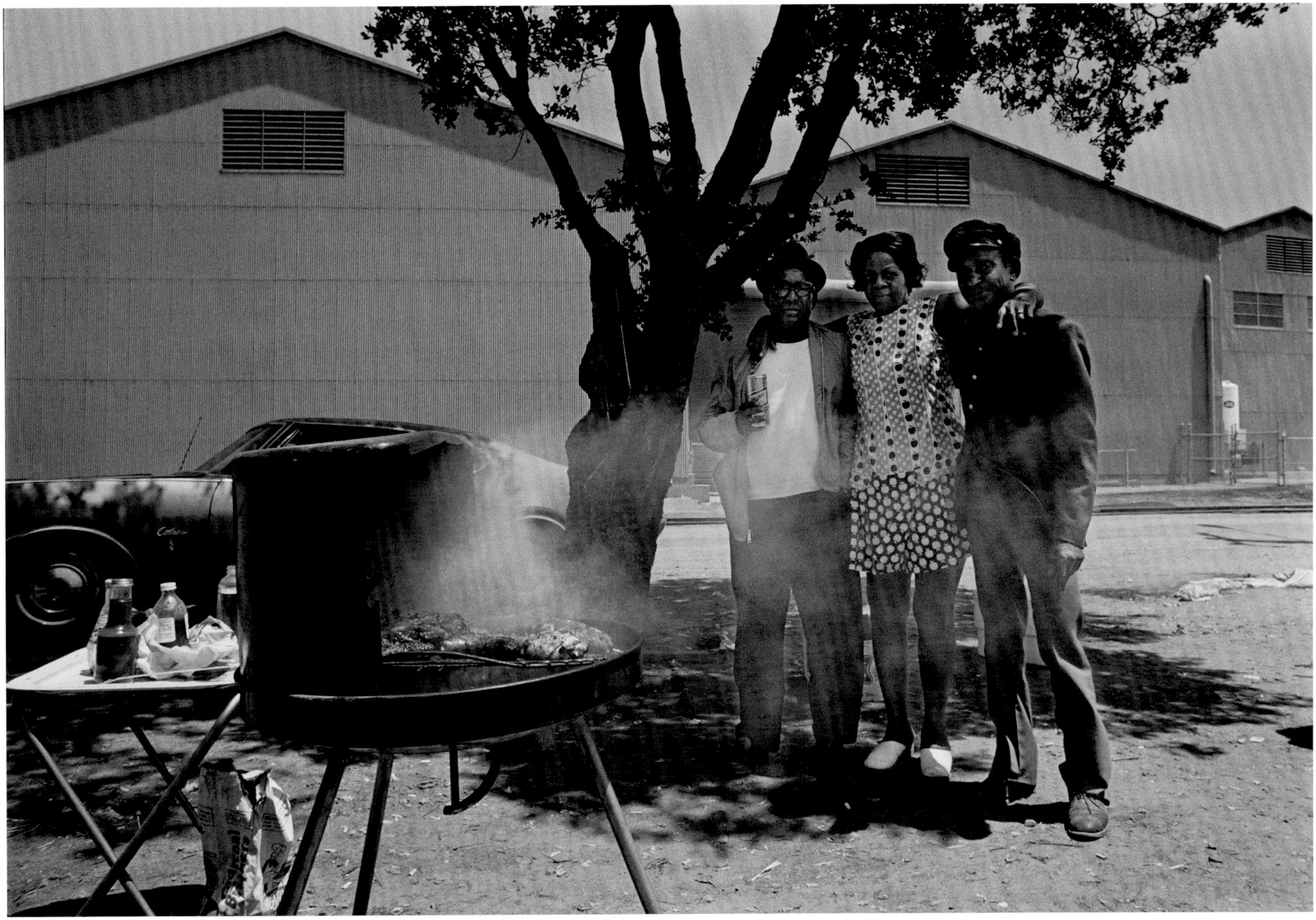

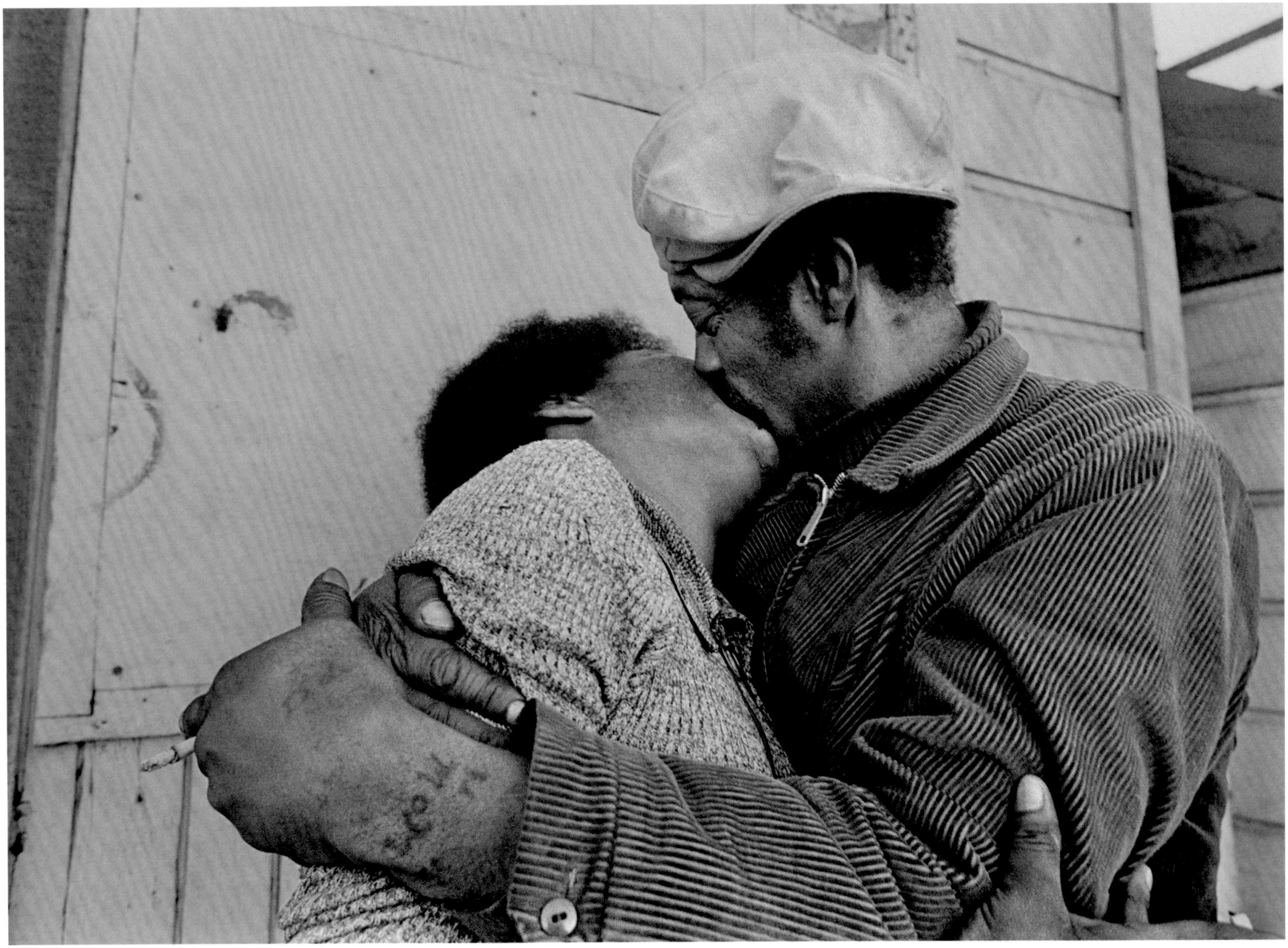

Acknowledgments

This book would have not been possible without the support of the many community members who opened their homes, churches, and businesses to me. We shared a common belief that their stories, dignity, and struggle and their world portrayed within these pages needed to be seen. Some who helped include Minnie Payne of ACORN Community Television; Elder Calvin Davis; C. L. Dellums of the Brotherhood of Sleeping Car Porters; Clayton Russell, president of the Phoenix Iron Works; Father John Maxwell; West Oakland residents Mr. Pipper, Mr. Davenport, Mrs. Zemmons, Mame Evans, Mr. and Mrs. Medcalf, Mrs. Michaels, Hatti Figgins, Mr. Topete, the Sousa family, Frankie Huffein, Raymond Johnson, Mr. Thomas, Joe Gomez, and Ralph Williams; and Father Richard Mangini of the *Oakland Catholic Voice*. This is just a small number of people whose names remained in my paper files from decades ago; many more were lost to time. I only apologize that it took decades for these photographs to be published.

I need to thank Carmen LiSing, my girlfriend back in 1973, who traveled with me to California to start a new life. As I began photographing in West Oakland in 1974, she supported my aspirations as a twenty-three-year-old photographer even though we had few resources and struggled to support ourselves in our new home in the Bay Area.

The digital files were prepared by Brian Shapiro and Sophia Cutino, who spent many hours scanning the old negatives and perfecting the files. Jeffrey Smith, my friend and agent at Contact Press Images, has been a constant advocate for my photographs.

I am especially pleased that Ishmael Reed, whom I have long admired, has written the foreword. Makeda Best, Leigh Raiford, April Martin, and Waldo Martin all looked at the photos and offered their thoughts, which helped shape this book. The team at Heyday—publisher Steve Wasserman, general manager and editorial director Gayle Wattawa, managing editor Emmerich Anklam, and art director Archie Ferguson—has been enthusiastic about this book and a pleasure to work with. Thanks for helping birth this book.

Most important, thanks to my dear colleague and friend Jon Logan, whose Jonathan Logan Family Foundation supported this book, and to the foundation's board and staff: Susanne Zuerbig, Barbara Raab, Stewart Owen, Lilly Quinn, and Theresa Boylan. Without them, we may have had to wait fifty more years for these photographs to be published. Their belief in my work, and that the foundation can be a catalyst for ideas and actions that illuminate the world and create positive change, can be seen within these pages.

THANK YOU.

About the Author

Ken Light has worked as a documentary photographer and filmmaker for over fifty years, focusing on social issues facing America. His work has been published in more than a dozen monographs, including *California Anonymous*, *Course of the Empire*, *Midnight la Frontera*, *What's Going On? 1969–1974*, *Valley of Shadows and Dreams*, *Coal Hollow*, *Delta Time*, *Texas Death Row*, *To the Promised Land*, and *With These Hands*. He is also the author of the text *Witness in Our Time: Working Lives of Documentary Photographers* in its second edition and *Picturing Resistance: Moments and Movements of Social Change from the 1950s to Today*.

He is the recipient of a Guggenheim Fellowship, two National Endowment for the Arts photographers' fellowships, a National Endowment for the Arts survey grant, and the Dorothea Lange Fellowship, as well as grants from the Hasselblad Foundation, the Open Society Institute, and private grantors. His work has been in numerous magazines, newspapers, and a variety of electronic and film media, and has been presented in over 250 exhibitions worldwide, including one-person shows at the International Center for Photography (NYC), the Oakland Museum of California, the Southeast Museum of Photography, Visual Studies Workshop, Visa pour L'image Perpignan (France), and the San José Museum of Art. His work is part of numerous collections, including at the San Francisco Museum of Modern Art; the Museum of Fine Arts, Houston; the International Center of Photography; and the Smithsonian American Art Museum.

Light was cofounder of the Mother Jones International Fund for Documentary Photography, which annually gave seven grants to documentary photographers worldwide, and a founder of Fotovision, a San Francisco Bay Area nonprofit documentary workshop and book program. He is the Reva and David Logan Professor of Photojournalism at the UC Berkeley Graduate School of Journalism. Light is associated with the photography agency Contact Press Images.

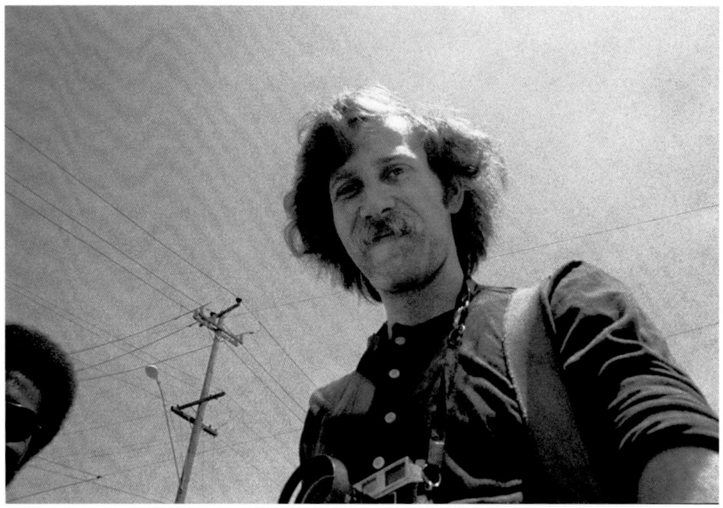

kenlight.com @kenlight_photo_

JONATHAN LOGAN
FAMILY FOUNDATION

The Jonathan Logan Family Foundation supports organizations that advance social justice by empowering world-changing work in investigative journalism, documentary film, and arts and culture.